Whose Heaven, Whose Earth?

THOMAS AND MARJORIE
MELVILLE

Whose Heaven, Whose Earth?

Alfred A. Knopf   New York   1971

To

MONSEÑOR HELDER CÁMARA

of Brazil

and to the memory of

PADRE CAMILO TORRES

of Colombia and

COMANDANTES LUIS TURCIOS,

CÉSAR MONTES, and YON SOSA

of Guatemala

Is it the prophet's thought I speak, or am I raving?
What do I know of life? what of myself?
I know not even my own work past or present,
Dim ever-shifting guesses of it spread before me,
Of newer, better worlds, their mighty parturition,
Mocking, perplexing me.

—from *Prayer of Columbus*
by Walt Whitman

Foreword

This book has been written because of a promise we made to some Guatemalan peasant leaders and university students in 1967—a promise that we would do all in our power to help them in their struggle for cultural, political, and economic liberation.

We hope that our effort to explain the reasons behind the struggle, its causes and its goals, will serve as a partial fulfillment of that promise. We are convinced that Guatemala—and, for that matter, all Latin America—will soon be caught up in a conflict not unlike that now ravaging Southeast Asia. And the people of the United States clearly cannot afford to be indifferent to its outcome.

We do not expect to be able to instill a complete understanding of Guatemala or the revolutionary struggle there; nor can we assume that every reader will sympathize with our conclusions, which are, after all, the fruit of intense personal experience. Nevertheless, if we create in a few minds some doubts about the absolutes by which many people judge the world, we will have accomplished at least part of our objective. For our experiences in Guatemala have convinced us that the values of our own society cannot legitimately be applied as a gauge of another society's successes and failures.

The identities of many of the people mentioned in this book have been disguised because we fear for their safety; some have been concealed simply because public recognition might be embarrassing and no useful purpose would be served by identifying them. We have named others correctly because their contributions to Guatemala and her people deserve public recognition, and they would not be put in greater danger than they are in already; others have been identified because their activities and declarations in the past have confused many of the issues with which our book deals.

If we have offended anyone either by identifying him or by not giving him the recognition he deserves, we apologize.

We wish to express our gratitude to the Maryknoll Catholic Foreign Mission Society and its many members whom we still count among our personal friends. Our parting has not diminished either our high regard for them or our appreciation for our many years of beneficial association with them.

Very special thanks go to Barbara and Will Inman for the difficult but rewarding hours we spent together unraveling the threads of two people's lives and reweaving them into a coherent narrative. Without their invaluable assistance, and above all their patient understanding, insight, and sensitivity, this book might not yet have seen the light of day. No less can be said for the devoted efforts of our editor, Regina Ryan Deutschman.

Finally, and most importantly, we acknowledge our eternal debt of gratitude to our parents. For even though they themselves have not always understood or condoned our actions, their Christian example and charity were the fundamental influences that led us to choose the difficult paths we have traveled. And their trust and ultimate confidence in us have provided a much-needed support at a time when many of our countrymen question our patriotism and many of our fellow Christians doubt our commitment to Christ.

Thomas Melville
Marjorie Melville

Contents

*8 pages of photographs will be found
following page 114*

Whose Heaven, Whose Earth?

1

If This Is Catholicism, What Am I?

Tom   The nine of us sat in a ring of chairs in the Catonsville, Maryland, police station, talking to one another. Five FBI men came in and glared at us. They seemed to want to make us feel ashamed of the fact that we had burned the town's draft files.

The agent in charge grabbed an empty chair from our circle, pulled it over to his colleagues, turned it around, and sat with his back to us.

Then in a voice charged with hate, he said, "Well, after this, I think I'm gonna change my religion!"

We had made it clear in our statement that we were all Catholics. His words profiled my dilemma. I had found many people in the Catholic Church, particularly among those in authority, whose beliefs were opposed to mine. Were they, with their set of beliefs, and I, with mine, to be considered members of the same Church? This FBI man, and those like him, identified the American flag with the Cross of Jesus Christ; Western cultural values with the message of the Gospels; the productiveness of the American economy as proof of God's blessing over and against all adversaries. While I believe that Christ had one message—the Brotherhood of all men in the Fatherhood of God—I also think that the institutionalized Christian churches of the Western world, and especially the

3

Roman Catholic Church, have so distorted this message that Christ's Spirit often seems stronger among people who have never heard of Him or who make no pretense of being His followers.

Yet, not too many years ago, I held beliefs that I now largely reject. I went as a missionary to Guatemala, where I was forced to compare what we Catholics taught to others with what we actually did ourselves. We preached patience and fortitude in the face of terrible human suffering and deprivation, while we lived in comfort. I also began to weigh what we taught in the name of Christ—a myriad of esoteric doctrines and dogmas—against what Christ Himself taught: the simple message of love.

As I examined the causes of the dehumanizing conditions under which the masses of Guatemalans lived, and discovered that the Catholic Church was most often morally responsible for such conditions by its insistence that "the poor you will always have with you," I began to re-evaluate my own position. It led me to ask the question that obviously now troubled our FBI agent: If this is Catholicism, what am I?

M arjorie If there was any one thing that had brought me to the Catonsville police station from a Maryknoll convent in Guatemala, it was my Catholic faith, the faith that made Christ's message the motive power of my life. Many of us get so caught up in the need to see Christ as a figure in history that we miss the meaning of His life as something working in us. The historical Christ means just another human life unless I let His Spirit come alive in me. This Consciousness comes to us first like a very young child, and as it grows, it absorbs more and more of our energy and understanding, finally developing into an Awareness that makes us feel immediate connection with other human beings, especially those who have been cut off from complete self-fulfillment. This can only come from the recognition that all

4

human beings are sisters and brothers of one another, all are the children of a Living Father. This is what Christ means to me, it is what being a human individual means to me. When you help individuals to recognize the Brotherhood of all men, you are helping Christ come to life in them. In Guatemala, we found many people who knew how to do this, though not consciously in the name of Christ. At Catonsville, we tried to show that others who claim to act in the name of Christ are working against Him, sowing death instead of life, using people for their own profit, power, and prestige.

Tom   I looked out the window of the police station as we waited for the FBI to take action. I marveled at my situation. Since being ordained in 1957, I had traveled a long road: I was now married to an ex-nun, excommunicated, and accused of being a Communist guerrilla; and at this moment was preparing to be confined in prison as a felon. I realized that many of my friends who had supported me in my missionary work would feel threatened by all this, that the transformation in my standing would be incomprehensible to most of them; yet my path was utterly logical and clear to me.

Marjorie   I stood next to Tom and put my arm around him. I didn't want to say anything. I had to stand close to him and let my thoughts loose to wander among distant memories, as I knew he was doing. I wondered if I could ever realize my dream of being a bridge for people: between those who believe in God and those who don't; between Christians and Communists; between Americans who believe themselves highly moral and Guatemalans and Vietnamese who suffer the consequences of American policy. So much of this separation and struggle between people is due to a lack of understanding.

5

Tom   The rights and wrongs of such a struggle don't often come in white and black; there are many hues of gray involved. Yet, in our experience, the Catholic Church and the United States government have inevitably failed to recognize this.

We hope that by explaining who we are, what we saw, and how we responded, people will understand why we have lost faith in the hierarchy of the Catholic Church and in the U.S. government, and why we feel that both only exacerbate the struggle, and hinder the quest, for human dignity in so many parts of the world.

II

The Making of
a Missioner

Tom the Priest I can't remember when I first wanted to become a priest or what suggested the idea to me. I know that it was preceded by the usual childish ambitions of wanting to steer the back end of the block-long "hook 'n' ladder" fire truck or else to roar through town with siren open as a motorcycle cop. Yet, by the time I was in the fifth grade, I was openly proclaiming my intention to enter the priesthood.

One day my teacher, Mrs. Hurley, expelled me from school because I told her to "shut up." My mother tearfully called her to find out what the problem was and how it could be resolved; she obliquely mentioned my ambition to become a priest—hoping, I suppose, that no one would want to punish too drastically a boy destined to serve God. Mrs. Hurley was delighted with the news, since she herself had a son in the seminary. I was readmitted to school without further ado.

Perhaps my religious inspiration came from the high esteem everyone in our family had for my Uncle Bill, who was a priest in the archdiocese of Boston. Perhaps it was the Catholic atmosphere of our family. Or maybe it came from my own religious instinct, curiously emerging along with a stubbornness that sometimes was to hinder, sometimes to further, my spiritual growth.

My family was always uncommonly religious, and I had more than my share of piety. Every night after supper we

7

would pray the rosary together and make a novena to the Infant Jesus of Prague. Every Saturday afternoon we went to confession, for which I often had to leave a baseball or football game early. Sunday we attended Mass and received communion, of course. Late Monday afternoon was reserved for the parish Novena of Our Lady of Perpetual Help. These were all musts so far as our family was concerned, but I also assisted at daily Mass with my sister Eleanor. She was the third of my parents' six children, and I, two and a half years her junior, was the fourth. Although daily Mass became a family custom sometime later, Elie and I went for years all by ourselves.

I can't account for this extra degree of piety—it didn't seem to manifest itself in other ways. I was always considered the troublemaker by my parents, and my mother never dared leave me at home alone with my brothers and sisters, since she knew that would immeasurably increase the possibilities of sibling confrontations. As a result, I was always taken on shopping tours into Boston, while the other five were left at home—an unintended stimulus for me to maintain my troublesome nature.

My conflicts did not stop at the edge of the family circle. Neighbors' broken windows, illegal rides on the undercarriage of horse-drawn delivery wagons, bloody fights with local toughguys in our West Roxbury Irish ghetto, were all incidents that tended to overshadow if not obliterate my piety as far as my parents were concerned. Still, my expressed desire to become a priest was often weighed by them against my behavior, while my brothers and sisters looked upon my priest notions as a clever subterfuge to escape or at least to lessen the punishments I so richly deserved. Art, my junior by two years, used to mimic my mother in front of our companions, taunting me in a falsetto voice as "my little Maryknoller." This would often earn him a fist in the nose, which in turn would merit me more than a few blows with the paternal strap across my bare backside. I never managed to figure out why he or any of the others considered my desire to become a priest as a put-on to escape parental wrath, for I received at least my share of punishment, if not more.

Yet, I was always aware of my parents' affection. We had a very close family relationship, and I usually felt that I got only what I deserved. Dad would always explain to us why he felt obliged to punish us physically; and although sometimes we might not agree completely with his reasoning and questioned that it really hurt him more than ourselves, we never doubted his love and were fully aware that his discipline was not administered in anger.

Also, by accepting his whippings with a minimum of protest, we proved to him that we were of his mettle. Strength was a quality Dad openly admired. I can still picture an incident which occurred when I couldn't have been more than four or five years old.

Mary, my oldest sister, came into the room to tuck me into my bed. I hid under the sheet. She pretended to search, then found me, loved me with a hug, kissed me. Dad called to her from the door to his room, "Mary, he's a big boy now. . . . He doesn't need to be kissed any more."

Four or five years old. No more kisses for a big boy.

Once, when I was in third or fourth grade, Art and I were playing baseball with some other boys down at Billings Field. I must have said something, and one of the O'Brien boys from up on Sanborn Avenue turned on me angrily. I didn't want to fight him—the O'Briens had the reputation of being the toughest fighters in the neighborhood. I knew that this one would lick hell out of me, in front of the other kids.

I started walking away, but he came after me. I began to run across the field. I thought I would never get to the other side. I imagined everyone was snickering at me. I ran into the big hardware store, and hid so that I could watch the window.

The O'Brien boy and his gang ran by, looked in, and kept on going.

I grew angry at myself. When Art came by, I went out to

meet him. I was so ashamed I nearly cried, but remembered that Melvilles must not cry. The Irish aren't supposed to show any emotion but anger.

Art tried to help: "There are too many of them. It was all you could do."

"But I shouldn't have left you there alone. Suppose they'd decided to take it out on you?"

My breathing still came in gasps. If Dad found out, what would he say to me? I swore that I'd never again run away from any fight—never.

Billy Cunningham once bloodied my nose, but I won the fight. My mother was angry over the blood on my shirt, but Dad was proud I had not backed off. I was knocked down in fights, and had my head split open. Dad called me "Stitches," and pretended he was angry. Mom shook her head, worrying. If Mom worried, that meant she loved me.

One day when I was working in an ice cream parlor, I tried to carry four gallons of syrup up from the cellar. I tripped and wasn't able to throw the bottles free in time. I broke them all and slashed one of my hands. The manager drove me to the hospital, where my hand was stitched up and swathed in a big bandage. I got home about ten that night.

I stood at the door of the living room, my bandaged hand behind my back. Dad and Mom had company.

"I'm going up to my room for some reading," I said.

"Okay, Tom. See you in the morning. God bless you."

Then, as I went up the stairs: "How many stitches, Tom?" Nothing more.

He wanted me to know that he had seen and cared, that he liked my not making a fuss over my injury, that he wanted a man for a son.

"Fifteen," I called back down the stairs, without stopping. I smiled. Dad didn't say much, but he encouraged me when I carried my own hurts. It was good.

By the time I was in the eighth grade, I knew I wanted to go to the seminary at Maryknoll, the Catholic Foreign Mission

Society of America, as soon as I finished grammar school. My parents contended that I should wait until after I graduated from high school. Their desire to keep me at home surprised and pleased me.

Once I tried to run away from home, but when I reached the local railroad station, I discovered I had no can opener among my supplies. I returned home to get one and was chagrined to find that my father had already read my explanation of filial disillusionment and was not at all upset over my departure. When I told him why I had come back to the house, he offered me his own pocket opener. His parental wisdom antagonized me to the point that I decided to stay at home and "get even."

Now that I wanted to go to the seminary, my parents thought four more years at home, plus a high school education under Jesuit auspices, would be what I needed to clarify and solidify my vocation to the priesthood. Maryknoll agreed that thirteen was too young an age for me to enter their school, even though it did accept other students at that age. I was told that few boys had as good a Catholic family environment as I did, which would make my continuing education at home better than seminary training. I was very disappointed.

The four years at Boston College High School dragged by. The Jesuits were tough on me. I spent at least two days a week in detention classes after school, often just for playing some practical joke. Sometimes I received the strap across my knuckles or my backside.

During high school, when not wrestling with the intricacies of Latin, Greek, and French, I spent my quieter moments reading all I could about Maryknoll. It had been a love of mine ever since I'd first discovered its existence. My desire to go to the foreign missions dated from the day I assisted at a novena in honor of St. Francis Xavier, the great missionary to India and Japan. The preacher had brought along a first-class relic of the Spanish nobleman-turned-Jesuit: his withered right arm sealed up in a glass case. As he described to us the rigors of St. Francis's wanderings in the Orient in search of souls for Christ, I knew that I wanted to be like the man who had raised this very arm to pour the saving waters of baptism over the heads of hundreds of thousands of the heathen. The life of a priest at home didn't attract me—it was too soft, I felt. My contact with Jesuit teachers did nothing to turn me away from Maryknoll, especially since such a small percentage of their order went to the missions, most remaining in America in teaching positions. I was determined not to take a chance on being assigned in the States. Maryknoll was exclusively for foreign missionary priests.

I read about Bishop James Anthony Walsh, the Boston Irishman who had founded Maryknoll in 1911 at Ossining, New York, and his saintly cofounder, Father Thomas F. Price of North Carolina, the "Tar Heel Apostle." They believed that Catholics must provide religious for the foreign missions, and there were as yet no native American orders with foreign missionary goals. *Men of Maryknoll* was a book I thumbed through many times, almost memorizing the heroic deeds of those first spiritual giants who had set out for Manchuria in 1918. Father Jerry Donovan, the Pennsylvania youth who died in China at the hands of bandits in 1936, became my modern-day St. Francis Xavier.

I began practicing mortification myself so that I would be tough enough to take whatever came. I saved my lunch money and sent it every month to Maryknoll toward the support of a missioner. I, too, would be a saint, or another Father Donovan, if God so willed it.

Sometime during high school, I began denying that I wanted to become a priest: It got to be too much of an embarrassment, being held up to me every time I stepped out of line, which was quite often.

I was beginning to notice girls, to be attracted by them; yet the celibacy that I knew was required by the priesthood made me want to keep them at arm's length. I consulted with my confessor over a problem with "impure" thoughts about girls. He told me that if I valued my calling to the priesthood, I would stay clear of the opposite sex. This wasn't difficult, since my heritage was one of strict Irish Catholicism. Sex was a taboo subject in our house—not only had we never had the facts of life explained to us, we knew enough not even to ask about such a matter. Distance from the opposite sex was expected of all of us; though such contacts were not openly opposed, they certainly were not encouraged. Bill and Mary, six and five years older than I, never had a date until college. Elie broke tradition occasionally in her senior year in high school, but the restrictions placed on such activities tended to discourage her. Except perhaps for Dave, the youngest of my brothers, high school dating was the exception rather than the rule in our family, and the fact that I didn't date did not in itself associate me with the priesthood in anyone's eyes.

Upon graduation from high school in 1948, I joined Mary-knoll, and was sent to its Junior College in Lakewood, New Jersey, an old, converted prep school that had been used by the Navy during World War II. Most of us slept in the decaying military barracks, where the heating system often would not function; in freezing weather we went to bed in overcoats, stocking hats, and woolen socks. I enjoyed those two years immensely, but some of my teachers indicated doubts about my "attitude." I managed to pick up demerits over broken windows in the swimming pool room, after-dark raids on the pantry, and the fire-extinguisher crusades I helped undertake against the recruits from opposing barracks.

After Lakewood, I went to Ossining to study philosophy and theology for six years, with one year sandwiched in for spiritual training at the Novitiate in Bedford, Massachusetts. I wasn't a good student; and, although the studies were not difficult for me, neither were they very stimulating. The cold logic of Thomistic syllogisms provided concrete answers for all problems, but it left most of us unconvinced sometimes, and uninspired almost always. Only the most philosophical and scholarly members of our class seemed to enjoy the studies.

Outside the classroom there was plenty of enjoyment for everyone. Maryknoll had never put tremendous emphasis on studies—the Order maintained that life in the foreign missions demanded a special character, a special kind of spirit, and it was this that was sought in us rather than the speculative mind that characterized students of other seminaries. Perhaps, also, it was this emphasis—the constant orientation toward the foreign missions—and the type of person that would even consider going to foreign missions, that gave Maryknoll its particular *esprit de corps*. Visitors to our seminary never failed to remark on its uniquely warm and joyful atmosphere. We ourselves noticed the difference when we went to other seminaries to play basketball or baseball. The somber and studious mood we found elsewhere never failed to make us grateful for being Maryknollers.

We were obliged to perform an hour of manual labor each day, and another hour was designated for athletics. Everyone participated in three or four different sports. I earned my battle scars in football, hockey, and basketball.

Time was also devoted to automobile repair, study of short-wave radio, classes in electricity and plumbing—all subjects in which we were encouraged to obtain a smattering of knowledge for future use in the missions. We also had song-fests, performed plays and skits, watched an occasional movie, and had television for watching sports events, Bishop Fulton J. Sheen, and the investigative hearings of Joseph McCarthy's Senate subcommittee.

Senator McCarthy became a big hero to most of us for his anti-Communist crusades, as did Bishop Sheen for his philosophical dissection of Communism. Maryknoll developed its own anti-Communist campaign, in which we all joined at least vicariously. China had been Maryknoll's first mission field; and, although the Order began sending more and more men in the twenties and thirties to Korea, Japan, Formosa, and the Philippines, in the minds of most people both inside and outside of the Society, Maryknoll signified one thing: the foreign missions in China. During the Second World War, most of our Asian missions were closed down, and Maryknoll turned to Latin America. But China remained our prime concern—a huge and fertile field for missionary endeavor—until the Communists took power. Then stories began to come out from China. Our missioners, such as Bob Greene and Bishop James E. Walsh* (no relation to the cofounder), were in prison, betrayed by some of their own parishioners. Bishop Frank Ford died in another prison. The Church was broken, destroyed, or at least driven underground, and we were identifying with the sufferings in our own flesh.

The stories we heard at spiritual reading from those missioners who had been expelled made our blood boil. Shortly thereafter, following mutual displays of hostility, North Korea went into South Korea. Bishop Byrne and Father Booth were marched off to North Korea, and there Bishop Byrne died from the hardships of the march. I was all for leaving the seminary to join the United States Army, but my spiritual director dissuaded me by pointing out that the United States had enough soldiers, while the Church had too few missionaries.

My desire to join the Army had not been entirely prompted by noble motives. I looked upon it as a chance to see the world, to get a glimpse at the life I felt I had missed before entering the seminary. About once a year, the desire to pull out would come upon me and would last a month or two. Usually the feeling arose in the fall after I returned from summer vacation, where activities were controlled but not regimented (though dating was outlawed), or in the spring after getting a close look at some of the postulants for the sisterhood who came from their motherhouse across the road to work in the seminary kitchen. My thoughts and dreams

* *Released July 10, 1970.*

15

about girls had accompanied me into the seminary. When I would talk over the matter with my spiritual director, Father Jake Driscoll, an old China missioner, he'd snort and tell me I was normal. He said that Maryknoll didn't want priests who didn't find women attractive, that the Order rejected only those who couldn't deal with the attraction. He said that the missioner in South China who wasn't tempted to take a second look at the women bathing in the streams was in more trouble than the fellow who did take that second look. I found his advice consoling and always managed to get over my pining after a few weeks.

In 1955, President Ngo Dinh Diem of South Vietnam came to address the student body. He was an old friend of Maryknoll's, stemming from the days when he had been given lodging at our Lakewood Seminary, in 1948–49. This had been done at the request of another old friend, Maryknoll's "protector" at the Vatican, Francis Cardinal Spellman, Archbishop of New York. I became acquainted with Diem at Lakewood because we were refectory tablemates. Many seminarians used to parody his name, calling him "Go Ding Ding" because of his adamant refusal, in defiance of seminary custom, to wash his own dishes. Diem was considered a protégé of Spellman's by the American Catholic hierarchy, and in Washington as well, where the Cardinal's political connections were of great value to the new President. Spellman had also been instrumental in generating, both here in the U.S. and in Vietnam, the religious enthusiasm that made a virtual pilgrimage out of the 1954 southward migration of 850,000 North Vietnamese Catholics into the waiting arms of President Diem. The President had now come to New York to thank the Cardinal, and decided to pay his respects to Maryknoll at the same time. He spoke to us in French, standing on the steps of our main altar—an honor that no layman except a head of state could expect to receive. His visit stimulated in many of us a renewed determination to become front-line warriors in the spiritual and ideological struggle against Communism that our Church was waging across the globe.

In June 1957, when I was twenty-six, I was ordained, and committed to Maryknoll for life. Six weeks before ordination, I had been assigned to Guatemala along with my buddy Denny Kraus. We had no say in our assignments, and mine came as a pleasant surprise. The third member of our rough-housing trio, Bill Kruegler, was ordered to Bolivia—where he was shot to death a few years later while trying to quiet a raucous mob in a bar next to the church. All three of us were excited by our assignments, because both Guatemala and Bolivia were known as tough missions. Denny and I were especially happy about Guatemala because we knew that much of the mission travel was by horseback and motorcycle —pastimes we enjoyed together.

Another plus for Guatemala was the struggle that was apparently being won there against Communism. In the early fifties we had read the diaries of our missioners there, telling of the difficult time the "Communist" government had given them. Entrance visas for new missioners assigned to Guatemala were often held up for months while the applicant was supposedly being investigated. One of our priests remarked that the Guatemalan government ranked missioners with thieves and prostitutes on the list of undesirables.

Maryknoll had first gone into Guatemala in 1943. In March 1945 a revolutionary-minded regime under Juan José Arévalo was inaugurated, which pursued many forward-looking policies aimed at improving the lot of Guatemalans educationally and economically. Then, in 1951, Jacobo Arbenz Guzmán was elected president. His basic program was agrarian reform. In both these regimes, revolutionaries and Communists worked more and more openly, and organized labor became the central force behind their political power, a role which had traditionally belonged to the military.

From what we at Maryknoll heard, the government was becoming under these regimes progressively more anticlerical and anti-United States. Historically, Latin America has exhibited a significant strain of anti-Church sentiment, dating from the liberal movements and Masonic influences of the nineteenth century. But this new brand of anti-Catholicism in Guatemala, though not so direct in its attacks, seemed all the more dangerous because it was Communist-inspired. Then, in 1954, we were all delighted to learn of Colonel Castillo Armas's successful invasion from Honduras, with the aid of the U.S. government. He established a regime that was strongly pro-U.S. and pro-Catholic Church and began a campaign to stamp out all vestiges of Communism. By 1957 the battle was largely won; yet I felt that an assignment to an area so recently dangerous gave me a front-line position in the fight against atheistic Communism, the greatest threat to the teachings of Christ.

I arrived in Guatemala in September of 1957, and was sent to language school in Huehuetenango, capital of the department* of the same name, to study Spanish for six months. I use the word "school" loosely, since there were only three students: Denny Kraus, myself, and an older priest, Father Moe Duffy. We had two teachers, neither of whom spoke English, and we alternated between them for individual tutoring. The classes were held in two storerooms in the city's main parish.

Despite the lack of formality, we learned the language quickly. All the cooks, houseboys, and neighbors spoke only Spanish, and we could speak English only to each other. Every weekend, we would go out to help with Mass in one of the sixteen parishes that Maryknollers ran in Huehuetenango department. We were soon preaching, hearing confessions, and baptizing in our broken Spanish.

* A *department corresponds to one of our states. In Guatemala, which has a more centralized government than the United States, the governor of each department is appointed by the president, who usually assigns army colonels to such posts.*

Huehuetenango, one of the most backward areas of Guatemala so far as relative progress is concerned, is located in the country's northwestern mountains. Its capital city is nestled in a valley at the foot of Guatemala's highest mountain range, the Cuchumatanes.

There were perhaps thirty-five Maryknoll priests and brothers in Guatemala when I arrived. Denny Kraus and I soon earned the nickname "Rover Boys" because we made it our primary concern to visit all the Huehuetenango parishes before we finished our language study at the end of February 1958. We knew we wouldn't have the opportunity to do so once we received our own assignments, and we both felt the need to get an overview of all Maryknoll work in Guatemala. Many of the missions could only be reached after a motorcycle or jeep trek of several hours followed by a five- to eight-hour horseback ride. We rode over dusty mountain roads and horse trails that often skirted beautiful canyons with no more than a few feet from mountain wall to precipitous drops of hundreds or even thousands of feet. When, by mid-May, the dry season turned into the rainy season, the dust was converted to mud. We experienced motorcycle spills, with skinned shins and hips, and rides on weary horses that had to fight against the suction of belly-deep mud.

The 250,000 people of Huehuetenango were largely of Mayan Indian ancestry. Every village had its own special dress. The men in the more progressive villages wore Western clothes, with only a colored sash at the waist to mark their Indian heritage and identity. In the towns with less *ladino** influence, the Indian dress for men often consisted of white coarse cotton trousers, covered from the waist to the knees by a *delantal*, or woolen apron, and a *capushai*, a woolen pull-over jacket with slits for the arms. Since altitudes in Huehuetenango varied from 2,500 to 12,500 feet, differences in temperature were extreme and necessitated clothes that could be easily

* Ladino *refers to people of Western cultural heritage, usually of mixed Indian–Spanish ancestry.*

shed or easily piled on. The varieties of women's pull-over *huipiles*, or blouses, were equal to the number of towns, and one had no problem identifying any woman's native village by her dress. The ankle-length, wrap-around skirt came in three colors—blue, green, and red—and was called a *corte*. It forced on the women a short, shuffling step that made them appear to be running.

My strongest first impressions of the Indian people were of their tremendous endurance and their attitudes toward modesty. The men carried loads of up to one hundred pounds on their backs, supported by a *mecapal*, a leather strap about 2½ inches wide and a foot long and worn across the forehead. It is tied at both ends with a rope that runs under the load. The load can thus be supported for eight-hour treks up and down mountain trails, with the upper part of the carrier's torso constantly inclined forward at a 45° angle. Considering that the men often weigh no more than 120 or 130 pounds, this feat of strength never ceased to amaze me. The women were no less adept at carrying a sleeping child strapped to their backs, besides a load of twenty-five or thirty pounds balanced precariously on their heads. The husband always walked first, bent under his load, with his wife a few steps behind, straight as a ramrod, her fast shuffling pace and swinging arms moving as if she would run right up her husband's back. The children marched behind in single file, each with his load, the boys with their own junior-sized *mecapals* and the girls balancing burdens on their heads.

As regards modesty, it took me a long time to realize that this characteristic is not an absolute laid down from all eternity but is relative to the culture in which it is practiced. I was often taken aback to see grown men urinating publicly against a tree or adobe wall or to find a woman squatting discreetly near the side of the road. Children, especially the boys, went uncovered from the waist down in the hotter areas until they were four or five years old. Modesty had nothing whatsoever to do with female breasts—babies were nursed at all times anywhere. Women took off their blouses and bathed themselves in the streams, and in the hot country they sometimes worked around the house wearing nothing above the waist. Whenever I saw such scenes, I would remember old Father Driscoll's advice, and once in a while I would steal a second look at the women washing in the streams. All the same, the women were exceedingly shy and usually hid their mouths with their shawls and found it difficult to speak up. It was a style of modesty I found very hard to accept.

By the time my six months of language study were over, I was fairly proficient at Spanish and was aching to be assigned to a mission of my own and to get down to my life's work. In February 1958 I was sent out as assistant pastor in San Miguel Acatán.

III

Sister
Marian Peter

Marjorie the Nun Some of my earliest and happiest recollections are of our family visits to my grandparents' home in Irapuato, Mexico, where I was born in 1929. My father was an American electrical engineer involved in putting up power lines through central Mexico. My mother was the daughter of an Englishman who had come to the country when he was seventeen and married a Mexican. My grandparents' house, identical with those I had seen in the storybooks in my grandfather's library, looked as if it had been transplanted right out of the English countryside. It was a two-story wooden structure that had a mysterious attic with gabled windows and a basement full of nooks and crannies that was perfect for playing hide-and-seek. In the afternoons we would sit on the large porch that ran along the front and one side of the house. The butler would serve us lemon sherbet, and we would enjoy the afternoon sunshine as we looked out over the rose garden in front. All the other houses on the street were typical of a small Mexican town—one-story buildings forming a continuous solid wall along the sidewalk, huge front doors, and bars on the street-level window.

I remember the persecution of the Catholic Church in the 1930's. I saw church doors closed and barred. I went to Mass secretly in private homes, and attended first grade in a Catholic school-in-hiding. The sisters who taught in the school did not wear the customary long, black garb. Each grade held classes in a different private home, and the sisters had secret hiding places for the crucifix and catechism books in case the police came. We were dismissed in twos and threes in order not to cause suspicion as we walked out.

What really fascinated me were the stories about underground priests and about those who were martyred.

When I was fifteen and the danger had passed, my granddad showed me a secret place in the basement that I had never discovered for myself. In the basement pantry there was one small cupboard with only three shelves. When pressure was put on the back corner of one of the shelves, the whole cupboard moved like a door, and inside there was a small room with a bed and a chair. Here, Granddad told me, any number of priests had been hidden during the persecution. They moved secretly at night to administer the sacraments and to say Mass for individual families. In the attic there was a small chapel with an altar and several kneelers, and Mass had often been said there.

One of the biggest disappointments of my childhood came with the confiscation of my grandfather's farm during the agrarian reform carried out by President Cárdenas. I loved to ride horses, and these went, too. I couldn't understand why the farm had been taken from my grandfather, who always treated his peasant workers very well. It didn't seem fair. But then, that was the way things were.

When I was eight, we moved to Chihuahua in northern Mexico. My sister was only three, and my three brothers were born there. We lived in a colony of about forty homes built for the managers and engineers of a large smelter. We had a two-room schoolhouse and American teachers. There was no dearth of activity, what with the swimming pool, tennis courts, and large lawns.

The happiest times were Christmas, the Fourth of July, and Halloween, great get-togethers for all the people in the colony. But I think the best was the Fourth of July. We had a huge picnic, races with lots of prizes, and a parade of decorated bicycles, all punctuated with firecrackers. I was very proud to be an American.

It was clear to me that Americans knew how to do things, especially when we drove up to Texas every year or two. I loved to see the clean streets—everything was so orderly and neat. I used to save my allowances because there were so many wonderful things to buy. And it seemed to me that it was Americans who had done the most for Mexico. People like my dad's father had come there to put in the railroads. Americans had brought in electricity, and the automobiles, airplanes, radios, stoves, and even clothes and shoes were American-made. I felt that Mexicans owed much to us Americans.

I finished seventh grade in the American school; there was no eighth grade, and since my parents didn't want to send me away as yet, I went back to the sixth grade in a Mexican school. This was the last grade in grammar school, and the classes were more difficult than in the American school. I had never studied world history, cosmography, or Spanish grammar, and even the arithmetic was different. I made new friends, but I felt a bit superior: My schoolmates were all Mexican girls; I was an American, and I was going to go to high school in the States.

Even before arriving there, I had felt that Loretto Academy in El Paso, Texas, was *my* school. It was a convent school for girls, and I was a boarder. I enjoyed the classes, though I did miss the freedom of home.

I played the saxophone in the orchestra and participated in sports. I taught catechism on Sundays and became a Wing Scout. From the time I was about eight, I had decided that I would one day fly an airplane, and being a Wing Scout was one of the most wonderful school activities for me. At home I plastered the walls of my room with photographs of planes, and I hung from the ceiling a model plane I had painstakingly made. My parents, torn between amusement and dismay, agreed that I might take flying lessons when I became eighteen. I bought the magazine *Flying* once a month, took a course in aeronautics, and did a lot of daydreaming.

The priest who taught our senior-year sociology class was tiresome, a soft and uninspiring man; but the subject was exciting. We learned about how society is organized, and about relationships among people. We talked about the role of priests and sisters in modern society.

One day Ruth, a classmate, said, "Excuse me, Father, but I don't think they do very much. What can priests and nuns do for people that professionals don't do better?"

I found myself standing up and defending priests and sisters. I had just read two books about Catholic missionaries in China, and I described their total gift of self to the people. No professional could be as dedicated as a priest or a sister, I insisted.

Later, as I was working in the principal's office, another girl in my class, Emma, said to me, "That was some speech you gave today."

"What speech?"

I had already forgotten about sociology class.

"You're thinking of becoming a sister, aren't you?"

"Who, me? You'd never catch me being a sister."

What a miserable existence, I thought to myself, *being locked in a convent!* Yet, when I was alone, I felt the thought rise in me. *Why not? Why not me? No,* I pleaded inside me, *please God, don't say me.*

In November we had a three-day retreat of spiritual conferences, reading, and meditations. We kept silence during the three days. Since it was our senior year, we took this retreat very seriously—it was a time to think about our lives and where and how we were going.

My dad had suggested that I consider going to college. I continued to think about my desire to become a pilot but recognized it as an impractical dream. And now I had to face this new question about becoming a nun. The thought scared me, but I wanted my life to be worthwhile and I had to admit that being a missionary sister would take courage, a giving of myself, that it would mean a lifetime of working for poor people who wouldn't have anyone else to turn to. I had seen many poor people in Mexico. I had marveled at the contrast between our homes in the colony and those dreary, long, dusty blockhouses where the smelter laborers lived with their families. I couldn't get around the sense of destiny I had begun to feel. If I were to live to be sixty-eight, I had already lived a fourth of my life. What had I accomplished or done for others? Being a nun would give me a chance to share some of the advantages of the education I had received. I hurried to the school library, where I had seen a magazine about some missionary nuns who worked for the poor far away and under all kinds of hardships. I found it again: *Maryknoll*. It was a religious order for American missionaries, with two branches, one for priests and brothers and the other for nuns. They worked in China, Japan, Africa, South America. In my mind's eye, Maryknoll was in technicolor, while the orders of Mexican sisters came on in black-and-white, in spite of the many stories I had heard of courage and commitment during the time of persecution in Mexico.

That night I wrote a letter asking to join the Order. After all, what did God make us for if not to help people? The catechism question I had drilled so often with the children in my Sunday classes kept coming back to me:

Why did God make you?
He made me to know Him, to love Him, and to serve Him here on earth and thus to be happy with Him in heaven for ever.

I wondered what my parents would say. My mother would understand; she was religious. Her father was a convert who took his faith quite seriously, and her brother, Charlie, was a priest. I would write to my Uncle Charlie and, with his help, be able to tell my mother and father.

Charlie wrote back with warm congratulations. I didn't wait for Thanksgiving vacation to tell my parents personally, but wrote to them right away. They reacted with considerable skepticism—they hadn't been aware of any exceptional piety in me. My father reminded me that I liked to have good times: I enjoyed dances, and I had often organized hikes and picnics in the colony. He felt he had been too sharp in insisting that I pursue a career other than flying, that he might have driven me to the convent. But nobody could have *driven* me to become a nun.

As for my mother, she just couldn't picture me as a nun. I was always ready to play jokes on people; I was stubborn; I just didn't have that demure, quiet aura she associated with nuns. But she finally accepted my decision.

I was very disappointed when Maryknoll suggested that I wait two years and in the meantime go to college or to work. I had made up my mind and I was ready right then. This was to be my first exercise in obedience. Dad, of course, was glad of Maryknoll's answer—he figured that in two years I would change my mind.

I didn't want my classmates to learn of my plans; the nuns at school, even less. I had seen the kind of attention other girls had received: a fawning deference that disgusted me. One was expected thereafter to be pious, demure, retiring. So I asked my parents to keep it a secret.

There was a strange blending inside me of calm decision, almost inevitability, and a sense of loss. I felt fine and noble having made up my mind to give my whole being to God, and there was adventure in the prospect of going someday to a faraway land to help people who needed me. But I dreaded losing the possibility of flying, and of meeting some exciting man and getting married. I wished sometimes that this calling from God would dissolve and leave me free.

During my senior year I won a scholarship to Webster College in St. Louis, Missouri, run by the Loretto nuns I had studied under in high school. It was like an extension of my high school experience: the classes, the boarding, the activities; we were treated as children, not adults. The next year I decided I would rather work while waiting to go to Maryknoll, especially since I felt that expenses would be too much for my father now that my sister was about to go to Loretto Academy high school. I became a gym teacher and part-time secretary back at Loretto.

I had begun to go steady with Luis, a Mexican boy, after graduation from high school—with some hesitation, because of my plans to enter the convent. I didn't tell Luis this, because I had decided there really was no problem: Ours was to be a passing relationship, nothing serious. Besides, I wanted to know more about boys, he was a terrific dancer, and a girl needed a date for most events.

My parents, though, objected to Luis. He lived in one of the houses outside the colony, and although they didn't say so in so many words, I sensed that they didn't consider him as belonging to "our class." They couldn't understand why I wanted to date if I were serious about becoming a nun. I wasn't in love with Luis, but we enjoyed being together. As the date for my leaving for Maryknoll approached, I had to tell him. At first, he didn't believe me; he argued with me, he tried to convince me not to go. I remember sitting on the porch at home one day and saying to him that I couldn't stand the prospect of some day setting up a home like one of those down the street: "How boring!" I didn't want to limit my love to one person. I wanted to be free to love many, many people.

In October 1949 I was assigned to the Novitiate training program in Valley Park, Missouri. It hurt saying good-by to Mom and Dad, to my sister and three small brothers. It hurt, too, to say good-by to Luis, who wanted to marry me. He had tears in his eyes and told me that he would wait for me to come back. I realized he had never accepted my determination to become a nun. In not convincing him, in having him feel that I returned his love, I had summoned forth his manhood;

and now, in rejecting him, I hurt him very deeply. I still regret that.

Dad gave me six months, said wire him and he would come to get me. I smiled—I knew how serious I was. Mother tried to seem happy. She said she was going to have my blue jeans framed, torn seat, faded knees, and all, because these were what reminded her most of me.

I loved Maryknoll; but the task of learning to be a nun was hard and exacting. We had to keep silent except during the few recreation periods. We learned to walk with downcast eyes. We reported our daily failings to the Superior. There was little we could do without asking permission. We studied and shared the work of the kitchen, the laundry, the sewing room. Several times a day we went to the chapel for prayers: Mass and meditation in the morning, the recitation of the divine office. We learned Gregorian chant and Church music. Although I put my whole heart and soul into these activities, they certainly didn't fill my hunger for adventure, and they took dogged determination. But all of us shared that dream of going to the missions. One of my heroes was Father Vincent Lebbe, a Belgian missionary to China. I wanted to be as dedicated and as hard a worker as he had been. And Father Jerry Donovan, a Maryknoller, had been a martyr. Maybe someday I'd be called on to give my life for Christ.

Although we were discouraged from making special friends with any individual sister, we were a happy group and enjoyed good times in sports, singing, long walks through the woods. But I distressed some of the older sisters. I walked like a sailor—couldn't I please try to be a lady? I was bossy—how could anyone live closely with such a person? I skipped and hopped—did I want to be called Sister Rabbit? I was hasty, I learned quickly and sometimes flaunted it—wasn't I aware of this, couldn't I show a little humility? But I was so charged with joy, for my life had meaning. Everything confirmed my direction and purpose, and I knew I was in touch with my real lifework.

At last, after two and a half years of novitiate training, *Marjorie* became *Sister Marian Peter*. Each of us was allowed to indicate three alternative names, one of which she would be given on the day we received the long gray tunics and black veils of Maryknoll nuns. The new names signified the new persons we had become. I was moved by my new name—St. Peter had been impulsive, generous, had made mistakes; he had loved Christ enough to die for Him head down on a cross. He would understand my need to be myself.

And so I took my vows, promising God poverty, chastity, and obedience for three years, after which the vows would be renewed for life. I was then assigned to the motherhouse in Maryknoll, New York, for two years of teachers college. I hadn't wanted to be a teacher; but then, I wasn't sure just what it was I *could* do as a missionary. My Superior said to me, "Go on to get your degree in teaching. It will be your door to many young people. Be a teacher." After studying at Maryknoll, I did my practice teaching at Corpus Christi School, on 115th Street in New York City.

In the spring of 1954 I was assigned to Guatemala, a new mission for the Maryknoll sisters, who had started a school in Guatemala City just the year before. My assignment came just after the overthrow of President Arbenz by Colonel Castillo Armas. Castillo Armas became a hero to me: He had achieved the near-impossible by liberating his country from Communism. Cardinal Spellman, in fact, had invited him to New York to receive an honorary degree of Doctor of Laws from Fordham University. I was thrilled to be going to an area where so much was happening, and I felt a joyous sense of special mission.

My practice teaching ended, I busied myself with obtaining the papers necessary to get into Guatemala. I also went shopping for clothes, because at that time sisters weren't permitted to wear their habits in Guatemala.

In August my visa came through, and I took a plane to

Guatemala City, where I was met by four sisters. Although they were in civilian clothes, I picked them out of the crowd immediately. They looked very American, and a bit dowdy, in their sober, long-sleeved, long-skirted dresses.

There were only five sisters in the convent—a good family number, especially after having lived as I had with two hundred and fifty sisters back at Maryknoll. We lived in Guatemala City in a house rented from a German family, away in Europe for a year. But as we entered the driveway and I saw my new home for the first time, I was astonished—and my excitement and joy at having arrived at my first mission were mixed with confusion: Was this to be the setting of the rugged missionary life I had dreamed about and prepared for during the past four and a half years? I wondered how we were supposed to live the poverty we had vowed. We even had two maids, Teresa and Olivia, to cook and clean so that we could be free to give our time to teaching and to our prayers. I was glad to speak Spanish again and felt at home with the maids right away.

I went to the cool, quiet room the sisters had prepared as a chapel. I knelt down to talk to Our Lord.

"Well," I said to Him, "You sure like to play tricks on me. You know I went to Maryknoll so that I could work with the poor in some God-forsaken place, and You go and bring me here—a fancy school where we teach English to little rich girls. This isn't being a missionary. Sure, I'll do it. And I'll do my best. But I'll be frank, Lord. I tell You right now I don't like Your idea of a joke."

After my prayer, I walked out of the house and into the garden. The profusion of flowers took my breath away. There were brilliantly red and yellow tropical *cucuyus*, delicately pink and white azalea bushes, roses, rows of snapdragons. Even the trees were blooming. There were some that looked like weeping willows with hanging red bottle brushes; one—called, appropriately enough, *llamarada*, "flame tree"—had branches

like sprouting flames. I gazed at all the tropical color and lush-
ness behind this beautiful house, and again I felt troubled. Yet
why should anything so lovely disturb me?

Through the trees I could see the four volcanoes on the
horizon surrounding Guatemala City. I felt something in myself rise in response to them. They seemed to hold a promise
and a hope that reached out to a secret yearning in me. Agua
rose in a perfect cone. Fuego smoked like an angry bull poised
to charge.

I was not certain if the wind I felt just then was inside me
or in the garden around me—or if there were any difference.
I had arrived in Guatemala, and this was my mission. I hoped
I could do great things here. I hoped I would love much.

IV

Whose Heaven,
Whose Earth?

The Priest San Miguel Acatán was a prize assignment. The town itself has only about a thousand inhabitants, but the parish covers more than twenty thousand souls spread throughout three municipal districts. Lying in the Cuchumatán mountains at an altitude of about 4,500 feet, the town is a five-hour ride by jeep or motorcycle from Huehuetenango. After twisting and turning over the mountain road that winds its way at times to a height of nearly thirteen thousand feet, one comes around a bend in the road, and there lies San Miguel. The climate at such an altitude is neither very hot nor very cold—it is this climate that has made Guatemala as a whole justly famous as "the land of eternal spring." The close-packed adobe houses with their white-washed walls and orange tile roofs line the narrow cobblestone streets and give the impression of having all been fitted into the three-sided valley with a shoehorn. The town seemed to sit on the mountain's lap, and I had the feeling that if Old Man Mountain ever wanted to stretch himself, all San Miguel would slide off his lap into the river a thousand feet below.

Above and below the town, hundreds of tiny, square, one-room huts cling to the sides of the mountains. These are usually made of poles plastered with mud and with roofs of straw, and it is obvious that their owners are not as well off as the people in town.

Besides having some of the best weather in the department,

33

the San Miguel parish is ninety-eight percent Indian. This I considered a blessing, since I had already picked up the prejudice of most of the Maryknollers working in Guatemala, preferring Indians to *ladinos*.

The Mayan Indian is a stoic and humble man who suffers much and complains little. He is also very religious and, though his expression of religious feeling mostly takes what we consider "superstitious" and "pagan" forms, he always holds the "padre" in such high respect that it borders on fear and awe. The *ladino*, on the other hand, looks down on the Indian and often shows contempt for him and even hatred, calling him *indio* in a context which implies "stupid" or "brute." *Ladinos* brag of their Spanish ancestry, whether or not they possess any, and they consider themselves guardians of Spanish traditions and civilization. They usually don't come near the church except for a baptism, marriage, or death, and many of them make little effort to hide their contempt for the missioners. They are by nature very polite, but much of our difficulty with them stemmed from the fact that we openly sided with the Indians against the exploitation that most *ladinos* practice against their less fortunate countrymen. We could see very little difference between the life styles of the two groups, other than the fact that the *ladinos* speak Spanish and their women wear Western dress. But these distinctions are enough to make them feel superior to the Indians and antagonistic toward the missioners. Still, where conflict between Indian and *ladino* did not exist, we found it relatively easy to get along with the *ladinos*.

In San Miguel, the two percent *ladino* population lived in town and owned most of the stores, ran the telegraph and post offices, taught school, and held the appointed municipal positions of secretary and treasurer, whereby they usually were able to manipulate the elected Indian mayor.

Father Jim Curtin was pastor at San Miguel, and I was to be his curate. He had the reputation of being a friendly man and an intelligent missioner. Standing about five feet ten and weighing over two hundred pounds, he didn't carry his weight very well and had a potbelly and round, droopy shoulders. He walked with a shuffle that barely raised his feet off the ground and never moved his arms, so that he had the appearance of being forever tired. He usually had a smile and some little observation for everyone he passed. His understanding of the Indian character was said to be unequaled. I considered myself fortunate to be working with a man who would obviously be a fine teacher.

I was assigned to the two outlying municipalities in the parish, San Rafael and San Sebastián. Each of these consists of a town of perhaps five hundred people together with ten smaller villages, called *aldeas*, populated by from fifty to five hundred people each. Altogether, there were some ten thousand people under my spiritual care, or about half the parish. These towns and villages were accessible only by horse or mule and visits to them entailed rides from the San Miguel center ranging from two to eight hours. My job was to visit both towns once a week and every village once a month, to hear confessions, celebrate Mass, perform baptisms and weddings, distribute communion, and teach Catholic doctrine. I also visited any sick person, anointing him with the holy oils, the Catholic sacrament for the dying; and I gave out medicine, stitched up machete wounds, pulled aching teeth, and tried to settle family squabbles that usually centered around mothers-in-law or the use of land privileges. For doctrine classes, a small five-hundred-watt, one-hundred-pound gasoline generator was lugged to the outlying villages on a catechist's back so that a projector might show slides about the life of Christ or some point of doctrine. Since there was no night life in these villages, a slide show was bound to bring out every ambulatory inhabitant in the area and afforded a golden opportunity for teaching some solid points of religion. Most of the Indians were not what we considered orthodox Catholics, though they themselves never agreed with that assessment. We called them "baptized pagans" and knew that some of them confided to each other that our insistence on Mass attendance and our campaigns against drinking were "protestant" practices.

The Spanish conquistadores had never really converted the Mayan Indians to Christianity, but had forced them nonetheless to take the Christian label. Now most of the Indians have a religion which is neither Mayan nor Catholic.

One Spanish priest, Fray Bartolomé de las Casas, worked intimately among the Indians at the time of the conquest and learned to respect their customs and beliefs. He later tried to intercede for them against the ruthless tactics of the conquistadores, but his compassion and insight did not prevail. Now, ironically, his face appears on Guatemalan coins.

Although the original Indian idols have been replaced by statues and pictures of Christian saints, the Indian attitudes toward them are little different from those they once held toward their original god-idols. In San Miguel, for instance, the name of the god that was supposed to have created their town is now long forgotten; today the founding of their town and the creation of their world are attributed to a picture of St. Michael—not the invisible presence of St. Michael, but the old picture itself. It has no relation whatsoever to St. Michael the Archangel except in the origin of the name. There is also a statue of St. Michael, of more recent origin; but because of the age difference, it is not only considered less powerful than the picture but constitutes a completely different deity.

To many of the Indians, Christian baptism is simply a substitute for an ancient pre-Columbian rite that was once performed by a local prayer-leader or Indian priest, called a *chimán*. A *chimán* is to some extent comparable to a witch doctor in other tribal cultures, being called on to cure sicknesses of supposedly supernatural origin. He will seldom baptize children now, unless there is a problem getting a priest to do it. But in former times, he would take the newborn child to a *fuente*, a virginal spring which ran right up out of the earth and near which no woman was allowed to go. The child was washed in the spring, and this bath changed the child from an animal to a human being. Essentially, the Indians still have the same concept: When the child is given a name in baptism, he ceases to be a thing and becomes a person.

Priests sometimes tried to take advantage of the Indians' sense of urgency about baptism in order to reach the people. We knew that, according to Indian belief, the couple chosen as the infant's *madrina* and *padrino* (godmother and godfather) were often closer to the child than others with blood ties. We would insist that parents and especially godparents, who were assuming spiritual responsibility for the young child's soul, come to catechism classes. They would therefore attend two or three days of classes, sitting stoically through the lessons, largely indifferent to what was being taught: If we were foolish enough to force them to go through such motions for the changing of a child from a thing to a person, then they would do as we insisted. The catechism lessons were usually taught by an Indian who knew both the local dialect and the articles of faith in Spanish. We punched cards for each person as a means of checking on his class attendance. I was unable at the time to see that this forced and mechanical approach to the teaching of Christian truths was hardly more meaningful than simply performing a baptism or celebrating a Mass for anyone who wanted it, with no questions asked.

Jim Curtin had more understanding of the Indian mind and customs than most of the other missioners and never indulged in such teaching by rote. He had obtained a working knowledge of the Indian language, K'anjobal, and inspired me to study it myself. Many of the priests felt the unwritten Indian languages to be beyond their abilities and contented themselves with their acquisition of an imperfect Spanish. Curtin translated the "Our Father," the "Hail, Mary," and the Apostle's Creed into K'anjobal, along with twenty-five basic catechism questions. However, the Maryknoll Superior, Father Hugo Gerbermann, condemned this, saying that none of us knew the Indian dialects very thoroughly and so we couldn't be certain we were translating the prayers correctly. Suppose, God forbid, we were teaching conceptions that were not even Christian?

We had, anyway, to try to teach the catechism in Spanish and to see that the people memorized the questions and answers. They might not know the meaning of the Spanish words, but they could say them and were thus assured of salvation. Hadn't I learned prayers in Latin that I didn't understand? You simply have to *say* them; it's not important whether you comprehend them. It was rather like a Tibetan prayer wheel.

One day a woman came in to take part in a baptism as a *madrina*. I insisted she learn the catechism questions: "You promised last time you'd learn the catechism. You didn't learn it. I'm not going to give the baptism this time unless you do."

She became angry. How could I deny the child a name because of its godmother's failure to learn some Spanish words? She went to the mayor to complain. The mayor was Indian, and for the Indians, religion is a way of life inseparable from politics.

The mayor called me over to his office and insisted I baptize the child. When I replied that I didn't tell him how to perform his mayoral duties, he looked at me as if I were from another planet. What I failed to understand was that the mayor's responsibilities extended to all the concerns of his fellow Indians—as leader, he was as much a spiritual father as a political elder. But the conceptual categories of my own culture filtered reality before it entered my consciousness, so that I saw separation where he saw indivisible connections.

Finally, the mayor flatly demanded that I perform the baptism. Meanwhile, the father of the child had gotten drunk. When he returned to the mayor's office and found that I was still refusing to baptize his child, he shoved me in the chest. I knocked him down right there and stormed out.

I went back to the rectory, leaving behind a stunned silence.

I was angry at the father and the godmother for their lack of respect for the Church and doctrine I represented, and furious with myself for having lost my temper. They did not come back to me, but went to another priest and told him they were members of his parish to get him to baptize their child. This sort of thing happened quite often, even though it was against the Church's canon law for a priest to baptize anyone from outside the boundaries of his own parish.

I was determined that these people were going to learn about Catholicism and that I was going to save their souls in spite of themselves, even if I had to knock people down or get killed myself in the process. I had the special mission of taking God's undiluted word to the heathen. They *would* hear me, and I would settle for nothing less. For I was convinced that most of the Indians, even those who took part in Catholic services but who did not learn the teachings in the catechism, were in peril of everlasting hellfire. I thought I had no right to compromise on questions of faith and that I had to insist, before giving the Eucharist or before baptizing a baby, that all the participants—and most certainly the parents and godparents in baptism—study the catechism.

But I never felt superior to the Indians. I visited them, talked with them, ate as they ate, enjoyed their company, and liked them very much. It was only on religious questions that I was inflexible.

The Indians had their own traditional marriage rituals, and if and when they chose to be married in church, the priests took this as a clear sign of actual conversion from the Indian religion to the Catholic faith. The conversion would then be sustained by weekly attendance at Mass and by the reception of Holy Communion, acts of faith that often entailed a walk of four to five hours from an outlying village to the center parish.

When an Indian or an Indian couple showed interest in the Church, either by joining or by getting married by a priest, we required them to burn their familial pagan cult objects.

Like their dress and language, both these objects and the Indians' ritual practices varied from village to village. But the most common pagan symbol, ironically enough, was a cross, representing the four wind-directions, and hence the four points where stood the Four Earth-bearers who sustained the world. A day in honor of one of the Earth-bearers, each in turn, was celebrated every five days—an Indian week. A month was twenty days.

When a couple married in the Indian faith, the *chimán* would help them choose a special tree for wood to make their cross. They would place it in their home. When they died, their spirits were believed to invest the cross, and their children would venerate it as the sacred abiding place of their ancestors. For a young couple to burn the cross was considered by the rest of the community to be a complete break with the past and an insult to their parents' spirits.

The priest in one village allowed Indians who took part in church services to keep their pagan crosses. He said it was too much trouble and not really necessary to have them burned. Other priests claimed he was trying to build up his attendance statistics by not requiring the people to make a clean break.

Since many priests did not bother to learn the Indian dialects of their parishes, they often could not understand what was being told them in confession. But I had studied K'anjobal, and as a result could do quite well at hearing confessions in the native tongue.

I would sometimes get angry because often the Indians I heard in confession told me only their sicknesses. "Don't tell me your sicknesses, tell me your sins!" I would insist.

But the Indians believed that sickness was a result of sin— more often than not, some transgression of ritual propriety: Perhaps a man hadn't walked around a house three times before entering when a sick person was inside; perhaps he hadn't said a prayer and burned incense before planting; perhaps his parents had done something, known or unknown, years before, that he was being held accountable for now that his parents were dead. It was difficult for an Indian to keep always in mind the manifold obligations and rituals he was supposed to carry out, and so he might not even know the sin he was being punished for. To confess a sickness, therefore, was to confess the sin, whatever it might be, that had caused the sickness.

I had no comprehension of such values. The Indians were guided by their own customs, taught by their own pagan spiritual leaders; but I wanted to save their souls according to *our* rules and regulations, as prescribed in Europe or the United States a hundred or five hundred or a thousand years ago by men of a vastly different culture. Why did my parishioners refuse to see that it was these rules and regulations that were the only true means of salvation?

In one of my first months in San Miguel, we recorded more than five thousand communions. Father Curtin was very proud. But some of the priests took a more jaundiced view: "We're nothing but sacramental gasoline station attendants," one said to me. I was hurt, and I thought about this; but I felt I was saving souls, and I persisted.

We could never be sure what we were getting across to the Indians when we told them that reception of Holy Communion meant partaking of the body and blood of Christ. We didn't know what they really thought, nor did we have any way of finding out. However, I could not buy the concept, held by some priests, that inducing such sacramental reception was simply swapping one set of superstitions for another.

Besides the view of ourselves as dispensers of God's mysteries, many of us had another image that was more human, less spiritual, and almost a contradiction to the first: The missioner is a tough guy. A priest who could go out for eight days, eat what the people could spare him from their own near-starvation rations, smoke cigars, ride horseback for hours, and cuss, whether or not he turned up many catechumens, heard many confessions, or married many couples—he was tough.

Since the Indians knew no English, we felt free to use foul language without worrying about being overheard or considered vulgar. I saw no contradiction in my insisting on Catholic ritual being practiced to the letter by poor Indians, while I developed a vocabulary that would have stunned the faithful back home. That was not the point. We had to be John Waynes, doing he-man things. Sometimes the Indians who worked around the rectory would make direct quotes from one priest or another, always with an accent, but the intonation and intent of the original expletives were unmistakably accurate. We comforted ourselves with the thought that the men could have no notion of what they were saying.

I would celebrate 5 a.m. Mass on Sunday; ride a horse for two hours to San Sebastián to hear confessions, say another Mass, and give out communion; ride a horse to San Rafael, two or three more hours away for more confessions, another Mass, and more communions, usually ending by 8 p.m. John Wayne had nothing on me. He certainly, in any case, never got the satisfaction I gained from my work. Nor would he ever labor with a people so friendly and secure in themselves and in their beliefs as the Maya Indians.

Inwardly, even then, I was already beginning to question the premises of much of what we were doing; but outwardly I was becoming a seasoned missioner—held in some affection by the people for whom I worked, grudgingly respected by the priests with whom I lived, and thoroughly enjoying the fruits of my own labor. I had much to learn.

V

A Teacher Begins
to Learn

The Nun   When I first arrived in Guatemala, I heard many stories and rumors about the atrocities the Communists were supposed to have committed before being thrown out by Colonel Castillo Armas.

We were visited one day at our school, Colegio Monte María, by Señora Ibárgüen, a member of one of Guatemala's wealthiest and most socially prominent families. "Can you imagine?" she began to complain. "Now President Castillo Armas is going to tax us more to pay his liberation army."

"But he did overthrow a Communist government, didn't he?" I asked. "It's only fair that you pay him now."

"Oh, he doesn't need our taxes. He receives American money to pay his expenses. No matter who is in power, we who have shown initiative in economic matters are always the ones victimized."

"How do you mean?" I asked.

"Under Arbenz, we were on the verge of having our estates taken away. You weren't here yet."

"Did he really take away lands?"

"Yes. That was the worst of his actions. He confiscated thousands of acres from the United Fruit Company."

"That must have been a tremendous loss—all those banana plantations!" I sympathized.

"Well, no. The lands he took were actually in reserve. But," she hastened to add, "the cultivated lands were next, I'm certain."

I began to feel a little anxious. I wanted to be reassured that the Communist Arbenz was as evil as I had been led to suppose.

"Still," I said, "that was terrible, taking land away like that. You can't serve justice by distributing land to the peasants with one hand while stealing those same lands with the other."

"It wasn't really stealing," she acknowledged. "Arbenz paid for the land in government bonds. But he paid only the declared value. You know how we do that here. In order not to pay too high a tax, you declare the value of your property at a low price. Well, he used that legalism as an excuse and paid United Fruit much less than the property was worth. And what with property values going up!"

Misgivings began to arise in my mind. The actions of Arbenz as described by Señora Ibárgüen actually sounded right to me. I dared not say so. But, I kept reminding myself, the Communists had tortured those who opposed them.

Señora Ibárgüen interrupted my silent questions.

"You know, I think the greatest fright of my life was last June, two days before Arbenz was defeated. All the ravines around the city were crowded with peasants armed with machetes. They were awaiting Arbenz's orders, ready to march into our streets. We'd all be dead if Colonel Castillo Armas hadn't come and defended us."

"Did he march on the city?" I asked her.

"No, it wasn't necessary. By the time he reached Chiquimula, Arbenz had conceded defeat. The bombing by the *sulfatos* helped a lot." She giggled, then grew very serious again.

"What are *sulfatos?*"

"Small planes flown by gringos. They strafed the peasants and dropped bombs. They called the planes 'farts' because they gave people the runs."

"It seems to me," I observed, "that it took mighty little military strength to defeat those people."

"Our liberation wasn't really due to military power. That's why I resent their taxing us now. It was thanks to our Archbishop, Monseñor Rossell. He's a saint. He carried *El Cristo de Esquipulas*, the miraculous Black Christ, in procession through the villages and towns of eastern Guatemala. He preached that the Black Christ wouldn't return to the capital until the country was set free from the atheistic domination of the evil Communist government. Everyone, rich and poor, rallied behind him. Actually he only used a replica of the statue that is kept in the cathedral here in the City. The original is in Esquipulas. The people have a great devotion to their Black Christ. Really, the Archbishop saved us."

I admired the courage and decisiveness of Monseñor Rossell. He did not just preach, he acted. I was also proud of the help our United States ambassador, John Peurifoy, had given Guatemala. I did not dream that another United States ambassador would later directly interfere with my life and work here.

The school year ended in October, and I wondered about a vacation. I wanted action, not rest. Sister Martina assigned Sister Ana María and me to work for two months in an Indian village, Jacaltenango, at the invitation of the Maryknoll Fathers. I had heard about Jacaltenango—it was a mission Maryknoll had established deep in the mountains in the department of Huehuetenango. No sisters had ever been there before.

This was my idea of mission work. Flying from Guatemala City to Huehuetenango, we passed over Quezaltenango, an area of a thousand scattered huts on green matted hills. A row of volcanoes stretched into the clouds.

At the grass runway we were met by Father John Lenahan, who lent us each a pair of trousers, which we wore under our long skirts for the horseback ride. First, we had a four-hour ride in a pickup truck. Father Reymann and Sister Ana María were in the cab up front with Father Lenahan, while I rode in back under the canvas top with Father John Breen and three Indians who had asked for a lift. Father Breen looked like a marine, with his crew cut and his square jaw. He puffed incessantly on a cigar. He spoke to me, but I was too busy holding on to make more than snatches of talk. We seemed to be whirling along the highest rim of the earth.

After hours of fighting off car sickness, I was glad to mount a horse. The trail ran through steep mountains and over rough bridges that spanned crashing rapids. Four hours later, we saw the tiny huts, mud-brown and lime-white, of the far-off village. The view was overpowering; but I was so worn out I could hardly enjoy it.

In Jacaltenango I was plunged into an Indian world, a shoe-less world, where Spanish was almost a foreign language. The work was good. The people were elemental, sincere, full of unsophisticated love, generous in their gratefulness—so different from the worldly-wise and patronizing attitudes of the rich people of Guatemala City.

We taught catechism and played with the children. Sister Ana María taught songs to the choir while I sewed vestments and altar cloths. The girls laughed at my attempts to learn their Indian language because I couldn't imitate some of the sounds. I wanted to stay there forever.

On our way home from the assignment, Father Breen said, "You sisters aren't doing missionary work. That's easy living you have in the City in that fancy school with all the comforts of home. Up here in the back country is where you're needed."

"Yes," I came back, "all this is hard. But it's not so bad when the people are receptive and loving and look up to you. You should try it with the city people—rich, aloof, used to having their own way without thinking about you. Try to get under *their* skin. I think physical discomfort is easier to take than the psychological pressure of people's indifference."

"Well," he answered, "that's the way you feel after a short visit here. It might be different if you made the rounds of villages for a week, riding in the rain, talking with uneducated people months on end. No entertainment, no distractions but reading."

"Believe me, I'd love to try," I assured him, "but you've given me a new reason to return to the City and work there. You can encourage the Indians and help educate them. Yet, if the politicians and plantation owners who live down in the capital don't see the need and begin to help, the Indians will always be exploited and held down. I'm going to work for them from the other end—with the young girls who are the future wives of politicians and wealthy landowners."

In trying to answer Father Breen, I had clarified my own purpose. Working in the City with the comforts of civilization didn't appeal to me as much as the physically exacting work in the mountains. But I realized that missionary work wasn't supposed to be what is more personally satisfying, but rather what is more effective for the good of people. I didn't have to be ashamed any longer of the comfortable life in the City.

VI

A Share of
Infallibility

The Priest After a year in San Miguel, I was assigned
to San Pedro Soloma, and Jim Curtin was
given another assistant. Father Hugo (Tex) Gerbermann, our
Maryknoll Superior, had come up to San Miguel shortly before yearly assignments of language school graduates and had
asked me about going to Soloma as John Breen's assistant. I
assured him that such an assignment would please me very
much, since Breen represented in many ways the kind of
missioner I wanted to be. He was a controversial topic of
conversation for everyone on the mission; you couldn't be
neutral about him.

John Breen stood about five feet ten and weighed perhaps
160 pounds, none of it soft. His face was angular, with a
jutting chin, sharp nose, and protruding cheekbones, and his
light-brown hair was close-cropped in a military cut. His blue
eyes took in everything; and when he spoke to you, he looked
straight into your eyes as if he were reading your mind. He
often had the stub of a cigar clamped between his teeth, and
his language was a match for any sailor's. Overall he gave an
impression of hard-working, no-nonsense determination, and
of a willingness to scrap, verbally or physically, with anyone.

There were many stories about his exploits, which he enjoyed recounting himself. Once, taking a sledge hammer, he
had completely demolished a wood shack used as a meat market which had been built on church property without his

permission. He was also known to have manhandled more than one anticlerical *ladino,* and his mission trips into the mountains for weeks on end with no more supplies than the clothes on his back were almost legendary. He expressed his opinions openly on everyone and everything, a quality that endeared him to a few but antagonized many.

I had met Father Breen only once or twice, but I liked him. I had become somewhat disillusioned with Jim Curtin, as I had discovered that his friendliness was merely a cover for insecurity and that his missionary activity was greatly limited by a lack of endurance that bordered on weakness. He was very sensitive and often took our parishioners' lack of religiosity as a personal insult. Every problem, big or small, sent him reeling, and he would sit in the great armchair in his room and gasp for air as if he had asthma. When the local musicians insisted on playing their marimbas near church during a service, he went out and took their playing sticks away from them and then worried for hours over the coming confrontation. Every few days, the pressures would get too much for him, and he would go to Guatemala City for a rest. Soon he was only at the mission on weekends.

After a year of attempting to cover Father Curtin's half of the parish in his absences, as well as ministering to my own half, I jumped at the chance to go with John Breen.

Soloma sits in a valley surrounded on all sides by high mountains, about two and a half hours by jeep from San Miguel. Often trapped under a cloud cover, the town is colder and wetter than the surrounding area, and the altitude, over seven thousand feet, makes the cold more biting. The houses are of the same pole-and-adobe construction as in San Miguel but are not as tightly packed together. In the Soloma area there is none of the special clay needed to make roof tiles; the materials used instead are straw and wooden shingles, both of which soon turn black, adding to the gloomy atmosphere of the town.

Soloma is larger than San Miguel, with perhaps fifteen

hundred people in the town and more than ten thousand throughout the parish. The language and dress are similar, but the variations are unmistakable. Soloma's *ladino* population is much more numerous than San Miguel's and also more aggressive.

Father John seemed happy to have me as an assistant, and I was pleased, because I knew his standards to be exacting. He had gone to Soloma only the previous year and was still in the process of remaking the parish's spiritual life. He told me that at least one of his predecessors, and probably two of them, had permitted the Indians to practice their pagan customs and receive the Church's sacraments at the same time. He was convinced that such leniency on the part of the priests was due to their interest in improving the statistics of confessions, communions, and marriages that we had to send to the local bishop and to Maryknoll, in New York, every year.

The pagan cross was the great bone of contention in Soloma. John's predecessors had performed weddings for hundreds of couples without insisting that they burn their family crosses, as was required in all the surrounding parishes. When John came, he set a time limit within which everyone had to burn his cross, or his whole family would be excluded from confession and communion. There was much resentment over his edict, and cries that "the other padres didn't make us burn our crosses" were heard from all sides. John tried to ease matters by rewarding all who complied with a big picture of the Sacred Heart of Jesus, which he himself placed in the house with a special blessing. It was accepted grudgingly at first; but as time went on, more families began to comply.

Confessions and communions dropped off at the beginning of his campaign, but after a time they began to climb again: 4,500, 5,000, 6,000—each month the number increased. John said he wasn't interested in numbers, but there was no other way to measure the spiritual life of the parish, and we were there to make converts and to save souls. We hoped the people knew what they were doing when they received the sacraments. We told ourselves that they did.

Despite my qualms about the nature of the Indians' faith, I enjoyed being with these people; I cared about them—it didn't matter if they were dirty or if I was dirty, whether they smelled bad or if I did, whether I was comfortable or not. But even as my respect for the Indians deepened, I felt threatened by their approach to God. They had any number of rituals for pleasing God, for getting good crops, for warding off sickness. I tried almost desperately to stop the practices that I considered rank superstition; I wanted to teach them new rituals for reaching God, some that were not very different from their own.

Sometimes I was met with: "You have your way, we have ours."

At other times, they would object: "What's the difference?"

I found myself occasionally raising the question in my own mind: "What *is* the difference?" The line was not easy to draw. The difficulty lay in distinguishing where pagan worship began and Catholic worship ended. For example, an Indian was considered a pagan if he burned a fistful of candles before a statue, because the pagans believed that the candles were food that the statue-god consumed through fire. But burning only one candle before a statue was acceptable, a custom practiced by Catholics all over the United States. Yet what was meant by it? Incense burned by priests at Mass was all right; for the Indians to do it was superstitious. What was the difference?

Father Breen was responsible for another village, San Juan Ixcoy, half an hour from Soloma by jeep. The two towns were very similar, although San Juan was much smaller, with six hundred people living in the town, five thousand on the surrounding hillsides, and only two *ladino* families. But unlike the inhabitants of all the other towns in the area, the people of San Juan Ixcoy wanted nothing whatever to do with orthodox Catholicism, beyond the baptism of their children. Two priests had spent a year apiece in San Juan, but had converted no one. Four marriages had been performed, but all four couples had relapsed into paganism—if indeed they had ever given it up.

One day, Father John said to me: "Why don't you go over and see if you can break San Juan Ixcoy?" I was challenged by Breen's confidence. He was a priest's priest, a tough man. Here was my chance to prove myself.

When I went to live and work in San Juan Ixcoy, I observed some disquieting things. In the church, 150-year-old Mass vestments were still being used by the *chimanes*, as were ancient chalices and ciboriums. I considered this sacrilegious. There were some seventy ancient statues in the church, most of which looked as if they belonged in a museum—some were missing limbs, some had no heads. I noticed that different groups of people knelt to different statues. I wondered just what their prayers meant to them, and how they related to the Catholic saints to whose statues they prayed.

Out in front of the church, there was a great wooden cross. Termites and dampness had rotted it nearly through at ground level, yet still it stood. But it was not a Christian symbol—it carried no image of the crucified Christ nor did it represent Christ's death; it was a pagan emblem, right at the very door of the church.

There was an oven in the middle of the church floor. On special occasions, the Indians would kill a chicken and burn its blood, along with incense, as a sacrificial offering.

I wondered what to do. Why was this pueblo holding out? Why did the people not come in to be married in the church?

John and I decided that the problem lay chiefly with the *brujos*, the witch doctors, whose strength was such that those who no longer believed in the old ways were afraid of reprisals by neighbors. If the rains came late, a majority of the people blamed the Catholics. San Juan or San Pedro is angry, they would murmur. Someone might even kill a Catholic who was foolhardy enough to flaunt his disrespect for the ancestral ways by failing to practice the ancient *costumbres*.

How did the witch doctors terrorize the people? In this connection, it is important to understand a crucial distinction in the kinds of psychic control exercised by Indian religious leaders, a distinction that is not dissimilar to that in tribal communities in other, widely separate parts of the world. The *brujo* is a practitioner of evil spells and can curse the kinsmen, livestock, crops, or life of an individual who strays from the fold. The *chimán*, or medicine man, is the one who heals, who names children after washing them in the virginal spring, who helps choose the crosses and other symbols of faith and health and good fortune. The *brujo* masters the secrets of night-darkness and inner mystery; the *chimán* is special child of the sun, of light and openness. Nonetheless, both powers might often be joined in the same person—as, for example, in a conflict between two enemies, when one man's *chimán* might act as *brujo* to the other man.

The manner of a man's becoming a *chimán* differs from town to town, but usually he does so by proclaiming publicly that he has received a "call" from God. Then he finds a *chimán* willing to teach him the rituals and the practices, including the uses of special medicines. A *brujo* is most often a man declared to be such by his or her neighbors, and this characterization may be the result of a harsh disposition, some physical deformity, or a number of unfortunate coincidences that can be related to the given individual.

New village leaders are elected every year, including a priest-mayor—the *alcalde rezador*—the top man in San Juan's hierarchy of authority. He is elected by the town elders; and though his authority is not recognized by the central Guatemalan government, it is accepted by all the people. For them he takes precedence over the civil mayor, who himself, in practice, recognizes the priest-mayor's superior authority. When I was in San Juan, the civil mayor was better educated than the *alcalde rezador*, and did not believe in all the Indian *costumbres;* yet he was expected to take part in many of the traditional rites and ceremonies and in fact held his own authority by virtue, not of representing the civil government, but of his participation in the Indian religious hierarchy. He was afraid to buck old customs, which had behind them all the force of ancestral loyalty and tribal trust. Anyone who broke with the old practices was seen as a betrayer of his people or at least as in contempt of the powerful *chimanes* and *brujos.*

Back there in the Cuchumatán mountains, the laws reflect what the people believe and want. The central government is not represented except by a resident of the region itself. Therefore, although I was a priest, I couldn't get the keys to the front door of the church. The local Indian leaders—to whom San Juan and San Pedro were gods, not Catholic saints —held the keys, and sometimes the people would stay in the church all night, performing rites of their own.

The rectory, however, opened directly into the church through a door to which I alone had keys.

Finally, after sizing up the situation for two or three months, I told the leaders that I was *jefe* (boss) of the church and would close it around 6 p.m. I felt it was time to begin to assert my authority as appointed representative of the Catholic Church. The people disagreed, but the first time I went down to Huehuetenango city for supplies, I bought a new lock. One night, after the people had closed the church and gone home, I broke off the old lock and put the new lock, to which I alone had keys, on the inside of the main door. Then I returned to the rectory through the inner door.

Next morning, when the people found the church locked from the inside, they didn't like it. But there was nothing they could do about it, as they had no way of getting at my lock. I tried to make the new opening and closing times correspond as closely as possible to the former hours and left the church open all night on special occasions in order not to antagonize them. Nonetheless, I controlled the closings and openings of the church doors and thus began to build up my authority on religious matters.

My next action did not go as smoothly. After another month had passed, I went into the church one night and took a sledge hammer to the adobe oven in the center of the nave. A carpenter came in and built some benches across the church to fill the space where the oven had been.

When the people saw that their oven was gone, they complained to the civil mayor, who called me in for an explanation. I told him that we needed benches for Mass, and that the oven had been in the way.

The mayor stared at me—probably wondering whether I was a fool or took him for one. In a culture where people didn't use chairs but sat on the ground or squatted on their haunches, to speak of the necessity for benches was obviously a fabrication. Neither he nor the people were convinced, and he told me they might have to remove the benches and replace the oven.

I warned the mayor that if they did so, I could complain to the governor, who might send in troops in support of Mother Church. I wonder now if I realized fully what I was saying, or thought it right that the Church could depend on the state to uphold its authority. My actions and arguments certainly indicated that I knew my own authority finally rested on that connection.

Thus we went at it. I refused to yield: The benches were not removed, the oven was not rebuilt. The people fought back: Three women and a man accused me before the civil mayor of having deliberately kicked one of the women while she was praying in church. I was surprised that the mayor paid any attention to such a patently false accusation, making me answer the charges. I did so by demanding that the witnesses be separated; then I showed that their stories conflicted as to time, exact place, and chronology. The mayor laughed and dismissed us all. I didn't know whether he had taken part in trumping up the charges, but I realized I could not trust him very far.

After a few weeks, the open anger over the disappearance of the oven abated, and people began greeting me again in the streets. But under the surface, there was resentment.

Next, I began removing some of the old statues, because I felt that, in their ruined condition, they played a superstitious, even fetishistic, role. The first night I took three or four of the more decrepit statues, without heads or limbs, and hid them in the attic above the rectory. I hoped no one would notice their disappearance.

However, people *did* notice. Different groups of worshippers were in charge of various statues, and even the broken ones were considered sacred. When people asked me what had happened to this saint or that saint, I said I didn't know where they were or who had taken them. They knew only I would *dare* to touch them, but what could they do? The statues were gone.

I had no problem justifying my denial. I had learned in my seminary classes of what Thomistic theology calls a "mental reservation"—which only means that the whole truth need not be revealed to one who has no "right" to that truth. Thus, what I was actually replying to their question was: "As far as your rights are concerned, I did not touch those statues." And the Indians, though they had never studied Thomistic theology, understood me well enough. For in their world, where the natural and supernatural constantly interact, the nature of reality is complex, subtle, ever-shifting. The perception of reality, therefore, may readily vary from one person to the next; truth is in the mind of the beholder. Americans pride themselves on being more scientific, more objective; but I think that, in terms of how we relate to one another, we are not very far from this Indian concept.

I shall never know the prayers said against me, the spells placed on my name, or the people's anguish and amazement that I should continue to survive and to prevail in my sacrilege against their beliefs. I was to get a certain inkling, however, when it came time to elect a new priest-mayor. For, after the election, the new mayor announced publicly that I would be dead within twenty days—by the end of his first Indian month as mayor. He was going to launch a campaign to induce God to get rid of me because of what I was doing.

In fifteen days, word came to me that he was dead. He was just an old man, and he died. The thought did occur to me, fleetingly, that he was punished by God for his arrogance, but I dismissed such an idea as rank presumption on my part. The Indians, however, do not believe in coincidences. Their new priest-mayor's death, coming so soon on the heels of his pronouncement against me, frightened them, and they were convinced that my power was stronger.

In a week or so, some young people began to study Catholic doctrine. They agreed to burn their pagan symbols. The four couples who had been married by previous curates there, then had later relapsed, came back to the Church.

My confidence grew, and Father Breen encouraged me. I removed more of the old statues until there were only twelve of the more important ones left. I repaired these and fixed up the church. Many of the people were angry with me, but more came around to begin studying doctrine. In my first year and a half, forty couples were married in the Church.

One night I was sitting in the rectory conversing with five or six young Indians, unmarried men with little else to do at night, who often came over to talk. Some of them were studying doctrine and visited me because I had a gasoline engine for electric light. As we sat around talking, skyrockets suddenly started going off.

"What's that noise?" I asked.

"Well, tonight's the changing of the *caja real*."

"What? What's the *caja real*?"

"Oh, just a box where they keep all the old books of the church."

"Where they keep—where is it?"

"My father has it at our house."

"Your father has it?"

The youth nodded. He was one of the Indians who had made his first communion in the Church, then had relapsed, but had recently returned.

"How come you never told me about it?"

"You never asked me, Padre. We had to keep special candles burning all year for the special spirits inside it. Anyone who opens the box or looks inside will die."

"You believe in all that?"

"Of course I don't believe in that."

"Well, how come you had it in your house?"

"It's my father—it was his turn to take care of it."

"How do you think we can get it back?"

"Get it back? Aiiee, Padre! There are fifteen or twenty men down there. They've been drinking. At midnight, they are going to transfer the box to another man's house for his family to take care of for a year."

"Then now's the time to take it back."

"Take it back to where?"

"It belongs to the church. Your father is friendly. It will be easier to do tonight."

I looked around at the youths: "Let's go get it back!"

They were frightened. Two of them ran off, but three young men, including the one at whose house the books had been kept, stayed with me. The others who remained were in their teens. They said, if I would get the box, they would help me carry it away.

I said I would go into the house, open the box, and bring out an armful of books at a time for each of them to carry.

"Run when you get your armful," I told them. "Then put them in the rectory and leave. The older people mustn't know you've helped me."

The young fellows were nervous, but they agreed to go down

to the house with me. I wore my priest's cassock to emphasize my authority. I wanted to show the Indians that they didn't have to worry about such rites as taking care of books and keeping candles lit to ward off evil spirits. Besides, the books belonged in the church.

As we approached the house in the dark, we heard the men chanting inside. We could hear clearly now and then a *"Jesu-cristo . . ."* or a *"Comam Dios San Juan . . ."*

I went inside. The young men waited out in the darkness. There were about fifteen older men in the house—the town elders. Each held a burning candle. They had been drinking, as is customary at religious feasts. I began to worry that I might have taken on more than I could handle. But I knew it was too late to back out.

Aloud, I said, "Good evening, Señores."

They all stared at me, but only Pascual, the young man's father, answered me: "Good evening, Padre."

He looked ashamed. None of the other men spoke.

"I hear you have books that belong to the church."

Still no answer. I plunged ahead: "You people have been wonderful. You've taken care of the church's books all these centuries. Now that you have a priest again, these books belong back in the church. When your ancestors used to have a priest, the books stayed in the church. When the priest had to leave, back in the time of the Independence, the Fathers turned over all these things to your ancestors."

Still no word from the fifteen Indian elders.

"I'd like very much for you to give me these books, for they belong in the church."

This monologue, with pregnant pauses, went on for about five minutes, still with no reply.

Then I opened the cover of the box. A great gasp went up; the men didn't know whether I would die or whether they would die. This was sacrilege beyond belief. The atmosphere in that small house grew explosive.

59

I picked up one of the books and unwrapped the kerchief around it. The book was handwritten and was dated around 1750. It was signed by a Spanish priest.

The men faced me, but their eyes seemed almost glazed, as if they were trying to disappear—or were hoping desperately that I would.

I spoke again, my voice constricted: "As a priest of the Holy Church, I thank you for these books."

I picked up about five of them. Each was wrapped in a scarf the size of a kitchen towel. I carried the books outside and handed them to one of the youths hiding in the bushes. He ran off up the hill with them.

I returned, took out another armful, carried them to a second youth. Then a third armful to the last young man. All the books were gone, and I returned to the house to give the boys time to get away. Still no one said a word or even gave a sign of hearing what I was saying. In a few minutes, with an elaborate *"Buenas noches,"* I walked out of the house and began climbing the hill to the rectory. I was about half-way up, walking, when I heard a terrible scream—a man's anguished and desperate cry. The spell was broken. I ran the remaining distance in about three minutes.

When I reached the rectory, the young fellows were waiting for me. "Get the hell out of here! I don't know what's going to happen," I told them. They took off.

About an hour later, I heard a knock on the door of the rectory. Several of the older men stood there. They were still drunk, and crying. They asked me for the books.

I explained again that the books now had to stay in the church. They hesitated and then turned silently and walked off into the night.

I never found out exactly what happened during the rest of that night; but from that time on, I could never be certain they weren't planning revenge.

The next day, the civil mayor and about twenty-five or thirty people came to the rectory. Intellectually the mayor was above the others. He knew that behind me were both the civil authority and the Church and that he was responsible to them for my safety. Still, he was also responsible to his own pueblo. I explained patiently but firmly to him that he would have to make it clear to the people that the books belonged in the church but that they were still in the pueblo—still, really, in the care of the villagers.

They went away. The *chimanes* and the elders were furious. Yet, a few weeks later, still more people came to study the doctrine of the Church.

In the meantime, I had set up a clinic in one of the rooms of the rectory, where I gave out aspirin, administered injections of penicillin, and pulled hundreds of teeth. I distributed powdered milk to the sick, the elderly, and nursing mothers. I also established a small merchandising cooperative for sending some of the local potato crop to the capital for sale. All these things created goodwill among a sizable number of people. The couples that had been married in the Church since my arrival were solidly behind me, though they sometimes worried about how far the elders would let me go. I thought that many others, though not agreeing openly with what I was doing, would be on my side or at least neutral in any showdown.

I was counting on my understanding of the Indian way of thinking to avoid any such showdown. There was much hatred toward me, and, although I greeted one and all, the majority of the people would not return my greetings, often turning their backs to me as I passed them on the trails. Still, I hoped that I could break down this attitude a little at a time.

My next undertaking was to knock over the great pagan cross in front of the church and replace it with a crucifix.

When a man from another culture and another faith interferes with the religious symbols and practices of a people in their own home territory, it is as if he is trying to shift the earth on its axis. And when any man is so certain that he alone knows all the answers for a people alien to his own culture, he had better study himself and his situation and meditate on what is really before him.

There I was, in Guatemala, trying to impose ideas and practices, not merely of the Church but also of America—which I considered superior—upon a people whose basic values, life style, and outlook I did not yet really understand in depth.

VII

When You Push Down a Cross, Be Prepared to Carry It

The Priest My arms were extended, and I was pushing on a great wooden cross. On a black night, in front of the church.

Had I come to Guatemala to push down a cross? Or was I trying to carry it? Did I find it an affront that a cross, the symbol of my life and work, should mean something other than what I understood and taught?

Had I been brought up a Catholic in Massachusetts, toughened in fist fights, and disciplined in seminary, to come to this outpost beyond the edges of civilization to push down a cross? My ears sang. Or was it the crickets? I was afraid.

I had been waiting for hours, reading a book and glancing now and then from the rectory window. The church was locked at night now, but people would still come and pray outside, sometimes before the tall, leaning cross. Finally, it was very late, and everyone had gone home.

I went out into the darkness and listened. No human sounds. Only crickets. I walked over to the cross.

The limbed piece of wood made a great *whoomp* when it hit the ground. I thought it must have wakened the mountains. I stood looking at it, hardly able to see. The feel of the wood, the weight of its resistance to my push, burned the palms of my hands. I had chosen a moonless night on purpose, but I felt the whole night sky tremble with the weight of the fallen cross. Did I really know what I was doing? That cross was to the pueblo what smaller individual crosses, made carefully from wood chosen by the *chimanes,* were to the individual family homes. It held the spirits of the community saints and of the ancestors of the village. *Our Father, the Cross,* the Indians would say.

The Cross of the Four Wind-Directions. Four Earth-Bearers. This was superstition to me. I could not let these people worship an unchristian symbol at the doorstep of a Catholic church.

There was an ancient and beautiful corpus of Christ in the church, hand-carved. Someone had later painted it in lurid colors. I had tried to persuade various young men in the village to sand it down, but none of them would touch it. Finally, a youth came over from Soloma and did the job, then applied a beautiful protective finish. He built a new cross and fastened the corpus upon it. We stood it up and planted it firmly in the earth outside the church, near the Cross of the Four Earth-Bearers.

I had told the civil mayor that the old cross must come down, that it was a menace. Rotted at the base and leaning over, it was liable to fall on someone. But the mayor would have no part of it.

I left the cross where it fell. When the people asked me about it next morning, I said, "Well, look. It rotted where it stood in the ground. It fell over."

But they knew I had done it. Some of the villagers went to the governor, who told my Superior at Huehuetenango that this was the last straw.

According to canon law, we were primarily responsible to the bishop of San Marcos, a Spaniard. But he was an old man, who found it difficult to visit us. He therefore left the administration of the Huehuetenango area to our Maryknoll Superior, Father Gerbermann, who gave him monthly reports on our activities. This arrangement came close to giving to

64

Tex Gerbermann the powers of a bishop. I heard that Gerbermann was coming up to San Juan Ixcoy to see what had happened and that he had said he might allow the cross to be raised again.

To prevent his undercutting me, I drove down to Huehuetenango in the jeep and explained to Tex about the cross. I told him we had made great strides in breaking the power of the *chimanes* and the priest-mayor, and if they were led to think that they could use the Superior against me, we would be back where we started. He told me he would let the Indians have their say, that he himself would do nothing but try to ease the tension.

When word spread that the Superior was coming to the village, a crowd of three or four hundred Indians began to gather to demonstrate their anger to him. Usually quiet and even subservient, the Indians are not submissive when it comes to questions concerning their land or their religious beliefs. These are the two matters over which they will confront *any* authority.

Although hard drinking is common in Guatemala, especially on religious occasions, the Indian leaders avoid it when they are holding some kind of audience. Yet some of the crowd had been drinking, which added to the tension. I was worried.

When Father Gerbermann arrived, he parked his GMC pickup wagon and came directly to the rectory. Together, we walked over to the civil mayor's office. About a hundred people, including the village leaders and *chimanes*, crowded in with us. Also present were some of the elders who had cared for the old church books and were there by right of age— among the Indians, age is treated with deep respect. In the back near the door were four young catechists from town whom I had taught. The rest of the people waited outside.

Gerbermann and I began talking with the mayor. As we spoke, the Indians also spoke—mutual monologues, with no one really listening to anyone else. A kind of magnetic field of sound was created. A council of simultaneous voices went

65

on in which what was thought and felt was expressed, and perhaps unknowingly absorbed. Some people began to yell.

In the back of the room, a commotion broke out where the catechists had been standing. I pushed through the crowd and saw that some men had the four catechists down on the floor, beating them. I pulled the catechists to their feet, one at a time, and led one of them back to where the mayor stood with Father Gerbermann—I knew the mayor would not dare allow anyone to touch the catechists in his sight. Otherwise, I feared they might be killed as betrayers of their ancestral faith. Such roughness was unusual for the Indians, but they were very angry.

I spoke sharply to Gerbermann: "Come help me get the other three before they're killed!"

I assumed he would follow me, but when I got back to the mayor with two more of the catechists, Father Gerbermann had disappeared.

"Where is Father Gerbermann?" I asked the mayor. "Where did he go?"

"Oh, he just said that we could put up the cross again. Then he left."

I went over to the door and looked down the road. The GMC was pulling away.

I turned back to the mayor: "He gave you permission to put the cross back up?"

"Sí, Padre."

"I don't believe it," I told him.

One of the other men spoke up. "Yes, he did say that, Padre. I heard him."

I stood there a moment staring at the mayor and at the other Indians. I must have looked like a fool. I was confused and furious.

The crowd began to break up. I walked back to the rectory. Some of the people came around to the church and apologized for the beating given the catechists. I wasn't afraid any longer, only angry. I kept trying to figure out why Gerbermann had left so suddenly.

Incredulously, I could only conclude that he had become frightened when the men began beating the catechists. Till then he had always impressed me as a really tough priest, as a prototype of what we all wanted to be. Even John Breen, who admires few people, admired him. Physically, Gerbermann was slight of build, and about six feet tall. He had a rasping cough that may have resulted from the cigars he constantly shifted from one side of his mouth to the other. He didn't look at you—he stared, daring you to outlast him— and he spoke very little. Yet he laughed readily and he seemed to be an easy person to get along with. He must have been about forty-five, and had been one of the first Maryknollers in Guatemala.

And now he had run out on me.

After much reflection on the situation, I drove down the next day to see him, and to find out first-hand what had happened.

I walked into his office. I had seen him angry before, but not at me. This time he started in before I could get a word out of my mouth: "You're sick. You're psychologically unfit for the mission. You have no business down here. They should know better than to send people like you to Guatemala. I've talked it over with my consultants, and I'm sending you home to the States. I've already wired to Guatemala City for reservations on a Pan-American flight home. You leave tomorrow."

These were not arguments, these were orders. What could I say? I left his office and went alone into the small chapel. I found myself crying.

Immature? Clumsy? Insensitive? All right. But *psychologically unfit?* Especially when I had been encouraged by both John Breen and Gerbermann himself? This was too much to take. I sweated and cried and tried to think things out. I felt numb. I must have spent more than an hour attempting to sort out the pieces into which my life had suddenly been shattered.

If I were made to return to the States, I would be ruined as a missioner. I remembered the feel of that cross in the palms of my hands. All those years of fights, learning to be tough; the reprimands and near-expulsions from seminary—for what? I prayed for another chance. Something had to give. I forced myself to my feet.

As I came out of the chapel, I met Father Henry Murphy. Henry had come to Huehuetenango a year after me. I stared at him: His face, his neck, his arms had turned yellow. Numb as I was with confusion and near-desperation, I realized at once that Henry had a bad case of hepatitis.

A month before, with much publicity, Father Murphy had opened the second Maryknoll parish in a new diocese. This parish, at Cabricán in Quezaltenango department, could not suddenly be deserted. Someone would have to be sent there to keep things going, and I knew that all the other priests were occupied. There would be no one to replace this man, and he would be out, ill, for at least two or three months.

In spite of my own state of shock, in spite of Henry's suffering, I started to smile inside. Henry's illness would create quite a dilemma for Tex Gerbermann. Tex was a tough Superior, but he was notoriously inconsistent. I could imagine how he would react to this situation.

Murphy went in to see Gerbermann. I waited, still feeling terrible. An hour later, Gerbermann called me into his office. He looked at me with a perfectly straight face. "Perhaps I should give you another chance," he said. "There's a parish in Quezaltenango. The priest is sick. I'd like you to go there."

He continued: "Now I want you to understand the people have their customs. Their own way of doing things. Don't interfere. If anybody *wants* a baptism, do it. If they ask for the catechism, teach them. Take what's already there. Do what the people want you to do."

These were strange orders from a Superior in the Catholic

Church, charged with bringing the True Word to the heathen. In other places when priests got rid of pagan symbols, they had been highly praised. Perhaps they had managed it less clumsily than I had.

Still, I now looked at Father Gerbermann as if for the first time. His inconsistency toward me was too blatant to be anything but what it was.

Gerbermann is really a failure, I told myself. He was first going to expel me from the mission only to cover his own weakness and error; now he gives me a contradictory mandate so as to be able to back gracefully away from that first decision.

Words rose to my throat. "Am I so quickly over my sickness? Does Henry's hepatitis heal my unfitness in just a few minutes?" I wanted to say. "And have I business in Guatemala after all?"

I said none of this. I told him I would go. Yet, I wondered, how was I to learn just what the people wanted, really needed, for me to do? Would I find this out in Cabricán? Or was the strange country I needed to explore, and perhaps to understand, rather *inside myself?*

I had no way of knowing that a few years more would find me asked to leave Guatemala because this time I was allegedly knocking over the Christian cross by associating with revolutionaries.

VIII

Roots into the Volcano

The Nun I had twenty girls in first grade. The trust in their faces absorbed my energies; and I concentrated on helping them develop and learn. They brought me a new awareness of how life grows and deepens. The year passed in a blur.

There was so much I wanted to learn myself. I wanted to study my new country, its Maya Indian heritage, its history. I also had to learn the hard lessons of living closely in a community of sisters, people with different personalities.

The rules of the Order, and our daily horarium with specified hours for rising, prayers, meals, and retiring, imposed regularity and routine on our life in the convent. But we often differed in the priority we would give outside activities. I wasn't attracted by invitations to tea at society ladies' homes. My childhood in Mexico had given me a transcultural background, and I sometimes found myself defending the Guatemalan way of living and thinking. My facility with Spanish gave me, although junior, an advantage over the other sisters, and this caused occasional friction. The fact that there were so few of us—six by now—made us like a family, for better or worse. We had the joy of sharing but were supposed to act as a group. Of course, total loyalty was expected, particularly in any disagreement with those outside the sisterhood.

I was scheduled to make my final vows in May 1955, promising God a life of poverty, chastity, and obedience until I died.

There was no doubt in my mind. I knew I would go through with it, as I had decided back in high school in 1947. No matter joy, no matter unpleasantness, no matter grief, I had made my own covenant with Christ: "Here I am, Lord. Just teach me to love—to love You and to love people." I almost felt my heart would explode, I wanted so badly to love. And I had a long way to go in learning to get along with people.

Vacation time came again, and once more, Father Breen invited us to work in his mission. This was the high point of the year for me. I was eager to share the openness and un-sophisticated friendliness of the Indians again.

We ate our meals with Father John. There was always much talk, unlike convent life where, in those days, there was silence at meals, and little opportunity for discussion. It was refresh-ing to get a man's point of view, so different from a woman's outlook, and certainly different from my own. I realized that I had come to be easily hurt by what might seem a harsh inflection of someone's voice, that I could react to words in an unnecessarily personal way. A man's direct language seemed so much healthier. Maybe, I thought, I can strike a balance between sensitivity and directness.

Talking things over with Father John helped me to under-stand the people in the mountains. John Breen was as keen in his logic as he was Spartan in his life. Having to defend my own ideas and approaches was a challenge. It forced me to clarify my motives and made me ask more pertinent questions.

Our discussions ranged from the problems of the assimila-tion of the Indians into the national life to more general consideration of how people relate to one another. Was chang-ing the Indians' native costume for Western-style clothing a measure of progress? Father John thought so. I was inclined to want them to retain their own cultural characteristics.

I returned to my teaching at Colegio Monte María invigo-rated, and with a much broader perspective on affairs in Guatemala.

The school was growing; each year a new grade was added.

We bought twenty-three acres outside the city, next to a Jesuit boys' school set up along the same lines as ours, and began building. Up to that time, the Colegio had been uncomfortably housed in one, two, and then three rented houses with bedrooms transformed into classrooms. I watched the new structure grow from the architect's plans to a huge, beautiful, well-equipped school. We looked for ideas in pictures of modern schools in magazines; and, when ours was finished, we felt it to be a match for any we had seen. It was a private American loan to the Order that had enabled us to bring it off, although we still couldn't afford to buy all new furniture and equipment. And ironically, it was because of cheap construction labor costs that we were able to accomplish as much as we did.

One day a lady came to see the Superior with inside information that President Castillo Armas was finally closing the huge gambling casino that had been built in the City's residential zone. He had been under pressure, on the one hand, from some of his army officers who, with American gamblers, had a financial interest in the casino, and on the other, from society women who were outraged by such blatant vice near their homes. Now all the casino's fine furniture was up for sale cheap, as the gambling operators had been ordered to get out within forty-eight hours. Two sisters from the school found solid bargains there: a huge kitchen range, a piano, furniture, and enough dishes for the large boarding school we planned. The seedy characters we bargained with seemed nice enough. We had no compunction about paying low prices. Perhaps we even felt a little self-righteous—this was a gamble *they* had lost.

In July 1957, President Castillo Armas was assassinated by a palace guard. I was riding a school bus, taking care of the children on the early morning run, when I heard the news. Rumor suggested two possibilities: It had either been Communists or enemies inside the government. Seventy-two thousand people had already been registered as Communists out of an estimated 200,000 party members, and at the time, many of the registrants were being arbitrarily arrested, generating unrest. Many people felt that the president had been taking political revenge and hunting for scapegoats. And even within the government, Castillo Armas had made many enemies.

The funeral was kingly. Thousands lined the streets as the procession passed, led by a riderless black stallion and a caisson-borne casket. I was very sad. Castillo Armas had been a hero to me in spite of the rumors that he had been a pawn of the U.S. Embassy and had permitted himself to be surrounded by brutal and selfish men. He had liberated Guatemala from the godless Communists; I could not forget that. The mystery of his murder was never solved.

The new president, Miguel Ydígoras Fuentes, came to the dedication of the school. The model classrooms were on display, punch was served, there were speeches. As the evening darkness descended, all the lights were switched on. The beautiful architectural lines of the buildings stood out.

Suddenly there was a blackout. Servicemen hurried to surround the president, women cried out in the confusion. Since we could not see what was happening, it seemed worse than it was. After a long wait, the lights began flickering back on, one by one. Someone reported that there had been an overload on the electric power lines, but people remained skeptical. Excited but hushed voices conjectured that there had been an attempt to assassinate the president. This sort of occurrence proved not to be unusual—Ydígoras's entire term was filled with abortive uprisings and rumors of coups.

Our work went on. The new school's nickname, "the Maryknoll Hilton," pleased the parents, who felt their daughters were attending the best school in Central America. For me, however, this name was an uncomfortable reminder of our ambiguous position. We wanted to educate the daughters of the upper class, but I wasn't sure we could achieve this by helping them isolate themselves from the rest of the population. Yet we found a high tuition charge unavoidable because of the debts we had incurred in constructing and equipping the school as well as having to pay lay teachers' salaries; this prevented low-income families from sending *their* daughters to us. Thus the students were separated from contact with people of other classes and deprived of a democratic upbringing.

Amid the whirl of teaching and construction activities, I had not forgotten the Indians in Huehuetenango. I wanted to make sure that my work among the daughters of upper-class Guatemalans would somehow lead to betterment of the lives of the poor; I gave much thought to how I might help build Christian consciences in my students so that they would want to work toward social justice for the less privileged. Then it occurred to me that scouting might have something to offer, because the ideal of service is supposed to be at the heart of the movement. The Girl Scouts' central office in Guatemala offered to send a leader to help us begin a group. The national commissioner was excited over our interest because it meant that scouting might have a chance to move from the middle into the upper class, where strong financial backing might be available.

I wasn't concerned with that; I wanted something that would help our girls learn to serve others. They were accustomed to having servants at home who would obey their every command, and this did not help them develop resourcefulness and self-reliance. They were rich in things, but they paid a price: Young characters failed to grow.

One night I was helping a ten-year-old boarder at the school to bed. She took off her shirt, dropped it on the floor, and said, "Pick it up." I did a double-take, as I felt anger well up inside me. I controlled myself and said softly, "Little girl, you pick it up yourself." I watched her face: She was as shocked as if I had struck her.

It was not enough to educate young children. Some of them

had been conditioned to values and ways of living almost beyond my imagination. It was too simple to judge and then to blame; I had to see the children as individuals, to understand the forces at work in their lives, to work with them as they were, before I could begin to help them see what they might want to become.

Every day, Berta, our scout leader, came to teach us. She worked as a secretary but was willing to come during her midday break. We would learn rules and knots and the history of scouting, between sandwiches. In a few weeks we were ready to form the nucleus of a troop. Our first activity was a hike, and some local City Girl Scouts came with us. We rode a public bus to the end of the line and I was happy when I realized that this was the first time most of students had ever ridden a public bus.

After a few short hikes, Berta judged that we were ready to climb a volcano. I was as excited as the children, for I had always loved mountain-climbing. We improvised most of our equipment. Those who didn't have sleeping bags took blankets and straw mats—the kind the Indians sleep on in their huts.

We warned the girls: "Bring your lunch, but don't bring too much. Remember, you each have to carry your own pack." When the bus reached the beginning of the trail, it was dark— volcano hiking is done in the coolness of the night, because the sun makes a climb exhausting. In the flash of lanterns I caught a glimpse of a girl named Nini struggling with her pack: She had filled her knapsack with canned treats from the recently opened supermarket. Nini couldn't even pick up her knapsack, let alone carry it. She was angry, but we relieved her of most of her treasure. I poked fun at her. I felt annoyed over her greediness and her having disobeyed instructions.

"Come on," I said, "I challenge you to reach the top without complaining!"

She didn't answer. She just pressed her lips tightly, slipped her thumbs under the shoulder straps, and turned determinedly to take her place in the single file.

We reached the summit after four hours, breathless, our faces wet with perspiration. Some youngsters literally had to crawl the last fifty yards. Nini was right up there with the rest. She looked away from me, then glanced back after a minute, and we both laughed. We had climbed together to the rim of the crater, and a sense of triumph united us.

Vapor fumes swirled from several fissures. The sun, a huge ball of fire, rose from behind thin white lines of clouds. Sunrise infused everything with wonder: The world seemed to rise out of its own sleep. The view stretched in all directions, and we felt the breadth and distance and openness. The ground we stood on was alive with tiny white blossoms. I breathed in the air deeply through my whole body. I felt I was flying.

Camping was next in our plans. We wanted the girls to sleep on the ground under tents. They had to collect wood, to blow with puffed-out cheeks till their fires caught, to peel potatoes and balance a frying pan on three small stones. I saw some of the girls furtively shake off the dirt from a piece of meat dropped accidentally and then eat it as if nothing had happened. I was delighted. They were learning what I had hoped they would—with no sermons from me. They were roughing it for fun, but the Indian huts nearby provided the harsh contrast of unavoidable hardship that they could not ignore. The girls saw the need to share with and to serve one another. They helped carry one another's packs, and they shared their food with another group that had burned its own dinner to a crisp.

Some of the badges we devised to give scouting a distinctively Guatemalan flavor required knowledge of the colonial culture and the Mayan heritage. One of the projects to earn the heritage badge was to build an Indian thatched-roof hut. Tono, the gardener at the school, directed our efforts. We used machetes to cut the tall grass, then tied it in bundles. Onto four poles stuck into the ground we built the framework for the roof. Sticks were crossed and fastened firmly together, then we balanced ourselves on the framework and painstakingly tied bundle after bundle of straw to cover the roof. I worked with the girls, and Tono would smile at our clumsiness; he wanted to do it for us. I wondered if he could see the sincerity of what we were trying to accomplish; I worried about seeming patronizing to him.

"Do you have permission for me to take time out from work to help you?" he asked me.

"Sí, Tono, please don't worry."

Still, I found him looking around nervously—he expected a reprimand. This was the result of a constant pull between the sisters' insistence on American efficiency and what I felt was the more human Latin American idea of combining hard work with reasonable pauses to converse and relate to others. I discussed this with the other sisters, arguing that sometimes our clashes with the workers around the school were cases of pragmatism versus charity. I hoped we would be for charity.

Not long after, Tono was fired, but not for helping us with the hut. Apparently his work wasn't up to par, which may have been so. For myself, I found it difficult to be boss and friend at the same time, and I was sympathetic to the workers' troubles. Did they come to me because I could understand Spanish, or was it because they had sized me up as a pushover?

Tono was given his terminal pay according to law; he had no legal complaints. But his wife came to see me the following week. "What are we going to do?" she sobbed. "He just can't find work."

"Has he been trying?" I asked.

"Oh, sí, every day he goes looking, but there isn't any work."

"Please," I advised her, "watch your money. Don't go spending it all at once."

"I am," she assured me, "but Tono has already spent twenty-five dollars to put a new thatched roof on the house. We needed it. It was beginning to leak every time it rained. This was the first time he had enough money all at once to get it done."

I thought of Tono's helping us to thatch the roof of our scout shack. We had cut the straw from the school fields, and it had cost us nothing. And our house was for fun. Tono, his wife, and seven children lived under *his* roof, and working for the school, he hadn't made enough money to repair it before then. I wondered what they would do when the money was gone.

"Look," I told her, "why don't you find some small business in which to invest your money? Like maybe buying some pigs."

"*Sí-i, sí-i*"—she was excited at the prospect—"maybe we can. We'll have to think of something." I could tell it was difficult for her to look ahead with any confidence, let alone with planning. For too long they had barely managed to provide each day's necessities. This was what living "from hand to mouth" meant. But even then I don't think I had any idea of what hopelessness truly was.

Sister Ana María and I were invited to a Scout leaders' course at Nuestra Cabaña, an international Girl Scout center in Cuernavaca, Mexico. Leaders from throughout the Americas attended, and at first we made them uncomfortable—our gray-and-black habits gave us a somber appearance, even though we didn't feel somber at all. But after a few conversations and songs and games, the atmosphere thawed. We learned much; and when I returned, I wanted to help the Guatemalan central office as much as I could. I was appointed national commissioner, which gave me a chance to repay the office for the help it had given us earlier.

As Girl Scout commissioner, I addressed many private schools and encouraged them to form troops. As a nun myself, I was able to break down some of the reservations that nuns' communities had held toward scouting, their vague fears that relationships between boys' and girls' troops were too free.

I organized a senior troop that mixed girls from public and private schools. They worked with a troop of blind girls and did volunteer duties at the hospital. Although there was little else the public- and private-school girls could share besides their work and camping—their social activities were different, their friends were different—they did learn to respect each other. Each group was surprised to find that it had falsely judged the other as being of loose morals. As their work went on, I could sense the mutual understanding that was growing between them.

I was deep into scouting when I received a new assignment to teach in the high school. This may have been all to the good—scouting took as much time as you wanted to give, and my time was quite absorbed by it. Besides, there were more sisters now at Colegio Monte María, and two were prepared and eager to take over the scout troops.

As my farewell to scouting, I decided to introduce some of these rich city girls to my Indian friends in Jacaltenango. I chose the ten most faithful Scouts, thirteen- and fourteen-year-olds. We crowded into a borrowed station wagon and set out.

The journey to the hills was an adventure in itself. After reaching Huehuetenango, we transferred to two jeeps, which could maneuver the rough mountain roads. A Maryknoll brother drove the lead jeep. A warm, friendly man, Brother Gus was a jack-of-all-trades in the mission. After four hours, he stopped. The road had simply ended. "Here we are," he smiled.

We were on a precipice; far below us ran a narrow blue ribbon of river.

"What is this?" asked Julia, a pert, freckled-faced girl with jaunty pigtails.

"Rosario."

"Rosario. You said—this isn't a place. Anyway, I don't see any houses!"

"Sure, it's a place." Gus was grinning by now. "This is where we switch from wheels to mules."

We listened. The deep silence was broken by the clopping, straining animals coming over the rise on our left. They were led by Chepe, a wiry Jacaltecan Indian, whose angular features were lighted by a huge smile. He and Brother Gus greeted one another warmly. Chepe and I were old friends from previous visits, but at the girls he only looked shyly; they were Guatemalans, yet to him they were foreigners—*ladinos*.

Rain was threatening. We watched Chepe, who had an uncanny ability to judge weights, dexterously pack rope-net bags. He quickly loaded the mules with balanced packs of sleeping bags and knapsacks.

The girls were chattering gaily as we mounted and started down the deep incline. Sidelong glances at the deep ravine edging the narrow path were now and then accompanied by gasps. Four long hours on muleback on twisting trails subdued my eager young friends. Slowly they began to droop and wilt.

Finally we came around a bend, and there before us was a long row of village girls in colorful wrap-around skirts, with flashing smiles and black braids dancing as they jumped up and down with excitement. They greeted us and thrust flowers into our arms. Some boys shot off firecrackers. We heard the resonant tones of a marimba—a strange mixture of melancholy and gaiety. We forgot how tired we were.

We were soon clopping on the village cobblestones. From the doorway of each adobe hut, two or three smiling faces saluted us. We wound past the village fountain, where women were filling their red water jugs, to the churchyard. There we slipped stiffly down from the mules and tried to walk on newly acquired bowlegs. I caught suppressed smiles among the Indians.

"But Sister, why did we get such a welcome?" Julia could hardly believe what she saw.

"It couldn't have been just for us," said Tita. "They don't even know us. I feel like a celebrity!"

Julia looked at me, then spoke very slowly: "I know. It's because of you. They know you, and you told them we were coming. Why, they kept saying, 'Madrecita, Madrecita!' as we rode past."

"Yes," added Lourdes, "it's because of you. We're just basking in the light of your sun!"

I laughed. "Getting poetic, aren't you? The welcome is for you. You're an event in this village. You *are* celebrities! You're probably the first people from the capital to visit their village. Do you think you can accept this graciously—with simplicity and friendliness? Without being patronizing?"

They nodded seriously. It was a difficult assignment. To these girls, Indians had been storybook people you saw picking coffee off in the distance on your father's plantation, or else pictured on postcards—people you could otherwise ignore.

Next day, the village girls served a typical Indian dinner in one of the parochial school classrooms. I left my Scouts alone so they could be acquainted, and ate with the sisters who worked in the school and hospital, some of whom were old friends. But I was distracted during the meal, wondering if the girls would be able to break through the barriers of class and culture.

I needn't have worried. That evening, when I went to say good-night, the girls were still talking excitedly. Impulsive Lourdes had cut right through in her own direct and friendly way. Her black hair, long and straight, her dark-toned skin, her smile—all had served to dissolve the mixture of disdain and respect Indians feel toward *ladinos*.

They told me about their visit to some of the village homes. An Indian thatched-roof hut is one thing when it sits picturesquely on a hillside and quite another when you enter it as friend of the family to share a cup of muddy boiled coffee. The floor is well-packed earth, the sides are mud-covered slats, and the roof is made of straw. Your eyes take a while to adjust to the smoky gloom; there are no windows, and the fire is built in the center of the floor, right on the ground. There might be a rickety chair or two, maybe a table. Straw mats are spread around near the walls. Ears of corn, Indian pots, other odds and ends, hang from the rafters. A tall person has to duck. Possessions are too few to require cupboards.

The girls found such an elemental kind of existence hard to believe.

"And you know, Sister, they invited us right in. They gave us coffee and tortillas. We didn't know whether to accept the food and maybe leave the family short, or excuse ourselves and perhaps show scorn for what they offered us. We didn't know what to do!" María Elena still felt the strain.

"Oh, and Sister, they told us about their boyfriends!" This was plainly a novel idea to Julia. "A boy goes with his father to ask for a girl's hand. If the girl's father accepts him, the boy must leave a load of firewood by the girl's house every day. I can't remember all he has to do, but it amounts to his paying a price for her."

"And what if she doesn't like the boy?" I asked.

Lourdes answered then: "Some of the girls don't even know the boys except by sight. But most of the time they've managed to talk a little together on the side, just to get to know one another. There's no dating or anything like that."

"The worst part," put in Julia, "and the part I'd hate the most, is that the girl has to live at his parents' house."

"Yes," went on María Elena, "the girl is like a servant to her mother-in-law, and her husband is expected to take his mother's side in any disagreement. That really leaves the girl out on a limb."

Julia thought of something else: "It was funny hearing them tell about playing basketball. They wear skirts that are just a long piece of material they wind around and around and tuck in at the waist. They said their skirts come undone easily when they run and jump during the game, and it's awful to have to suddenly clutch your skirt when it starts to come off. Sounded as if they don't wear anything underneath. Aii, it's incredible they have so little. The clothes on their backs and maybe one more blouse and skirt for holidays—and that's it!"

I had wanted the girls to be exposed to a different kind of life, a starker kind of existence, but I hadn't really known whether it was possible to penetrate the barriers. These girls had found ways to break through. They had shared boy-talk and clothes-talk, had laughed together, had identified in spite of their differences. No adult could enter that world, least of all a sister or a priest. I was envious. As a nun, I could open certain doors; but so often they were opened only for others to go through. *Is this my life?* I wondered. *Am I to be only a catalyst?* I thought of Moses looking from the high pass over into the Land of Canaan. He couldn't go through either.

I'm being sentimental and dramatic, I told myself. *What more do I want? Who has a richer life than I?*

Still, something kept working at the back of my skull; a question was asking itself in me, of me.

Future Wives of
Future Leaders

The Nun I left scouting with no regrets—I was leaving the troop in good hands, and my new job offered another challenge. In the course of the previous seven years I had taught all but one of the six elementary grades; now I was to be home-room teacher for fifteen-year-old girls in the third year of prevocational school. This was a critical time for them; it was their last school year before they had to choose a career.

The school system gave the girls four choices: Three years more of high school would give them certificates as either teachers or public accountants; two years were sufficient if they wanted to be secretaries or to prepare for college. At our school, most chose the college-preparatory program. Girls would often come to talk to me after school, to tell me their dreams and their practical plans. They also wanted to talk about boys and parties. I tried to help them see what was possible, without discouraging them. It has always been difficult for me to set limits on life, and I have always been suspicious of those who did not trust, or who would inhibit, my own dreams. I was torn between wanting to protect some of the girls from romantic hopes which could only result in disappointment and trying to encourage their idealism in ways that would be meaningful as their lives grew.

We talked about values. What was most important for them to focus on in choosing a career? Was it how much money they could make, or what service they could do for people? Or was it their rank in society that would guide them?

Lily and Rosita, two of my most active students, ran after me in the corridor one day. Each grabbed one of my arms. They looked like twins, one brunette, one blonde, and both bright-eyed, short-bobbed, five-foot live wires. They skipped alongside me, matching my usual fast clip.

"We want you to help us," said Lily.

"Yes," went on Rosita, "help us to start a Sodality. Father Merino, a Jesuit, suggested it."

They stopped me. "Please?" they asked.

"Well," I sighed. "Let's sit here on the bench and talk about it."

I told them about the Sodality I had belonged to in high school: "It was purely religious, aimed at making us pious. The Virgin Mary was held up as our model and patron. Some of us taught catechism, and we all wore a medal on a wide blue ribbon when we went to chapel for Mass and other religious activities. But it was routine to belong. It actually was nothing too special or demanding."

Lily was undaunted: "Maybe so. But ours doesn't have to be like that." Rosita nodded.

Lily and Rosita were right; the idea had real possibilities. Instead of just talking about good ways of being and doing, the girls could begin to practice them. Practice, experience— these would do more for the building of character than any exhortations from teachers.

"The first thing," I suggested firmly, "will be to make the requirements for belonging difficult—so that being a member will mean something."

Rosita was thinking, too: "There are other ways to be religious besides praying. The Sodality motto is 'To Jesus through Mary.' We could meditate, but we could also have fun and learn."

We began weekly meetings where we planned action and nurtured motivation through reading and discussion. The

Sodality Handbook suggested we use *The Imitation of Christ* for this. But even in my novitiate days this book by Thomas à Kempis, a spiritual writer of the fourteenth century, hadn't appealed to me—he seemed to make Christianity a somber and self-obliterating way of life, whereas to me, the Living Christ was to give us joy and free us, fulfill us. We read and talked about the life of María Teresa Quevedo, a Spanish girl who had died in 1950 and had had a great devotion to Our Lady. We also read the book *Prayers*, by Michel Quoist, a French poet. One of his prayers was called "Lord, I Have Time," and went in part:

> *You understand, Lord, they simply haven't the time.*
> *The child is playing, he hasn't time right now....*
> * Later on ...*
> *The student has his courses, and so much work....*
> * Later on ...*
> *The young married man has his new house; he has to*
> * fix it up. He hasn't time.... Later on ...*
> *The grandparents have their grandchildren. They*
> * haven't time.... Later on ...*
> *They are ill, they have their treatments. They*
> * haven't time.... Later on ...*
> *They are dying, they have no ...*
> *Too late! ... They have no more time!*
> *And so all men run after time, Lord.*
> *They pass through life running—hurried, jostled,*
> * overburdened, frantic, and they never get*
> * there. They haven't time.*
> *In spite of all their efforts they're still short*
> * of time,*
> *Of a great deal of time.*
> *Lord, you must have made a big mistake in your*
> * calculations.*
> *There is a big mistake somewhere.*
> *The hours are too short,*

The days are too short,
*Our lives are too short.**

We decided that we *did* have time. What we had to look for were ways of effectively using that time.

Meanwhile, the Guatemalan Congress had passed legislation permitting the teaching of religion during school hours at the public school. José García Bauer, a dedicated Catholic politician, had triumphed over the outspoken newspaperman Marroquín Rojas, who called García Bauer the "Sacristan." The Church and the United States were Marroquín's prime targets.

The Sodality girls saw the new law as an opportunity for service. We felt it would give us a chance to serve children from a lower social class. The danger of paternalism was there, but we fought against that constantly by analyzing the reasons we might think ourselves superior, by considering man's true dignity, and by discussing the undermining effects of paternalism.

When my third-year girls began teaching catechism classes in two public grade schools, they were thrilled with the significance of what they had undertaken. Yet the weekly class was demanding. Some of them faced fifty or sixty squirming seven- to nine-year-olds who were used to being disciplined with a ruler. Other girls tried to teach students who were actually older than themselves and who weren't shy about making smart remarks.

The catechism classes taught by the girls each year ended with the children receiving their first Holy Communion. The ceremony and the festive breakfasts afterwards were full reward for the volunteer teachers' work. They found large white candles for the children to carry, and got the girls white starched veils. They soothed preconfession fears, they escorted the procession of wide-eyed urchins to the altar, they en-

* *Michel Quoist: Prayers. Translated by Agnes M. Forsyth and Anne Marie de Commaille (Sheed and Ward: New York; 1964), pp. 97–8.*

couraged the nervous little ones to swallow the communion wafers.

Afterwards, at long tables festooned with white crepe paper, the excited children feasted on tamales, fruit, bread, and hot chocolate.

A huge white, bell-shaped *piñata* was pulled up and down as the young students in a wide circle clamored at one of their schoolmates who, blindfolded and armed with a long stick, attempted to break the pottery belly to loose a treasure of candy and peanuts and surprises.

The Sodality also sponsored film forums. One of the pictures we obtained was *To Kill a Mockingbird*, whose theme of racial prejudice offered a good starting point for an effective discussion: *Were we or were we not, here in Guatemala, racist in our attitude toward the Indian people, just as white North Americans are toward black people?* The debate became heated.

Lourdes's words came through strong and clear. A *ladino* like the others, she looked around the room at her well-to-do fellow students and accused them directly. It was apparent that she was gaining a new view of herself as a person: "No one can ever know what it means to be poor like an Indian unless one has had to eat from the plate of the poor. And not just once, for a thrill. But every day—because one *has* to. You say we're not prejudiced like the gringos. That we don't look down on the Indians the way they do on blacks. Why, then, do you call somebody *indio* if he's stubborn or says something you consider stupid? Why is it an insult to be called *ishta*, which is just the Indian word for 'woman'? Even worse, why do some of you treat Elvira María the way you do?"

Elvira María was an Indian girl with straight black hair, a round smiling face, and a sweet manner. She had come from Huehuetenango and wanted to be a nurse. She was at Monte María on a scholarship, and she had to endure the snubs of the society girls.

Lourdes continued like a prosecutor summing up his case before a jury. Only this jury included those whose cases she was trying: "Think about what you do. You ask Elvira María to explain math to you. You'd copy her homework if she'd let you. You would love to get her grades. Yet I've heard some of you call her 'dirty *ishta*' to her face. You ostracize her from your socials. She's good enough to help you study but not good enough to be your friend. You criticize the gringos, then you dare to pretend you're innocent yourselves!"

No one could answer her. We drifted from the room in silence. I looked at the girls' faces. They didn't look back.

Some of the girls in Sodality lacked the confidence to face a class of restless children, so instead they organized a distribution center for food and clothing the Sodality had collected for the poor. They supplemented these with powdered milk and wheat flour from Caritas, a U.S. Catholic organization that sent surplus food and used clothing to needy people in other lands. Someone in Guatemala had to investigate the claims of the needy and handle the distribution. We received hundred-pound bags of powdered milk, along with detailed forms to be filled out for each family. The Sodality girls offered food to some of the poor who lived in shacks not far from the school. The contrast between their own homes and those they visited upset them. Once exposed directly and repeatedly to such human need, the girls found it difficult to solace themselves with the attitudes they had been brought up with concerning the poor. They came to realize that these people weren't lazy; and that their being accustomed to hardship didn't mitigate their suffering. The girls' frustration over not being able adequately to relieve people's needs made them restless and anxious.

Men, women, children would come begging at all hours. They would come to my classroom door where we kept the supplies and wait patiently for class to end. Then one of the Sodality girls would attend them.

María came one Saturday afternoon, a baby tied on her

back, two little ones by the hand, a basket on her arm. She was in her twenties, wore her hair in one heavy braid, had no shoes; her dress was halfway down her calves, covered with an apron. Her eyes betrayed her suffering.

"*Madrecita, por favor,* can you help me? Two days ago, my little brother died. He was twelve, just the age to begin to help. Besides our own four children, my husband and I have taken care of five of my sisters and brothers since my parents died. Manuelito was the oldest. He caught the measles."

"Did he die of the measles?" I asked her.

"No, *Madrecita,* he had a fever. Remember the storm three days ago? The walls on one side of our house were not covered properly. The water just poured in. Manuelito caught cold and died of the fever. All the money we were saving to fix the walls went to bury him. Three other children have measles now. Wouldn't you have a blanket you could give me?"

I was stunned. The price of a child's life was the price of a blanket. I longed to go up to my room and strip the blanket off my bed, but the blanket wasn't mine to give away. Here was the paradox of the vow of poverty, here it showed its teeth. You *own* nothing, yet you *have* everything—and *you have nothing to give away.* Then I remembered that, after a scout hike, a blanket had appeared, and no one had claimed it for over a month. I fetched it for María. I found clothes for the children, second-hand shoes for her, and a large bag of powdered milk.

After that, María came regularly to ask me for one thing or another. Sometimes I was impatient. I wouldn't always have what she needed, and I had no way of getting it. Nuns may take the vow of poverty, but it is people like María who *live* it. I had promised God to live poor, and I wanted to, but here I lived comfortably and lacked for nothing. And what I had most of was what the poor had least of—security. Sometimes María would come and, if I were out, she would wait four or five hours. No one else would do! She had to wait for the *Madrecita.*

I remembered all our talk about the dangers of paternalism and laughed wryly to myself; even the term María used to address me accused me—*Madrecita.*

More and more, I was beginning to see the impossibility of providing for Guatemala's hungry people merely by charitable donations. At the same time, I knew there was something important about the personal contact, maintaining the human dimension of charity. I knew that large, impersonal programs could not supply all the human needs of deprived people. I had so many questions.

What the Sodality actually did was of small and only temporary assistance to a very few of the thousands of poor. We educated a few rich girls to the desperation that abounded in their city. This all seemed pitifully little to me. I would think of Michel Quoist's "Lord, I Have Time," and I would wonder how much time remained to us Christians.

One day María came to thank me and to say good-by. Her husband had been given a job down south working on a plantation. She was beaming.

Great, I thought. At least this would mean food every day; besides, it's warmer down there.

A month later, back from doing errands in town, I found María sitting on the bench where she had always waited. I couldn't believe my eyes. I called to her.

"María! What happened? What are you doing here?"

I had thought I was finished with her, that she had been taken care of. In my helplessness, I boiled over with impatience. "I just don't have anything to give you right now!"

"*Madrecita!*" she smiled. "I didn't come to ask you for anything this time. I had to come to the city to see if I can get a checkup. I'm going to have a baby. Look here—it's my turn to give you something!"

She handed me a basket of tropical fruit.

Eh, Manuelito!

X

To Listen and, Perhaps, to Learn

The Priest I had now been assigned to the department of Quezaltenango, a new diocese, under a Spanish bishop, and with very strange instructions for a missioner to observe: *Let the Indians be themselves, and help them in any way they ask.* I had been kicked out of San Juan Ixcoy because, in my zeal to do what I thought we were supposed to do—to destroy the Indians' belief in their pagan gods—I had overreached myself. This experience had forced me to see that there was much I didn't understand, and I went to Cabricán in a reflective mood, determined to see with open eyes, to listen, and to learn.

To be honest, I must admit there was another reason for my change in attitude: I wanted to show Tex Gerbermann what would happen when I obeyed his instructions and the expected five thousand communions and the rest of the sacramental gas station statistics didn't come through. I figured his orders were designed to save his own face, and I resented the criticism implicit in them—that I was too imprudent to be allowed to act as a genuine missioner, and so was now to become a sort of clerical caretaker.

Still, however mixed my motives, my state of mind now permitted me to be open, vulnerable, to what I found in Cabricán. I no longer felt any compulsion to prove anything, either to the Indians or to myself. I listened in a different way to my parishioners now, for my reasons for listening had changed. And that listening changed me. I had set out, like Columbus, with one goal and, like him, had landed in another place, with a different set of conditions and with pressing questions about my original destination and purpose.

"Quezaltenango" means "Place of the Beautiful Bird" and is named after the quetzal, the bird represented on the flag of Guatemala. (There are no longer any quetzals in Quezaltenango, however—they now inhabit the lowland country.) Quezaltenango department borders on Huehuetenango and San Marcos, sharing the same mountainous terrain, but including as well an area of fertile plantation land along the Pacific coast. Its capital, which bears the same name, is the second-largest city in Guatemala, though only one-tenth the size of Guatemala City.

The Indians of Quezaltenango are the most colorful and independent in the country. It was an ancestor of theirs, the great king of the Quiché, Tecún Umán, who fought the fiercest battle against the Spanish conquistadores. He was finally killed in hand-to-hand combat with the Spanish warrior Pedro de Alvarado. Legend has it that, as Tecún Umán lay dying on the plains outside the town of Quezaltenango, a quetzal landed on his chest and bathed itself in his blood— whence the bird's red breast today. Tecún Umán is a national hero in Guatemala, and his descendants in Quezaltenango are determined that he not be remembered simply as a figure of legend, but as an ancestor whose spirit unceasingly demands that the proud heritage of the Quiché be vindicated somehow, someday. The Indians of Quezaltenango are unquestionably the leaders of their race.

My Cabricán parishioners were more open and outgoing than the people of San Juan Ixcoy, and we established a quick rapport. I learned about their lives, their beliefs, their relationships. I began to understand them, to admire them, to love them as a people and as friends, not as potential converts to a different faith. I sensed that it was important for them to be themselves and not to become mere replicas of a hard-nosed *Norteamericano*.

So often missioners go out to carry the Word, forgetting that the Infinite will always, somehow, be there ahead of us. The Indians told me about their beliefs, and asked in turn about my God. Gradually, we began to realize that our God was the same—He creates us, wants us to live together and to share our lives; he prepares our end. We discovered on both sides that we weren't too sure about our beginnings or the inevitable ending. And although we could never be certain we actually understood each other's concepts, we seemed to agree that people should find themselves through relationships based on love and mutual respect. We said it in different ways, but the essential elements were the same: love and trust.

As I learned about their beliefs, I became aware of a profound paradox: Their religion was based on fear and punishment and divine anger; yet they behaved with loving respect toward each other. My religion was one of love and charity toward others; yet, in the name of my faith, there arose fear and anger and the compulsive need to placate an implacable God.

And why were these people, who had so little, so unselfish? Why were people like me, who owned so much, so careful of possessions—although Christ has promised that our sharing will be rewarded a hundredfold? The contradictions struck me more and more deeply. I began to wonder and question.

For perhaps the first time in my life, I began to think for myself. And I listened to the people of Quezaltenango—to more than what they said on the surface. Like the quetzal, which is said to die in captivity, the Indians of Guatemala have effectively lived in captivity since the Spanish conquest, and their spirit has long seemed dead. Yet my experience in Cabricán taught me that there are levels in the human psyche in which life runs below the surface, waiting for a chance to break through. I heard the Indians' words, and I heard beneath the words the sound of the quetzal's wings, and I let those wings fly free in my own inner valleys.

I had been taught that the sacraments of the Church should never be approached in a spirit of superstition—that these sacred rites should be experienced as joyous and enriching, not performed out of fear. Yet we told the people that their babies would not go to Heaven unless they were baptized. Over a period of time I came to wonder about the actual differences in spiritual content between what we said the sacraments symbolized and accomplished and what their *costumbres* meant to the Indians. I gradually came around to the view that we were confusing differences in culture with differences in essence. For instance, I would raise my hand over a penitent's head, make the sign of the Cross, and pronounce a Latin formula—and, I believed, the man's sins were thereby forgiven. For an Indian, this same spiritual miracle was accomplished by burning a fistful of tiny candles or by confessing his sicknesses to a *chimán*. I wondered if there were only a thin line between many psychological and spiritual realities. God, after all, is infinite and is not to be bound by the particulars of our Graeco-Roman symbolism.

If the parents wanted a baptism, I baptized a child as I had been instructed when first sent to Cabricán. But I required that both a godfather and a godmother be present and that, with them, the Christian community take spiritual responsibility for the children as they were baptized. When I asked who would help see to it that this child was brought up in Christian charity and understanding, everyone present was expected to answer. Spiritually, the children belonged to the whole community, though more especially to the *padrino* and *madrina*.

When groups of children were to be baptized, there would ordinarily have to be four adults present for every child.

One Sunday a child whose parents were not practicing Catholics was brought in. When I asked, "Where are the father and the godfather?" the people answered, "Out in the plaza." That meant that they were drinking, celebrating the child's being given a name. I looked around the congregation and saw an elderly Indian Catholic, and asked him to stand in for the *padrino*. He stood directly behind the *madrina*. They didn't know each other—at least she didn't turn around to see whom I had asked to stand in as godfather.

For each child, I would ask the responsible adults, one at a time, to place his or her hand on the chest of the child. In Spanish, the word used is *pecho*, which means both "breast" and "chest." It was my sixth baptism that day, and I was impatient. I spoke to the elderly Indian.

"Put your hand on the chest."

No response.

Impatiently, I repeated, "Put your hand on the *chest*."

The old man hadn't seen what had been going on, I suppose —he reached over the shoulder of the godmother, put his hand inside her blouse, and took hold of her breast.

I couldn't believe what I was seeing. The godmother stood there absolutely expressionless; if she was surprised, she gave no visible sign. The two Spanish nursing assistants began to laugh. I gasped and turned around quickly to keep from laughing out loud. I kept telling myself, even while my shoulders were shaking with incredulous laughter, "This is serious! This is *very* serious! This is terrible!"

I turned around to face the congregation. There was not the slightest change of expression on the old Indian's face or on the face of the godmother. His hand was still firmly placed in her bosom. I finally got hold of myself and baptized the child. Then I told the old man, "Now you can take your hand off."

To people of Western culture, this seems hilarious. For a man to touch a woman's breast in public, especially in church, is beyond our wildest imaginings. But to the Indians in the mountains of Guatemala, there is nothing prurient or suggestive about a woman's naked breast. They found incomprehensible the shock expressed by the Spanish nuns when they would see a mother nurse her child while receiving communion. It was simple enough: A nursing child doesn't cry.

Silvestre, the catechist, assisted during baptism, and would explain in the Indian language what was going on. At a certain point in the service he also helped to put a few grains of salt on the child's tongue. This was to represent the salt of the earth, hopefully to give the child a taste for spiritual reality. If the child was nursing, Silvestre would say to the mother, "Take your breast out of its mouth." Sometimes he would simply reach over, take the breast in one hand, and pull the child's head back with the other. I would drop a few grains of salt on its tongue, then he would shove the baby's head back onto its mother's breast.

Sometimes while a mother was kneeling in church, her child, even one as much as three or four years old, would run up to her, pull her breast out, and suck a little milk. The child might otherwise get no food, for the Indians had so little.

It may well be a commentary, not only on the relativity of humor, but on how far we Westerners have allowed ourselves to become removed from the elemental nature of direct human touch, that we often laugh at the intimate touch of each other's flesh.

I went to the Indians to teach them about Christ, and they taught me about humanity. As I looked at the way the Indians approached their brothers and sisters, I wondered how I had ever accepted limitations on the ways of approaching Christ.

I slowly came to realize that religion is not a matter of taught and accepted principles so much as a way of living and being. A way of life means a way of relating with actual people. I had a deep sense of well-being when I was with the Indians. I ended up thinking their values were as good as mine, maybe even better than mine . . . certainly better for them.

When I had first come to Cabricán, I had asked: "What do you want me to do?"

They had looked at me strangely. "What kind of a priest are you?" they seemed to be wondering.

But they answered simply: "Baptize. Celebrate Mass. Sing the chants for our dead in the cemetery. What else is there for a priest to do?"

Now we both understood one language—and the man who speaks the language of brothers does not stop to read the name of a man's church outside the door of his brother's need.

I asked them what I could do for them besides say Mass, baptize children, and hear confessions. One day they finally said, "Do you think you could help us buy a truck, Padre? Like the *ladinos* have? To carry limestone and wood?"

Cabricán has a large limestone deposit, and the people have made lime from the stone for generations. But to reduce the stone to lime, wood approximately equivalent to the weight of the mined stone had to be burned under the ovens filled with limestone. The men had literally stripped the area of trees for firewood. Now they had to go a half-day's journey, one way, to get to a place where there were trees. The *ladinos* had mules, and two of them owned trucks to carry firewood and limestone to the ovens. All but a few of the Indians, however, carried the limestone and firewood on their backs—a hundred pounds at a time. Each ovenload of lime required ten tons of limestone and approximately the same weight in wood. The product was sold for between thirty and forty-five dollars an ovenload, which was usually divided among eight men—four who had gathered the firewood and four who had provided the stone.

The Indians wanted to buy an old truck for two hundred dollars or so. I suggested that we (or I) would spend most of our time repairing it, and that we should try to buy a new vehicle. I investigated prices in Guatemala City and found that trucks came high. The best we could find was a three-ton GMC for just under Q.6,000.* Luckily, the owner of the agency was a good friend of the Maryknoll Fathers, and he

* Q. = *quetzal, the Guatemalan unit of currency, which is pegged, and equivalent, to the dollar.*

told me that since I was involved, he would sell the GMC on good terms: Q.2,200 down and Q.276 a month for the following fifteen months. I did some figuring in my head, then told him I would let him know. "Don't mention this to any Maryknollers," I asked him. "Some of them wouldn't understand why I'd be wanting to buy a truck."

Back in Cabricán, I reported to the Indians, and we talked it over.

"Aiii, Q.6,000, Padre! That is too much. That's more money than all our land is worth. Where will we ever get so much money?"

I had been thinking of possibilities. "If we speak to the Banco de Occidente in Quezaltenango, maybe they will lend us the Q.2,200. We can make the monthly payments with the money we'll earn on the extra lime we produce by saving time with the truck," I suggested.

We did some adding and subtracting. Finally they agreed it was possible and worth a try.

Four of the Indians went with me to see the bank manager in Quezaltenango. Standing at attention in his office, they presented their proposition, which obviously amused him. I let them do the talking, which they did all at once. It reminded me of the mayor's office crowded with a hundred men at San Juan Ixcoy, their leaders all speaking at one time. Finally, the manager told the four he would see what he could do. He dismissed them and asked me to remain behind.

"Listen, Padre," he said, "those people are *indios*"—using the term equivalent in a *ladino*'s mouth to "nigger"—they have nothing to guarantee the loan. Even if they had legal title to their lands, those lots aren't worth Q.2,200. I can't lend them money."

The Indians had brought in their deeds, some of them handwritten, indicating that no one laid claim to the parcels of land on which they lived. Such deeds are used in local transactions but have no real legal value.

I was disappointed, and did not try to hide my feelings.

Then the manager smiled benignly: "Now, Padre, if you could sign the loan and find some plantation owner to cosign it, thus using your good name as a gentleman and a priest, and his plantation as a guarantee, I think we can do business. But not with just Indian signatures."

Driving back to Cabricán with my four companions, I was silent. Indians don't ordinarily talk much unless they are excited or disturbed, and now they were talking. They were excited about the prospect of the loan, the new truck, and who knows what other possibilities. I lacked the heart to tell them that the bank would not accept their land titles as guarantees. They had no idea that their deeds were not legal tender. They had been talking and arguing about means of getting a truck for two or three weeks. Of the first seventy or eighty men interested in the new truck, only twenty-four dared risk putting up their land titles as a guarantee. It was a fearful gamble for them; those small, dry plots of rocky soil were all they had. When we had left for Xela* with the twenty-four deeds entrusted to us, some of the men came to the village early to see their four brothers off and to remind them for the hundredth time, "Be careful of my title. Do not lose it. I'm a poor man, and this land was given to me by my father."

I had thought to myself, *I'll protect those deeds with my life if need be.* But how do you protect a poor man's place on earth when neither he nor his place have any legal standing in the eyes of the powers that be? I couldn't protect something that had no value. Then how do you go about giving a poor man's dignity any worth?

Now we were driving home. The men still had their deeds. They had left Xela under the impression that the deal would go through and that they would have to return later with their deeds. They knew I had stayed behind in the manager's office; they were too polite to ask me why, and at this point, I didn't want to disillusion them.

The trip from Xela to Cabricán is two hours by jeep, four

* *Indian name for Quezaltenango.*

by truck. By the time we reached home, I had decided that I would sign the loan "as a gentleman and a priest," and would ask a plantation-owner friend to cosign. He was not sympathetic to the Indians, but he trusted me. I wouldn't tell the Indians: They had lived too many years thinking their lives were somehow unworthy in the eyes of the *ladinos*. I had to help them believe that their word was as acceptable as any man's and their lands as good as any plantation—not to deceive them, but because I knew that their human worth was very real and very great. I believed also that, working together, they could develop a strength and a sense of economic worth to reinforce their belief in themselves and their dignity as human beings. Tecún Umán is not dead; he sleeps.

About two weeks later, the four Indian leaders and I went back to Xela. Arrangements were completed with the bank and a lawyer, and a contract was drawn up which I signed. The four men from Cabricán signed as witnesses for my signature, although they were told that I was signing as a witness to their signatures and that the bank manager was accepting their land titles as security for the loan. Nonetheless, beyond the legalities, what these men understood did truly reflect our relationship; for trust is a deeper law, a law beyond any court's power to enforce or nullify. Their land titles were turned over to me, and they were not told of the plantation owner's guarantee. We shook hands, received a bankbook with a Q.6,000 deposit in it, and set out again for Cabricán. We had decided to borrow the entire sum from the bank so as not to have to make two sets of payments.

A few days later, the five of us who had signed the bank note left for Guatemala City to buy the truck. We took along a *ladino* to drive the truck back, since as yet none of the Indians knew how to drive. Discussion before setting out had led us to conclude that a new truck probably would not be best for driving over old back trails with five tons (all three-ton trucks in Guatemala carry five-ton loads) of stone and firewood. The truck would therefore be used to carry lime to the plantations, and we would buy a farm tractor and hitch-trailer to maneuver across the mountainsides from the quarry to the ovens. This would require making the down payment on the truck and owing the rest, after all, but paying for the tractor (Q.2,300) and trailer (Q.600) completely. We also would have to set up an office with a safe and an adding machine. The bank's Q.6,000 loan was just enough to put us into operation.

When we got back to Cabricán the next day, a hundred people were waiting for us. We had completed the transaction that morning in Guatemala City and had left together around 10 a.m., myself and two men in the jeep, the driver and two men in the brand-new yellow-and-white GMC. By jeep, the trip took five hours from Guatemala City; by truck, it took eight. We stopped the jeep at the entrance to the pueblo and told the people waiting that the truck would take at least three more hours. Some stayed anyway, but others went home to work and to eat, then returned.

By 6 p.m., three hundred people were waiting for the truck. Finally, it appeared over the top of the last mountain above Huitán. I couldn't make it out myself, but the Indians have keen eyes. In another half-hour the truck rolled into town, and a fiesta began.

The air was charged with joy. For me, it was all my Christmasses in one. The twenty-four owners were out with their whole families. The sparkle of pride, of risk, of ownership, shone in their eyes. As soon as the truck stopped by the side of the church, everyone crowded around and looked. Then a child ventured to touch it. His finger left a big greasy smudge-print on the fender.

One of the new owners, with a reproachful look at the child, wiped the fender clean with the sleeve of his coat. I had never seen these people so exhilarated. They couldn't believe the truck was really theirs.

It was a day of deliverance from a life of walking with back-breaking loads. We blessed the truck. Everyone sang a song of thanksgiving to God.

XI

Finishing School
for the Consciences
of Rich Girls

The Nun Colegio Monte María had as its original purpose the training of leaders. To teach the
children of the rich is one thing; to help them begin to reach
out to the poorer people of a country that is seventy-two percent illiterate is quite another.

Josefina Antillón, a Guatemalan lay teacher, and I had between us the bulk of the teacher-training courses. She and I
had become close friends. We were the same age, thirty, yet
she seemed older to me. She was taller and stockier, and she
moved slowly. She didn't like to climb mountains. She method-
ically worked out ways and means of solving practical problems. But she did not stop with ideas; she was one of the
most generous individuals I've ever known.

One day in 1960 we were talking in the teachers' room about
our three prospective teachers.

"Next year, to finish their course, they'll have to do some
practice teaching," I said.

"Yes," Josefina nodded. "I've been wondering which of our
grade school teachers would agree to have practice instructors
observe them at work, and also which ones would really be
worth observing."

"Somehow, the idea of their teaching here just doesn't appeal to me," I said. "They would be instructing their own

sisters, and sisters of their friends. I can just hear the parents: 'I'm paying tuition so that my child will be taught by a regular teacher. I'm not paying to have some young girl practice on my child.' "

Josefina laughed. "Yes. It's funny, but it's no joke."

"The best thing would be to have a special school—a school of our own," I continued.

"You mean, a pilot school?" Josefina asked.

"We could set up our own school, with controlled classes. Then the girls could also learn about administration by taking turns as principal, secretary, and treasurer, and they could handle all the necessary paper work with the Ministry of Education."

Josefina thought a moment. "We could direct them in counseling children and in taking care of discipline problems."

"Ay, Seño Jose"—I called her by the abbreviated name the students had given her—"this can really develop into something. It could be a laboratory school, run by the students themselves. They could take care of enrolling the students. It could be their own school, really."

"But where do we find the money? We'd never get the administration to pay an extra salary for the demonstration teacher. And where would we set it up? In what building?"

Josefina was with me, ahead of me. "You and I can take care of the demonstration teaching," she said. "We can handle the required subjects for the student teachers in the morning and set up the model school to function half a day. I'm sure we can get permission to organize an afternoon-session school."

I knew she could get the official authorization. She seemed to be friends with nearly everybody at the Ministry of Education.

"Then that may solve the other problem," I said. "If we have our school in the afternoon, we can use the kindergarten classrooms, since those sections have school only in the mornings. I can get that permission from the Superior."

I had already figured out in my mind where we would recruit the children for the school. Five minutes down the road from Monte María was a colony called Castañás. Some speculator had sold lots there very cheaply, and the incoming residents had put up houses or shacks or whatever they could afford. Most were very poor. One water spigot served the whole area. Dirt roads. No sewage disposal system. There was no prospect of a public school there for a long time. I was certain we could get children from there to come to our pilot school. We would ask them to pay a nominal amount, maybe fifty cents a month, to give them a sense of independence in paying for their children's schooling and to give us some money to buy paper and pencils, and for general expenses.

Josefina and I worked out the details and then spoke to Sister Mildred. As I had expected, she listened with interest as I laid out our proposal: It was one more way of preparing our students for leadership; the girls would get broader experience in the pilot school, facing classrooms of underprivileged boys and girls, restricted deliberately in numbers but not by any standard of intelligence or good conduct. Sister Mildred approved the idea enthusiastically, and we went recruiting.

Recruiting, however, proved unexpectedly difficult. I had confidently assumed that the parents in Castañás would seize this chance to have their children learn; but unfortunately they had already been subjected to too many "good offers"— electricity, paved roads, water—only to find themselves in debt and with the same conditions when it was all over. We talked to family after family, we followed school-age children to their homes. We tried to allay the parents' doubts and skepticism.

Nonetheless, the day the school opened in January 1961, we had managed to sign up the maximum we had hoped for— twenty-four children for first grade. However, a new problem arose almost immediately: the indignant reaction of the parents of the Monte María kindergarteners, who used the same classrooms in the mornings. How could we dare permit these urchins to use the same bathroom facilities as their own darlings, the same desks as future wives of presidents, cabinet ministers, and industrialists? Why, those filthy little children probably had some skin disease.

The strongest answers to these attacks came from the practice teachers themselves, and Josefina and I let them handle the complaints. Let them explain to their own people what it meant to be willing to share their well-being. For a time, the problem subsided.

The three student teachers planned everything—the classes and the school programs. They really learned to teach. But they also learned to handle problems of discipline and to develop good parent–teacher relationships. The parents of the practice-school children were delighted and proud. Because we wanted the *Escuelita* (the "little school") to stand out, to shine, to show up well, the hardest thing for me and Josefina was to let the student teachers make mistakes, to have them do something and let it go wrong, to suggest and help, but not to take over.

When October came around, the barefooted children had learned to read. They could write a little. They could add.

We faced more serious problems, however, for the following school year. We would have to put in a second grade, since it wouldn't be fair to the first group of children to cut off their opportunity for schooling after just one grade. There were five aspiring teachers ready to begin their practice work, and we needed a second group of students. Also, we would have to change schedules—the practice school would function better in the morning, when there could be more teaching time and when the children would probably be more alert; while the formal classes for the fledgling teachers could more easily be held in the afternoon. This would require a separate building, which would cost money.

Again we went to Sister Mildred. The year's success was to

our advantage—she also wanted the *Escuelita* to continue, and she agreed to help us. She solicited money from friends, and designated a corner of the school property where a new building could be erected. Josefina and I spoke to an architect, who agreed to draw the plans for free. We were given cement blocks and floor tile. The school, with three classrooms, had to be ready in three months, in time for the January opening. Incredibly, it was.

The student teachers themselves bought plywood, and sanded and painted it for use as blackboards. They decorated the rooms. Now it was their very own school. I was moved as I watched them take registrations, talk with parents, work out the yearly schedule.

Some of the bus drivers, gardeners, and janitors who worked for the Colegio enrolled their children in the *Escuelita*. Several of the other sisters took an interest and planned aid projects with their classes. Sister Rose Angela took up a collection of shoes for the "poor children"; others gave gifts of food for the families.

The *Escuelita* children were given the right to use the bus facilities provided for regular Monte María students. Here was an opportunity to teach the little rich girls to share.

"You can't sit here next to me! You're dirty. Besides, my parents pay for me to go to school, and yours don't!"

When I heard this, I shuddered. I wondered how often the Castañás children heard that kind of remark or read it in someone's expression. At Monte María, we talked to the children about this in no uncertain terms: "That little boy doesn't have running water at home. He has to walk three-quarters of a mile to get a bucketful."

He got his seat on the bus after that incident. But this was the kind of lesson the privileged girls at Monte María had to learn over and over again. There are so many who close themselves off from awareness.

The practice school, meanwhile, was well launched. I was becoming deeply involved in my regular schoolwork and in other activities, and Josefina, too, had other plans. At our request, Sister Mildred put the model school into the hands of Sister James Agnes, an excellent, experienced teacher who had just come to Monte María that year.

Sadly, however, our hopes for the school were not to be fully realized. We had established it with great good will, but without a sufficiently long-range perspective, and eventually we had to pay the price for our shortsightedness. For, ironically, what we had started in order to help the poor—by teaching the Monte María girls how to be leaders—became a sore spot, a segregated, second-hand school built of cement blocks and a tin roof, standing in stark contrast to the elegant and sumptuously furnished girls' school next door. What we had built as a laboratory and a model was now known as "the poor school," had now itself become part of the problem.

True, without it the children who went there might never have had any education at all. Whatever else might be said, we had provided at least a small answer to part of the huge problem that enveloped the lives of the people of Castañás. Yet the parents of the Monte María students, and some of the sisters themselves, felt that even this partial solution had to be hedged about and restricted. The *Escuelita* children were forbidden the use of the swimming pool, and a fence was built to "keep them in their place" both physically and symbolically. It was at this time that I began to get some real insight into the attitudes of those who favored the status quo, the haves— some understanding of their drive to squelch all rising expectations of the less fortunate. The haves' great fear, I now saw, was that once the have-nots managed to breach the wall between them, an irreversible movement would start. The have-nots would no longer be satisfied with humiliating handouts, would no longer be satisfied to be beggars; but would demand that, at long last, they and their children be allowed to be men.

The poor you will always have with you. How little I had understood this saying of Jesus. The poor—ever at the experimental mercy of social workers and demagogues, vulnerable to disease, victims of their own ignorance, they crowd along the edges, or into the inner cities, of population centers. I had never been a cynic, nor had I ever expected to solve the world's problems alone. Yet I had always been suspicious of abstract schemes that sought to answer human questions without human involvement. Usually I tried to work wholeheartedly on whatever task was at hand. Only now I paused to take stock and to aim at a far wider view of what was going on.

I had many doubts about the worth of the projects I took part in. So many seemed eaten up with futility—band-aids on cancer sores. Yet I had no other way to learn, and neither did many others. Our good intentions often led us in unexpected directions, to destinations we did not know existed. Thus the *Escuelita* experience revealed to me my own poverty of perspective and of awareness; and it seemed that only by learning the hard way could I begin to experience my real, human connection with people in need, who so often, unless given hope and help toward organization, remained at the mercy of those rich in wealth and power.

I did not feel that my small projects were wrong. I simply realized that I shouldn't deceive myself about what they could accomplish. I prayed that I would be among the bearers of hope and that that hope would not be false.

XII

Patterns Under
the Surface

The Priest I have gone ahead of myself. Human lives do not work themselves out in neat chapters and rhymed stanzas. The rhythms in our being and doing have a beat, an irregular regularity, that is more of resonance than of mechanical symmetry. To recount fully the story of myself, a priest, at work in the back hills of Guatemala actually requires the interweaving of several narratives. So many currents are in motion in the life of every human being that he often loses sight of even his own continuity. And so I have to begin now, back at the edge of the Guatemalan tapestry, to bring along the fuller pattern of what was happening. In a piece of Guatemalan Indian weaving the colors are forceful, the figures are sharp and angular, the whole fabric is elemental, religious, charged with an earth-humor that reverberates with both innocence and terror. Life for me in those days had much of that elemental quality; but its patterns did not emerge so evenly.

It was in August 1960 that I had been sent to Cabricán to replace Father Murphy. Two weeks before Christmas I received word from Father Gerbermann that he was coming to see how I was doing. I decided to put on a big show for him: I would give a large group of children their first communion; I prepared more than twenty young couples to be married; there were babies to be baptized. And for all these, there were parents and godparents to be involved. Altogether, some three or four hundred people would participate that day.

The atmosphere in Cabricán was far different from that in San Juan Ixcoy. I had hardly any organizing to do, since there were many willing people to take part in the services and in the accompanying fiesta. Many of these people, literally thousands of them as the years went on, would have a strong impact on my life there. They taught me some of what I know of myself today and much of what I have learned of life.

Francisco was a fine man of sixty-five years—a very great age for an Indian in Guatemala; yet he acted and talked as if he were twenty-five. He was thin, about five feet six or seven inches tall, with very black hair and no beard. The image of energy and determination, he walked quickly and carried himself as straight as a ramrod. He was a mason and a carpenter, self-taught. He wore glasses for reading or, at least, for looking at the printed page, since I don't believe he could read. Francisco always looked you directly in the eye. He was a true patriarch, and everybody went to him with their problems. He spoke with authority, and everyone listened. Even the *ladinos* called him "Señor Francisco," and feared him. More than once he told off the mayor on account of some injustice perpetrated against a weaker member of his race. His anger was always right, never righteous, and people trembled if they were the object of it. Yet he never raised his hand against anyone and was known as a soft touch. If someone needed something, he would go to Francisco; if Francisco didn't have it, he would help the asker to get it. He always had some orphan, widow, or sick person in his house. Indians tend to be generous, anyway, but Francisco was an example for other Indians. When he had first joined the Church through marriage some fifteen years before, he had had to spend fifteen days in jail for being the first to convert. Since then, many others had followed him into the Church, as they followed him in so many other activities.

Francisco maintained that life was something you gave to others in so many ways. Every act of this man gave life to his fellow Indians and, often, while I knew him, to me.

Silvestre was a young man of twenty-five, very quiet, husky, with strong cheekbones. His black hair was always unruly. He was very intelligent, and smiled often, but I never heard him speak unless spoken to first, and I never heard a word of complaint from him during my six years in Cabricán. Silvestre seemed incapable of becoming excited over anything. He could never be hurried, yet he worked eighteen hours a day around the rectory and church. I grew very fond of him and his quiet, uncomplaining persistence. He was a young man but, because of his intelligence and quiet manner, when he spoke, even his elders listened.

Teodoro was a real gentleman, thirty-five years old, very stocky, about five feet five, intelligent, bright-eyed, always laughing or smiling. He spoke well of everybody and everything. He seemed incapable of thinking ill even of the Devil—an utterly uncynical man. Yet his approach to life was very philosophical; he told me he believed that God wanted his people to suffer for the sins of others. He worked harder than anyone else, except perhaps for Silvestre, even though he could not believe his labor would have any really significant effect.

When I would grow angry with him because he, as representative of the co-op, would allow himself to be pushed around, he would tell me, "Have patience with us, Padre. Perhaps God wants us to suffer this way. God is patient with us."

His attitude always took me aback, because I knew he wouldn't make excuses. He would try all the harder next time, but he would not hurt anybody. To him, there was no other explanation for the evils his people had suffered than, "Perhaps God wants it that way."

When my Superior arrived to see how I was getting along,

the people involved with the church services crowded around. Catechists were examining some of them in points of doctrine; I was hearing confessions; marriages and first communions were being recorded in the church registry by Silvestre and Teodoro. Father Gerbermann was dumfounded. I overdid my nonchalance.

"People getting married," I said.

"Oh, this is great! This is wonderful!" He was very excited. I was getting the credit, though I really didn't deserve it.

The people in Cabricán had decided to build a parochial school. None of this had anything to do with my presence. Yet, remembering the circumstances surrounding Gerbermann's sending me to Cabricán, I played up all the developments to him. I couldn't resist the pose, though I knew it was the people's spontaneous interest that was actually responsible.

Father Gerbermann was assured that they would build the school themselves. Francisco, as spokesman for the people, asked him to send some nuns to serve as teachers.

Gerbermann was delighted. Here was a parish opened only six months earlier, and he was being offered eggs, chickens, and flowers, and asked for permission to build a parochial school. He drove back to Huehuetenango and wrote me an enthusiastic letter of commendation.

I, however, still felt like a sacramental gasoline station attendant, using the people. My Superior had been ready to get rid of me after I had made errors while engaged in serious efforts on behalf of the Church in San Juan Ixcoy. Now I was receiving credit for good results I had actually very little to do with. I began to feel that we were playing games with the people. They were like pieces on a chessboard, to be moved by us, the players. A living Christ and real people didn't seem to have much to do with the value of my work just then.

I was still attached to the Church psychologically, as a be-all, end-all, system. Yet I had begun a period of questioning.

Meanwhile, the Papal Nuncio, Monseñor Paupini, came up from Guatemala City to Huehuetenango to consecrate an altar in the main parish there. I was astonished at his manner—he didn't want to touch the "dirty peasants." Later, Gerbermann told some of us that the Nuncio, an Italian, had promised to make Huehuetenango a separate diocese with Gerbermann as its first bishop, if the latter would write a letter to Rome praising him. Monseñor Paupini was apparently looking for a more important post. Gerbermann laughed about this and gave us the impression that he wouldn't think of writing such a letter. Not long afterward, the Nuncio was assigned to serve in Colombia.* He thanked Father Gerbermann "for what you have done." And Tex was made bishop of Huehuetenango.

This kind of thing was disillusioning to me, but it was not a gripe of mine alone. Many of the priests, especially the younger ones, also sweated out these problems. We talked about them when we saw one another.

I did not then identify the actions of Gerbermann or of the Papal Nuncio with the general policies of the whole Church. The Catholic Church was still, to my mind, the instrument of Christ's Redemptive Work. The hierarchy was primarily responsible for carrying out this mission; if certain individuals along the way were falling down on the job, that did not reflect in any basic way on the Church itself. Christ's Redemptive Work, if it were to be effective at all, would have to be done on many different levels.

Many of us felt threatened by Tex Gerbermann's indiscriminate manipulation of priests, the way he tossed them about from parish to parish, with no regard for personalities or programs, under the guise of "obedience." This greatly undercut the sense of continuity and concentration in our work. His inconsistency confounded us: A priest could break his back to increase the number of sacraments distributed in a given month and receive praise from Tex; the next month the same priest would be called on the carpet to explain why the mayor, or the sisters, or the sacristan, or some group of parishioners

* In 1969 Pope Paul named Monseñor Paupini a cardinal.

Father Thomas Melville in Cabricán, Guatemala, 1965.

Sister Marian Peter, 1964.

Chimán burning incense before the village cross.

Sprinkling the blood of a chicken on skyrockets
that will be fired to salute the saints.

[LEFT]   Village elders, with staffs of authority,
leading a parade commemorating the death of Tecún Umán,
an Indian warrior who fought fiercely against
the Spanish conquistadors.

Members of the Cabricán cooperative in their brand-new truck, 1965.

Father Tom discussing co-op problems with the Indian truck driver.

Members of the cooperative making lime.

Father Jalón

Titina

Sister Marian Peter
Father Aguirre

Father Joe Kelly

Sister Marian Peter and *cursillistas* in Medellín, Colombia, 1965.

Marjorie on a visit to
Petén in 1967 to investigate the
possibility of opening schools in
Pope John XXIII Colony.

¡Oh, Bendito Señor!

Hasta las MONJAS que creíanse "cristianas", han sido
tentadas por el demonio como colaboradoras de las F.A.R.

"Guerrillera"

Hermana
MARIAN PETER
de la Orden Maryknoll

The guerrilla nun.
Shortly after Marjorie and Tom
left Guatemala in December 1967,
the White Hand, a terrorist
organization, circulated a death list
that included Marjorie, Tom,
and Art Melville.

He aquí un raro espécimen que tras ayudar con dinero, ropas y medicinas
a las F.A.R. en la zona huehueteca, transpuso las fronteras patrias en
compañía de los sacerdotes norteamericanos hermanos Melville, rumbo
hacia México, después de haber "engañado al clero"... y a la catolicidad
guatemalteca.

Marjorie and Tom Melville in Washington, D.C., January 1969.

had complained about some aspect of parochial life. Gerbermann never investigated any complaint he received, but just took it at face value and reprimanded the priest accordingly. Often a priest was sent on his way to another parish to begin the game all over again.

After the Indians in Cabricán had built their school, the Maryknoll Superior sent in nuns to run it. Since Gerbermann had become bishop of Huehuetenango, the Superior was now Father Jim Curtin, the former pastor of San Miguel. About five or six of us who were former parish assistants of Curtin's had opposed his nomination, since we were familiar with his inability to withstand the pressures of a parish. But most of the other priests had voted for him, basing their judgment of him on his friendly nature. He barely survived his six-year term; the difficulties were too much for him, and his selection as Superior was nearly disastrous.

The sisters he sent to Cabricán were of the Order of the Religious of the Assumption, founded in France during the last century. Their particular interpretation of Catholicism was a revelation to me. At first, I was so happy to have their help that I tried to overlook what I considered the idiosyncrasies of their strict rules and their attitudes toward man—woman relationships. For their part, they were so pleased to be working in the mountains that they were restrained, if determined, in their efforts to prod me and the people in their direction. Friction existed, but it was very low-keyed.

The Assumption Order is rather upper-class, devoted to education of the daughters of the wealthy. They have sumptuous schools in various parts of the world but had recently decided to institute mission schools, in which they would teach children and do medical work among the poor, to parallel each of the elegant schools they operated. The Cabricán school was their first mission school in Guatemala.

The original contingent included a Sister Superior, who was in her forties, two younger sisters in their twenties, and two lay girls, also in their twenties, from Spain, to assist them.

There was also an auxiliary sister, a kind of second-class nun, who did not teach or treat the sick but did the laundry and cooking for the others.

Conflicts soon developed between the sisters and the two girls. Most of the difficulty seemed to revolve around the sisters' refusal to allow the girls to eat with them; instead, food was passed out to them from the kitchen, located in the cloistered area. Another sore point was that the girls were not allowed off the school grounds more than once a day, and only for a fifteen-minute period to go to the post office to pick up the mail.

The girls were not allowed to speak to me unless the Superior was present. Since I was not acquainted with the nature of their contractual relationship to the sisters, I did not think this strange. If that was the way Spanish nuns treated Spanish lay missioners, I was not going to interfere. Finally, however, the Sister Superior dismissed the two assistants in a rather high-handed way, meanwhile convincing me that the two were the cause of all the strife. I suggested that they be sent back to Guatemala City to work in the school for wealthy girls, and the Superior eagerly agreed.

The two girls were soon replaced by two more docile lay missioners, also Spanish. After a time, the Sister Superior decreed that one of the younger sisters should not go to confession to me. According to canon law, the pastor of a parish may not offer to hear the confessions of nuns in his parish; a special, approved, confessor must be brought in from outside. However, a nun, for her peace of conscience, may request any priest, including her pastor, to hear her confession. Although the Church is very strict about priest–nun relationships, it is forbidden for a Superior to interfere in the matter of confession. I had thus acquiesced to hearing the younger sister's confession on several occasions, and I was surprised when I learned that Madre Amparo, the Superior, had now forbidden this. She informed me that she could tell by the way the younger nun looked at me that she was in love and therefore would be unable to make an honest confession to me. I thought this exaggerated, but since the Superior was already beginning to question my attitudes toward the Indian women, I agreed not to hear Sister's confession again.

Finally, the Sister Superior removed the younger nun from her teaching post and brought in another sister, a Cuban. Some of the priests in the region told me they believed that Sister Superior was in love with me herself and just refused to recognize it. I laughed this off as absurd; but as the months wore on, Madre Amparo became steadily more vociferous in her objections to my talking to the lay missioners or to the other sisters, and in her insistence that I was leading the girls and women of the parish into sin. I began to wonder about this myself.

These nuns in general betrayed an obsession with sex that showed itself in a disquieting and destructive way. They seemed to consider any contact between men and women a sin. They explained to me in utter seriousness that, while North Americans do not have in their nature the weakness of the flesh due to original sin, hot-blooded Latin peoples and Indians *are* afflicted with this weakness. They considered themselves and our parishioners susceptible to excessive sexual arousal from ordinary displays of affection. After Mass, I was accustomed to sharing the *abrazo* (embrace) with the Indian women and shaking hands with the men; but the sisters exhorted me to keep my distance, insisting that such intimacies were not fitting for a priest.

In San Juan Ixcoy, I had tried to force people into a certain mold, and as a result had found myself removed from the parish. My dismissal, as I have said, had shaken me deeply, and I had reflected much on the meaning of these events, to decide the nature of the relationship I was trying to help establish between these people and Christ, and between these people and myself. When, therefore, the sisters began to correct me for being too friendly with the Indians, I took another look at myself. Was I wrong again, too impulsive in my approach to the people I was supposed to help lead? In San Juan Ixcoy, I had been blinded to my own instincts because of my will to convert the Indians. But now I *was* listening to my inner voice, and it assured me that an openness to *abrazo* was a valid human response. I could not believe that this was ugly or that it promoted sinfulness in people as sincere and direct as the Indians.

Indians, sometimes old men, would come up to me and ask me to lay my hand on their heads and bless them. This embarrassed me, not because I didn't want to touch them, but because they seemed to feel I had some special power. I finally began asking them to bless me in return.

I would often visit the school during lunch-time recess. I loved the young children and was moved by their eager enthusiasm over the new school. The love was mutual. They would crowd around me, trying to touch my hand, to grab my shirt. The sisters insisted that I should not allow the little girls to hold my hand.

They complained: "You never see a priest in Spain without his cassock on!"

I just laughed at that. I was deeply suspicious, and still am, of anything that separates religious leaders from the people they are supposed to serve. Communion is oneness shared two ways. Wearing a cassock during my daily work about the parish, I felt, created a separation, not a bond.

The sisters, however, convinced that anything to do with sex was sinful, did not relent. One of their explanations was that, since Indian girls marry so young, I might create confusion in their minds, and might make it difficult for them to accept an Indian husband if I allowed them to be affectionate with me.

Since I refused to stop being affectionate and would not reject the friendliness of the children, the sisters began telling the girls that it was sinful to touch me and that they must confess such acts as sins.

Imagine my confusion when the girls would come to me to

make their confession and say: "Padre, three times I held your hand."

"That's not a sin!" I would exclaim.

"Madre said that it was a sin and that I should confess it to you."

Was I supposed to assure ten- and twelve-year-old girls that they were forgiven for the sin of holding my hand?

The first time I heard that in confession, I was furious. I went storming down to the school and confronted the Sister Superior, who I knew was the source of most of the trouble. I repeated my protestations against the type of morality the nuns were trying to teach, and insisted that we straighten the matter out between ourselves before going to the people with such concepts. She shrugged off my objections with "You are a *Norteamericano* and a man. You do not understand the nature of women and even less these people." I bit my tongue and walked away. I considered making a complaint to the bishop of Quezaltenango, Monseñor Luis Manresa; but he was a Spaniard, and I wasn't sure that he would agree with me. Father Curtin, as Maryknoll Superior, had no jurisdiction over the sisters, even though he had been responsible for getting them to come to Cabricán.

On Guatemalan Independence Day, after the mayor and others had spoken in celebration of their country's independence, the sister in charge of the school stood up and gave an *ex tempore* speech. Why were they so proud to be independent from Spain, she wanted to know: "Everything good and holy and wonderful that you people have came from Spain. . . . And here I am, coming again from Spain, to bring your children some real civilization!"

The Indians were used to such talk in relation to their own culture. But the *ladinos*, Guatemalans of supposed Spanish extraction, were insulted.

One day I stopped at the school and found one of the girl students standing outside the building, crying.

"What's the matter?" I asked her.

"Our Mother is punishing me." The Superior insisted that the children call her *Nuestra Madre,* "Our Mother." She even signed all her notes to me and notices on the bulletin board "Our Mother."

"Punishing you for what?"

"For washing my hair."

It was the custom for the Indian women and girls to go down to the river, take off their blouses to keep them from getting wet, and wash their long black hair in the running stream. Their hair often grew down to their waistlines. This girl had not gone down to the river, where she might have avoided the Sister Superior's censure.

"What's wrong with washing your hair?"

"Because I washed it in the *pila* behind the school." (A *pila* is a big, well-like, outside sink.)

"What's wrong with that?"

"Well, I took off my blouse to wash my hair. It was so early this morning, nobody was around. Sister said I shouldn't do it in the *pila*. That somebody might see my breasts. But look, Padre, I don't even have any breasts!"

And, in all trust, she pulled open her blouse to show me her poor, frail, rib-stretched chest.

The sisters were convinced that I was unfit to be a priest. I was too familiar with the Indian women, too affectionate with the little girls, spent too much time on unchurchly interests of the men, and almost never wore my cassock. A gringo, a cold-blooded man without the evidence of original sin, simply could not or would not understand that he was leading these people into all kinds of transgressions. Time after time the Sister Superior went to Bishop Manresa to complain about me.

By canon law, however, a pastor is to his parish what a bishop is to his diocese. A bishop can curtail a pastor's authority only by removing him. But so long as I was left in charge of the parish, my authority, which covered the parochial school, could not be diminished. Despite my fears, Bishop Manresa apparently defended me against the sisters' charges. He explained to me more than once that he had tried to mollify them.

After the death of a horse I had used, another priest gave me a kind of motorcycle that we called a "totegoat." It had a huge back tire and a small front tire. It was chain-driven, very light, and could go up a rather steep grade in the mountains. I used it to travel into some of the remote areas.

In Cabricán, I let the schoolchildren ride on the totegoat behind me. One day, one of the girl students, about twelve years old, was riding with me, holding me around the waist. A sister walked by, stopped and stared, then turned on her heel and strode into the school building.

Later she accused me of misleading the children. She said that I taught them to be too friendly with me, that I was encouraging the girls to have impure desires for me. "You don't have such desires," she said, "but they do. I'll have to tell the bishop."

The sisters ran their own small residence with the rules of a cloister. No man was allowed inside. Regardless of emergencies, certain hours were strictly kept—for prayer, meditation, and recreation.

"We have our rules," they would say.

Once a leak developed in the sisters' sink.

"Father, can you repair our sink?"

"You don't allow men in your convent," I chided them with a straight face.

"We have our rules. As our pastor, you may not come inside. As a plumber, you may."

The sisters wanted to set no precedents.

It came time for the Cuban sister to make her vows, the final confirmation of her commitment to the Church as a nun. During the service she was crowned with a wreath of white flowers and a ring was placed on her finger, to indicate poverty, chastity, and obedience, thus making her a Bride of Christ.

I looked at the flowers around her head with something less than admiration. A few weeks earlier, I had celebrated a special Mass at the request of the Indian brotherhoods dedicated to the perpetuation of the ancient *costumbres*; and this same sister had been quite critical of the "silly superstitions" of the representatives of the brotherhood standing before the altar during the Mass, each with a burning incense pot in one hand and the staff of his office in the other.

I had begun to examine more closely our own Catholic customs. Many of them now appeared to me to be only slightly more sophisticated forms of superstition than those *costumbres* I had been trying to force out of the lives of the Indians in San Juan Ixcoy. I glanced from the crown of white flowers to the crowd of Indians surrounding her, congratulating her on her consecration. *They are the ones,* I thought. *They are the ones who live lives of poverty, chastity, and obedience.*

The schoolchildren thronged around the sister; there was a special greeting in Spanish that they had all been taught by the other sisters to say to her: *"En horabuena!"* (In [your] beautiful hour!) I wondered what they would have said had they chosen their own words, in their own language. Did they know what it meant to be a "Bride of Christ"? Did I know?

The night before, the sister's brother, an exile from Cuba, had arrived from New York to join in the celebration. He had brought a bottle of whiskey, but his sister took it away from him. He told her, "Give me my bottle, or I'll go buy one here."

The four nuns and the two girl assistants watched as he and I took a drink in the girl assistants' room. We all sang some songs in celebration of the event. The sisters sang also but refused the whiskey.

When the time came to retire, the Cuban nun grabbed the bottle. Her brother looked sadly at her.

"I've flown all the way down from New York. Don't spoil it."

"You watch yourself," she told him.

The next day, as the two or three hundred schoolchildren pressed around to congratulate the sister, she turned to her brother and said, "It is at times like this that I am most happy that I have given myself to Christ and not to any man. I have three hundred or more children, and you have only four."

The blood drained out of his face. When he could speak, his words came out in a tight kind of anger: "Three hundred children, eh? Tell me, Sister, how many nights have you spent pacing the floor when one of them was sick? How many times have you worried yourself half to death when one of them didn't come home on time? How many times have you been driven to tears when one of them did something wrong? You don't know what motherhood means."

I was embarrassed by his frankness, yet I felt a kinship with him. I could have told him she had been ordered "for the love of God" by her "holy rules" not even to interrupt her recreation period to give one of the children medicine.

"After all," their Superior once told me, "we love God first and man second. We can't let man interfere with our love of God."

I reminded her of St. John's saying that the love of God and the love of man are identical, that you can't have one without the other, and that the man who says you can is a liar. She stared at me with such a look that there was no mistaking who she thought was the liar.

Indians from the mountains would bring in their sick for treatment by the sisters. Once a little girl came in who was paralyzed. One of the lay girl assistants informed me that the sisters planned to send the child back that day.

"You can't send that child home," I told them. "She needs a hospital. We'll have to do what we can here."

"We're not a hospital," the Superior answered me. "We can't put her up overnight. We have our rules. Nobody can stay under the same roof with us."

"That's not true," I reminded her. "Sister's brother was here for her vows."

Still she refused. I made a place in the rectory for the child and her mother. The girl assistants came by and treated them. The sisters later complained to the bishop that I was trying to make them look bad in the eyes of the people.

I stocked extra medicines in the rectory to give treatments when the sisters refused to break their schedules even for emergencies. The new assistants (the second pair of lay missioners had meanwhile been themselves replaced), two older and less docile girls, also from Spain, had to give off-schedule treatments on the sly, because the sisters made them live according to the convent rules, as if the girls were preparing to be nuns. If it became known to the sisters that the lay missioners were coming into the rectory, even though it was to treat sick people, there would be hell to pay.

The sisters' complaints about me to Bishop Manresa eventually began to have their desired effect. At the bishop's request, Madre Amparo had been transferred to El Salvador by her superiors, after she had been in Cabricán for two years. Madre Teresa had replaced her; but she, a product of the same strict regimen, did not differ in her attitudes from her predecessor. When Bishop Manresa began to hear the same complaints about me from the new Superior, he paid more attention than he had in the past. He spoke to Father Curtin, my Maryknoll Superior, about it. Canonically, the bishop could simply remove me if he wished, but because of a contract he had signed with Maryknoll to retain our services for his diocese, he left that decision up to Father Curtin. Jim liked my work, however, particularly the tremendous success of the cooperatives I had founded. He told me to stick it out.

After a year of troubles with the new Superior, Bishop Manresa was getting tired of hearing complaints. The sisters were becoming more and more insistent about my supposedly unpriestly conduct in regard to women.

The two new lay missioners would often stop in at the

rectory on their way to the post office for a chat with me. Also, one of the girls who had returned to Spain to enter a convent began to write to me, and I to her. When we realized that we had developed a crush on each other, we decided to break off the correspondence. Unfortunately, I made the mistake of mentioning this situation to the Superior. I knew things would go badly for me when—as she was pretty sure to do—she told the bishop, so I decided to inform him myself. He was upset by my news, and afterwards told Father Curtin that he did not like my attitude toward priest–women relationships.

Curtin was distressed. In the seminary, it is taught that the good priest seldom if ever goes near women. Outside the confessional or apart from a women's Sodality, priests' dealings with the other sex are frowned upon, and even condemned. The anticlerical world delights in the story of a priest who appears to be unfaithful to his vows. The exaggerated emphasis placed on this matter often drives priests to great lengths to prove how "pure" they are, even if it means sacrificing charity and compassion in the process.

Father Curtin listened to my views, then maintained that the bishop was right and that I had better accommodate him. At the same time, he told me that I should send back to their villages the five young boys who were then living in the rectory. They were staying with me because I had wanted them to be able to study in the evenings, using my books and rectory light. I felt it was a shame that bright young minds should be neglected because of the lack of opportunity—no books or electricity to study at home. Now they had to be deprived because of "appearances." Curtin said they had to go because otherwise, "people will talk."

It was all so incongruous that it seemed like some drama of the absurd. Father Jim had come to visit me to set me straight on my dealings with women; he left instructing me on my relationships with boys.

All this preoccupation with appearances and proprieties that had little or no relevance to our work in Cabricán heightened the absurdity implicit in the Church's insistence on mandatory celibacy for priests. The Second Vatican Council, convened by Pope John XXIII, was meant to "open a window" in the Church to let in a breath of fresh air. As more and more policies of the Church became subject to critical examination, celibacy began to attract increasing attention in clerical circles. When Pope Paul succeeded Pope John, however, he forbade any discussion of the matter by the Council bishops. In addition, to forestall any speculation as to what he intended the Church's stand to be, he came out with a hasty encyclical reaffirming celibacy as the "glory of the priesthood of the Western Church." Few Catholic periodicals carried the story of the group of internationally famous theologians in Rome who tried to meet with the Pope and have him delay the issuance of the encyclical. They were blocked by powerful members of the Roman Curia, the rulers of the Church's bureaucratic machinery. There was to be no discussion of the subject, no thought on the matter other than that of the Pope himself and of Cardinal Pietro Parente, an archconservative. With that development, the bishops dropped the issue.

Living in Guatemala gave me insights into this question that I might never have come by in the States. *Machismo* is a way of life for the Latin man. The term means "virility" and refers principally to an individual's sexual prowess. Every Latin man brags of his many sexual conquests, whether real or fictitious. It is customary to be seen publicly every once in a while with a young woman other than one's wife. The Indian does not observe this custom, and this is another reason why the *ladino* despises him.

To most Latin men, true celibacy does not exist—it is a figment of the imagination. A priest is either a hypocrite or a homosexual, never a celibate. One Guatemalan priest told me that it was common for his father and brothers to kid him for being "queer," knowing that he was leading a celibate life.

Father John L. McKenzie, the great Jesuit Scriptural scholar of the United States, has written* about what he labels the Church's "breeding-pen theory" of marriage, in which sexual relations are sanctioned primarily for purposes of procreation. He criticizes the marriage formula used for administration of the sacrament of matrimony, in which the word "love" is not even mentioned. He lampoons the descriptions of married saints (who, incidentally, are few and far between) in the breviary, whose highest praise for them is that they never used their partners sexually: "The finest Christian marriages in the book are those in which the partners pretended that they were not married." Given such a theology of sex and marriage, I thought that the sisters' attitudes toward the Indians and myself were at least consistent with Catholic beliefs. It was my own belief on this subject that was no longer consistently Catholic. For it now seemed to me that in the Church, the primary importance of the charity of Christ had been replaced by concern for the chastity of the Brides of Christ.

* *John L. McKenzie: "Q.E.D.," Critic (Oct.–Nov. 1967), p. 10.*

XIII

Volcano:
CHI–RHO

The Nun If it were necessary to name one key ingredi-
ent of my spiritual growth and development
in Guatemala, I think it would be my taking part in *cursillos*.
Many things grew out of these "short courses" which, coupled
with my work at Monte María, brought about my own
awakening.

I had come to Guatemala hoping to work among poor
people, and instead had found myself assigned to teach rich
children. For a long time I felt that this was God's joke on
me. Now I'm not so certain. I was given the opportunity to
understand the mentality of the well-to-do; I had to hear about
the United Fruit Company from the landowners, and to see
how the Guatemalan elite treated Indians. Going from Monte
María one mile to Castañás, I covered the distance from haves
to have-nots, from wealth and power to despair and social
ferment.

One afternoon in June 1962, at a meeting of Catholic
school teachers, I heard that a series of lectures on social
problems would begin that evening. I invited four of the
practice teachers who were concerned with social problems to
go with me. They would profit themselves and also serve as
my companions, since as a nun I couldn't go out alone.

Father Aguirre, a Venezuelan Jesuit, was the chief lecturer.
He was a short, stocky man, whose black Basque beret crowned
a square face with crinkly eyes and a wide smile. He spoke,

with considerable power and eloquence, about his work as a union organizer among the oil workers of Venezuela. His forceful logic and erudite illustrations bespoke his experience in exhorting university students to assume their share of responsibility for making employer–labor relations more just. He was accompanied by a young architecture student and a young woman in the last semester of law school, both of whom also lectured.

I listened intently and took notes as they spoke of hunger and illiteracy in Latin America. It was the first time I had heard such statistics: Two-thirds of all Latin Americans go to bed hungry each night; every large city is surrounded by a "crown of thorns"—huge numbers of shacks thrown together along the sides of mountains and in the ravines by millions of peasants who were pouring into urban centers looking for a livelihood. Carmela, the law student, asked what *we* were going to do, if we were truly Christians, about conditions that forced human beings to live like animals.

The problems were obviously worse than I had realized. More than ever, I wanted to do something. After the speakers had concluded, a dark and handsome young Jesuit—surrounded by boys from Liceo Javier, a neighbor school to Monte María—asked them a number of questions that had occurred to me as well. His intense desire to find ways and means to resolve the problems was evident.

Father Aguirre described the *Cursillos de Capacitación Social*—eight-day courses designed to foster social awareness, which he had developed and which were being given successfully in Venezuela. The purpose behind them was to try and encourage the students to pursue the Christian ideal of a career as an opportunity to serve those less fortunate rather than simply as a means of earning money. Father Aguirre said that so many idealistic students at the university turned to Communism because they saw in this doctrine the only answer to social problems. He made Christian social doctrine relevant and infused the students with the enthusiasm to dedicate themselves as wholeheartedly to it as others did to Communism.

After the last session, I looked for the young Jesuit, Xavier Zavala.

"What do you think of the possibility of our having some *cursillos* here?" I asked.

"I was wondering that myself," he said. "Although they're designed for university students, I don't see why we couldn't arrange it for our graduating classes."

"What about having them mixed, boys and girls?" I wondered.

"Well," he answered, "if we can get permission, it would be an ideal preparation for the fellows and the girls, who will be together at the university. After all, we've kept them isolated from each other all through high school."

Father Aguirre was delighted by the idea. If we made all the arrangements for permissions, for food and lodging, and for the recruiting of the participants, he would send up a team of two Jesuits and two university students from El Salvador during the November vacation.

Sixty of us gathered together that first evening—mostly boys and girls in their late teens just graduated from high school, plus a few teachers, including Xavier and myself. The introductory talk explained the horarium, and we were staggered by the prospect of rising at 5:30 a.m., retiring at 11 p.m., and having just one hour-long rest period after lunch. Discipline would be semimilitary: The group was divided into squads of six members each which were required to stand in formation before every activity; punctuality was strictly enforced; all disorder was publicly punished by push-ups for the boys and sit-ups for the girls. A whistle marked the time for change of activity.

I looked at the students. Many faces fell, and I could almost read their thoughts: *To think I came voluntarily! But this is baloney. I'm going home.* But before anyone could actually voice such opinions, they heard the "commander" say, "If anyone thinks this is too hard and that he can't take it, we'll be only too happy to accommodate him with transportation home. We don't want children here. This *cursillo* is for those who have courage and resistance and who are looking for something worthwhile in life." No one opened his mouth, but everyone went to bed with misgivings.

We were awakened by a whistle and were given ten minutes to be outside dressed for physical exercises. Three of the girls dragged themselves out late. Everyone stood silently at attention while they did their sit-ups. One boy snickered and found himself up front doing push-ups. There was no longer any doubt in anyone's mind what the "commander" meant. After twenty minutes of vigorous exercise we were given a half hour to bathe, dress, and be in the hall for meditation.

Father Jalón's intense blue eyes scrutinized each person as he came in the door. He laughed easily, talked endlessly, had many jokes, and soon earned the nickname "Donald Duck." But he could also be serious. He led us in meditation on the "Our Father," taking one phrase a day: "God is Father to us—what does the word 'Father' mean?" Mass followed in the school chapel, and then breakfast. The first meal was served—to everyone's surprise—by Father Jalón, Father Sheifler, two students from the Salvadorean university, Xavier, and myself. Thereafter, the squads took turns serving their fellow *cursillistas* at meals, washing the dishes, sweeping, and cleaning the classroom and hall.

The classes, according to the syllabus prepared by Father Aguirre, covered the three areas in which he felt that Catholic high school graduates usually faced, because of poor preparation, their biggest crises—social doctrines, sex education, and Catholic faith.

Of the three, social doctrines received the most emphasis. We listened to a long descriptive lecture on the social conditions of the poor in Latin America; we considered the industrial revolution; we studied laissez-faire liberalism, capitalism, and neo-capitalism, and saw how these doctrines provided the rationale for the corrupt and exploitative labor practices of the early nineteenth century and how even to our day they had continued to legitimize and exacerbate the division between the rich and the poor.

We learned how Marx and Engels developed the doctrine of Communism to explain class struggle as part of the historical evolutionary process; how Communism came to be considered an answer to the sufferings of the poor. We sought to understand Communism's basic premises and then to refute them and point out the basic errors. "Communism will never succeed because it is based on error," we learned.

Finally, we turned to Christian social doctrine, as expounded in key papal encyclicals—*Rerum Novarum, Quadrigesimo Anno, Mater et Magistra*—finding in it a program of justice, equal opportunity, and charity to right the world's evils.

We speculated on a common phenomenon: Upon entering the university, students—boys, especially—are often shamed into hiding their religious observances and inclinations by the prevailing spirit of anticlericalism. Religion is often seen in Latin America as primarily a concern of women. When men go to church, they often stand in the back; and until recently a man would receive Holy Communion only on his wedding day.

Could this situation be an outgrowth of "liberalism"? We raised the question whether capitalism wasn't, after all, as atheistic as Communism. How could we hope to work for a more just social system if we didn't live our belief in God's common Fatherhood of all men? What is faith anyway? Who is God? Questions were raised that these young people had been led to believe were sacrilegious. Once the question of the existence of God was faced openly, stored-up misgivings and paradoxes in the students' minds poured out. For most of them had found that they could not harmonize the dogmas and doctrines in whose terms they had been taught about life, with what they saw actually going on around them.

There were other carefully thought-out activities. Every afternoon, in separate groups, the boys and girls learned self-defense tactics. Partisan politics is often violently militant in Latin American universities, where classes are usually in the evening because most students work full-time. They are older, on the average, than North American students, are active in their country's civil life, and usually constitute the bulk of its intellectuals.

Each student had to give a short speech every day. This practice was just as necessary as the self-defense exercises. Student meetings were important for policy-making at the university, and anyone wishing to be active and effective in them would have to be able to express himself forcefully and fluently. For many of the *cursillistas* this daily speech was one of the most painful and difficult aspects of the course—particularly for the girls, who were embarrassed at having to speak in public for the first time, and most especially in front of boys.

The topics for the daily speeches were designed to give the directors of the *cursillo* a more thorough knowledge of the participants, as well as demanding of the *cursillistas* self-analysis and even occasionally an emotional catharsis. The topics were simple and direct: why I came to the *cursillo*; the worst social evil I have witnessed or experienced; words at the burial of a student martyr; the person who has most influenced me in my life.

The preparation for this last topic stripped you down to a kind of existential nakedness, especially if you hadn't stopped to consider who you were, how you got where you were, and where you were going. To decide who most influenced you, you had to decide what you were really about as a person. Of course, you could choose some holy or famous figure that would help you prop up the mask behind which you liked to operate. But most of the students, being both quite serious and quite young, found the question bringing them initially a kind of dismay. Many discovered for the first time how empty their lives had been.

After this personal scrutiny, to attempt to answer the question "Who is Christ?" was far from an academic exercise. We tried to determine whether what we knew of Christ was only what we had been told from ancient writings and drilled into us by the Church, or if we had had personal experience of His reality. Could one come to know His Presence through study? through some kind of meditation? through Mass and Holy Communion?

In some extraordinary way I came to realize as never before that Christ *is* my living brother—He *is* the poor child in Castañás who needs food and medicine and water and wants to learn to read. Christ is not merely *in* him, He *is* the Indian who lives nearly starving and tries to grow some corn on a tiny plot on a hillside. He *is* the peasant leader who dares to resist the plantation owner and is beaten and killed.

This new-found insight into the real nature of Christ united all the *cursillistas* who shared it in a tight and warm bond of brotherly love.

Many of the pent-up questions of meaning in our lives had burst through during the week. We had been forced to open up, to break through the hard crust of old notions we had previously had concerning religion and social reality, to examine everything anew in the light of the presence of a Living Christ. We saw Him now both as a personal presence in each of us and as a generative, motive force in time of social revolution.

On the last day we stepped outside at dawn for the exercise period and watched the volcano, Fuego, belching forth its burning lava. The sky glowed with an eerie red-and-gray suffusion. We put our ears to the ground and heard the reverberations of the eruption. Instead of regarding this as an evil or destructive omen, we could not help but sense an identity between the eruption and the spiritual breakthrough in ourselves.

against allowing such activities to continue. He observed that the subject we had chosen was for adult audiences, while we had used high school actors.

A group of boys from the Jesuit school heard about the Nuncio's objections. They went to visit him and later reported their conversation to Xavier and myself.

"Why are you opposed to our presentation?" they asked the Nuncio.

"Because it is an immoral play," he observed.

"Have you seen it?"

"No."

"Then how did you make your judgment?"

"From the report of a Spanish drama critic who now lives in Guatemala."

The boys already knew about this writer.

"Did you know, Monseñor, that that man has personal animosity toward Sastre? In Spain, they are literary rivals."

The Nuncio seemed dubious. The boys continued: "We also hope that you haven't confused Sastre with Sartre. Would you read the play yourself if we brought you a copy?"

"Yes, but it is nevertheless immoral. Besides, this putting on activities with young boys and girls together is bad. Why, even a dance is bad. I know that from my personal experience. I was a boy once. Don't you feel immoral urgings at a dance?"

The boys looked at him in disbelief.

"No," they answered unanimously. They left his parlor wondering how a man like this could be expected to be an adequate moral guide for others. Meanwhile, they had learned something about higher authority.

After waiting a semester for things to cool down, we were able to put on two more plays. We were careful to choose milder topics.

Once a week the high school boys came over to our school to join our students for special lectures and discussions. Experts came to explain the Central American Common Market, the process of determining minimum wages, the workings of the Alliance for Progress, the effects of extensive malnutrition in Guatemala.

One day the girls brought the morning newspaper to class. It carried a story about migrant workers which destroyed any remaining illusions they might have had about the treatment of these laborers:

A truck was carrying Indian peasants to a cotton plantation for the harvest. It had been raining, and the back of the truck was covered with a tarpaulin. The driver heard someone banging on the back of the cab. Finally he stopped and went back to see what was the matter.

The peasants told him that one of their number was dead. The driver pulled the dead man to the edge of the truck by his legs, lifted him, then dumped his body over the embankment by the side of the road. He tied the canvas down, got back into the cab, and drove off.

The banging commenced again. The driver ignored it until finally he couldn't stand it any more. He went to the back again and dragged out two more dead men. The rest were near collapse.

They pleaded with him that they were suffocating from the exhaust fumes. He ignored them. They were too weak to help themselves. Over the course of the journey he pulled twelve dead Indians off the truck and threw their bodies into the canyon along the road.

The enormous evil appalled us all.

We talked about the value of work and of the men who performed it, about work as a source of capital, about human dignity. The girls began asking questions at home. During weekend visits to their fathers' plantations they started to notice actual conditions. One of the girls was so upset by the indifference of her family as she discussed these matters that she left the dinner table crying. The next day, her father came to the school.

Sister Mildred called me into her office. "Tone down your classes," she said. "You're upsetting the girls."

"I can't," I answered her.

"What do you mean, you *can't?*"

"I'm following the official course in sociology. I'm only pointing up actual conditions in their country. I'm not exaggerating a thing. How can they become real leaders if they are protected at this age, when they're hungry to know what is really going on? We should all know about these matters. We should all get upset."

Sister Mildred simply looked at me.

Angrily, I left her office. Why should I tone down my classes? Why did we keep sacrificing principle to avoid disturbing people, especially those in high society? I was angry at the girl's father, and disappointed with Sister Mildred. I had never expected her to react to a complaint that way.

In a later class, I gave a lecture on housing. I had often visited two slums, La Limonada and Castañás. I tried to translate dry statistics into the concrete human reality they represented, and tell the students about the despair I had seen. When eighty percent of the houses in the whole country had dirt floors and no running water, what kind of daily misery did this indicate for thousands of people? As I spoke, I noticed that María, a very sensitive girl, was becoming agitated.

"You have no right to talk like this," she sobbed. "You are a foreigner. You are criticizing my country. We know things are bad here. We are not blind. We are the ones who must do something about it. You stop talking like this. These aren't your people."

It hadn't occurred to me that the girls would regard me as an outsider, presuming to talk about "their people." I wanted them to be my people, just as I wanted to be one of them. Yet I was a *Norteamericana*, a *Yanqui*. I had no right to forget that. I had come to Guatemala to give my life to its people, expecting nothing in return except the satisfaction of knowing

I was doing meaningful service. With chagrin, I began to realize that I also expected gratitude. When María branded me a "foreigner," I was pained.

Soon afterward, I resolved to ask Sister Mildred if I could obtain Guatemalan citizenship. I knew that my allegiance to my Christian faith transcended my loyalty to the United States. I was proud to be an American; but if becoming one with the Guatemalans required me to forfeit my citizenship, I was prepared to make that sacrifice. After all, I had given up my family when I became a nun, yet I didn't love them any less. And giving up my citizenship wouldn't mean that I loved the United States any the less. It was only that I had come to love Guatemala more than any foreigner has a right to, and still remain a foreigner.

Sister Mildred agreed to write to Maryknoll's Mother General to ask permission. Two weeks later, the answer came back—in the negative. I felt hurt; my own motives had seemed good to me. The answer included an explanation that Maryknoll might someday want to send me to another country. I was shaken: I hadn't considered that possibility in a long time. I knew that I had pledged to Maryknoll that I would be ready to go anywhere, at any time. When I gave that pledge, I had even been proud to be available. In Guatemala, however, my work, my personal interchanges and relationships with the people, had deeply interwoven my life with theirs, and it was here now that I wanted to live and work for the rest of my days.

Suddenly the fear arose that my request for Guatemalan citizenship might precipitate a reconsideration of my assignment. I wanted no risk of that. I hoped they would forget about me. I resolved to be neither seen nor heard from for a while, so far as the Mother General was concerned.

XIV

God
Occurs

The Nun The weekly discussion between the girls from
Monte María and the boys from Liceo Javier
became very meaningful. One week they proposed to examine
the topic "What Boys Think of Girls and Girls of Boys."
Needless to say, this question interested our students as much
as it does young people everywhere.

I myself, however, felt inadequate to contribute to the discussion. How else, in all honesty, could I feel? My experience
with men—as men—had been limited to my short acquaint-
ance with Luis, my boyfriend back in Mexico. And while we
were dating I had already known I would be entering the
convent, and so hadn't allowed myself to take the relationship
very seriously. Now I tried to understand what was going on in
these students' minds and feelings, hoping to help relieve
them of guilt-ridden notions about sex and love. I always
answered their intimate questions in class as frankly as I could,
trying to put them at ease and inhibiting my own embarrassment. They sometimes asked me why the other sisters were
afraid to answer direct questions about sex.

The boys and girls argued vigorously and frankly from their
own experience. They considered the advantages and disad-
vantages of going steady. And it took all the courage they
possessed for some of the girls to stand up before the group
and speak their minds about boys' fickleness and about the
rigid supervision of young people's social life under the tradi-

tional chaperone system. I knew they would have to learn to face opposition and criticism in order to grow to be leaders.

By watching the girls' reactions and talking afterward with the boys and Xavier, I began to understand more clearly the basic psychological differences between men and women in outlook and emotional reaction. The boys expected to be able to speak the truth straightforwardly, "in hard words," as Emerson put it, and they assumed the girls would answer back in the same manner. But the girls expected the boys to be polite and not to speak so strongly. The boys felt there was something hypocritical in the girls' reluctance to speak out in front of the group. The girls struggled to overcome the social caution and restraint that had been enforced upon them. Modesty seemed more marked in Latin girls than in their North American sisters, and was compounded by a natural shyness about standing up and baring their souls.

One day I had a conversation with some nuns who questioned me on my concern about poverty in Guatemala. They suggested that the love of God and the love of our fellow-humans are not the same thing, that the love of God took precedence over love of people and concern with their needs. I insisted that the two were indivisible and that it was perilously wrong to separate them. This didn't sit at all well with the other sisters.

I went back to my room afterward and searched myself in the darkness as I meditated. I realized that I had been in part, defending my love for Xavier; I experienced Christ in Xavier at that time, and I knew it. I could not prove that to the sisters, and I would not try. But there was work to do that could not wait. I recognized that there were believers who were atheists and atheists who believed, though the words of both might tend to belie the true nature of their commitments. To me, Jesus Christ was not an abstraction. He was a Living Presence, incarnate in every human being I met. He did not go by the name of Christ, and He often did not follow any of the churchly paths of Christianity, but He worked and moved and gave Being to all, nonetheless. When Christ came alive in me, I recognized Him in others. I felt a kinship with all I met, my brothers and sisters. Was this heretical? Why did I have to justify such thoughts even to myself?

I needed to let Xavier know I loved him. I wrote him a poem from my heart. I was embarrassed when I gave it to him, yet I had grown to trust him and dared to show him my poem. Somehow, I was afraid that, with overt expression, the chaste beauty of my love would be shattered; and I was determined to be faithful to the promise I had made to Christ. In any case, my love would have been wrong only if I were to let even the thought of expressing it physically come to my mind. I was at peace in my feelings toward Xavier. I did not distrust love.

Brother, yes, I feel you to be my brother;
Not an older brother, nor a younger brother—
  Maybe my twin.

This is because we both have an older Brother,
Christ, who carries us in His arms;
He wants you and me to take by the hand so many
  younger brothers and sisters.

He wants us all to launch out into the sea of love.
A sea with waves of emotion,
  An infinite horizon, far away, and
    the peace of profundity.

To be brother and sister through the unity of ideals,
And of ideas that burst forth in accord.
To be brother and sister because of a common Mother,
Our Lady, who sees and arranges things.

To be brother and sister because God is our Good Father.

You have brothers that are yours alone, others are mine,
And some are both of ours.
Pray to Christ to help us carry them high.

The day that you take Christ in your hands,
The day that you'll be a priest,
I think I'll feel you to be raised up yourself.

You'll be another Christ, and thus more a brother of mine.
You'll be, still more, another reason to unite me to Christ.
  Speak to Him a little of me,
  And much of our brothers and sisters.

You've done a lot for me.
  Since I've known you, I am more of a Christian.
I hope you can say the same of me.

  Thank you for being my brother.

I could see he was pleased as he read it. He didn't say anything. We just smiled and walked away from each other. I knew my love was safe and that ours would remain a true friendship. I was happy to recognize and accept my womanly feelings.

Xavier and I invited students from other schools to our weekly discussions as part of a campaign to break down snobbism and competition among students. The discussions dealt mostly with the social problems that were tearing Guatemala apart. For example, a $14-million theater was being constructed in the shadow of the scaffolding for a huge new basilica—both within a stone's throw of thousands of incredibly miserable hovels. To spend great sums of money to fulfill the secondary needs of an elite while the basic needs of masses of human beings went ignored seemed clearly futile and wrong. Even after hours of fiery debate, discussion would continue in small groups of earnest students. Yes, we decided, the priorities of spending in Guatemala were all wrong; but what could we do? The answer seemed elusive. The only conclusion we came to was that they, as students, should prepare well to be conscientious professionals.

A much simpler question got me into trouble. I had brought

along with me to Guatemala many of my own notions about high school from the United States, such as the value of graduation proms and school rings. After several years, however, I began to look into some of the practices I had helped introduce at Monte María. Was it fair to buy expensive graduation rings that cost nearly $40 each, when there were innumerable families around who lived on $160 a year? I decided to present this to the students as a discussion topic. One of the boys acted as moderator, since I felt obligated to take part in the debate myself. For I wanted to make clear that although I had approved of the rings earlier, I no longer thought their use justified.

After much discussion of the many pros and cons, it was concluded that each individual had to decide for himself or herself; but many had come to feel that giving up a ring was at least symbolic of an awareness of the prevalent poverty and of a willingness to do something about it. The pragmatists in the group regarded this as self-deception: "You aren't going to feed anyone with $40. That won't solve the problem of Guatemala's poverty." The more sensitive and those responsive to the meaning of symbols came back with, "We have to show ourselves, if nobody else, that we do care how our less fortunate brothers live."

Some students were getting the message. The main thing was to begin to examine the habits and customs we had all grown so unquestioningly used to.

Next day in school the topic was still hot. Many felt guilty over their unwillingness to make a personal sacrifice and began to look around for someone to assuage their consciences. They found him in Father Pedro Carbonera. A Spanish Dominican who taught at Monte María, he was quite short, always dressed in his long white robes, young in age—thirty-four—but so rigid and conservative in outlook as to seem ancient. He agreed that giving up graduation rings was a meaningless gesture. Besides, he went on, it was God Who made the poor poor and the rich rich; we should learn to accept our destined roles and live graciously within them—the classic stance of Spanish Catholicism. Some girls were relieved by this argument; but others felt anger and frustration.

In class, they told me what Father Carbonera had said, and I went to argue the question with him at once. I found him in the teachers room, and we had one of our not-uncommon heated debates. (One notable earlier argument had concerned Teilhard de Chardin, the French Jesuit thinker, whom I had been reading at the time. Father Carbonera characterized Father Teilhard's works as dangerous and probably heretical. "You are not equipped to read him," he had informed me. "And you, who should be, are afraid to risk it," I had retorted.) I told him: "What you've just fed those girls is a distortion of the Gospel. You're comfortable and well off, like so many priests and nuns, so you can believe that those who are poor are so destined by God. That is not Christianity. That is not good theology. That doesn't even make sense."

The argument went back and forth furiously and ended, as usual, with neither of us budging from his own position.

Two girls from Monte María and four boys from Liceo Javier stuck to their resolution and refused class rings. Their refusal was kept as quiet as possible, but I was proud of them.

One of Monte María's requirements for graduation was a seminar on a socioeconomic topic. Our student teachers had decided on an investigation, under Josefina's guidance, of the lack of rural schoolteachers. The college-preparatory girls were planning a study under the direction of María Luisa Cajas, a close friend of mine who had just graduated from law school.

María Luisa's physical daintiness was an exterior reflection of her inner sensitivity. She came from a poor family and knew what it meant to suffer need. She was a teacher, but had gone on to study law because she knew how much the poor needed legal help. We discussed possible topics for her group and finally decided on cooperatives.

The cooperative movement in Guatemala had barely survived Castillo Armas's campaign against peasant organizations. When we visited some of the few cooperatives still functioning and talked with several leaders in the movement, we found that they were very excited about our interest and the help that the published text of the seminar might provide. In too many people's minds, cooperatives were classified as communistic. I hoped that the idea of individual work in this field would catch fire among the girls and open the minds of the wealthy.

Near graduation time, María Lara, the girl who had accused me of being a foreigner without the right to criticize her country, came to me and shyly confided, "I'm going to become a social worker. I know this is the best way I can help my people. Thank you for teaching me what you did. Please forgive me for talking to you the way I did at the beginning of the year."

I was as touched by this as I had been hurt by her outburst a few months before.

The girls in Josefina's seminar came to the conclusion that their country's illiteracy was so bad that all graduating teachers had a social obligation to teach in rural areas for at least one or two years. Four of them—Irene, Isabelle, Elsie, and Anabella—wanted to set the example. These were the student teachers who had gone with me to hear Father Aguirre's lectures on social problems. During the discussion following his talk, they had made vows to go to the mountains as volunteer teachers. Now, more than ever, they wanted to make that promise good.

"Do you have any thoughts as to where we could go?" they asked me.

I thought of Jacaltenango. Although I had been to other missions in Huehuetenango, this was my first love. The sisters there were starting a parochial school and needed Guatemalan teachers.

"Jacal, perhaps," I ventured.

Irene and Isabelle threw their arms around me in Latin affection and enthusiasm.

"Really? Really? Are you sure?" They had been to Jacaltenango with me on a visit, and they knew some of the people there.

"I'll write today and find out."

"Please, please! All four of us want to go."

Since mail took nearly ten days each way, we resorted to telegrams, which were cheap and had become the usual means of communication between the mission parishes. The sisters answered that they were delighted. I learned that Father Denny Kraus, the pastor there, had a special knack for working with people and that he loved company.

The only problem was with the girls' families. Irene's and Isabelle's parents were reluctant, but eventually relented. Elsie's and Anabella's parents were adamant—their daughters were not meant to work with that class of people.

The day before Irene and Isabelle were to go, another sister and I sat for several hours with Isabelle's mother. She couldn't bear the thought of her daughter's going. She was honest and told us frankly her anxieties about living conditions, about the village people with whom Isabelle would associate, about medical attention, and about what supervisory help she would receive, since she had no teaching experience. We were somehow able to calm her fears, and next morning, Isabelle was with Irene on the plane to Huehuetenango.

We continued having *cursillos* during school vacations. Xavier and I picked out four of the more outstanding students who had attended the first *cursillo* and prepared them to become *cursillo* teachers. Then, with Father Jalón, we formed a team. We were now recruiting candidates from the university as well as from high school graduating classes. I had made many contacts with university students during my year there, and this made it easier to invite them to a *cursillo*.

One day during a *cursillo*, I was directing the discussion on

Christ, and in the course of it I read the famous passage from St. Matthew XXV:

> I was hungry and you fed me, thirsty and you gave me drink; I was a stranger and you received me in your home, naked and you clothed me; I was sick and you took care of me, in prison and you visited me.
>
> The King will answer back, I tell you, indeed, whenever you did this for one of the least important of these brothers of mine, you did it for me!*

Most of us had been talking about Jesus Christ in one way or another, all our lives; and some of us had dedicated ourselves to doing His work. Yet during these days of intense sharing in the *cursillos,* the reality of Christ slowly became more palpable to us. This day, particularly, as we considered the words of Christ, a stronger meaning began to show through to me.

My heart began to beat very fast. I looked around at the others. There were so many different expressions on their faces—some were actually rapt, some seemed in pain. Suddenly, I understood. And my literal, geographical concept of the Kingdom of Heaven and the Lake of Eternal Fire fell away before the onset of this new revelation: The real Heaven is a state of communion, of compassion and loving concern, with all our brothers and sisters, all of them incarnations of the Living Christ; the real Hell is a state of alienation, a being out of communion with yourself and with other people and with God, distrustful, competitive, prejudiced, seeing others as things, sources of profit and gratification only. This was a completely new insight for me, and I was thrilled with its meaning. I saw Christ struggling to be born in other faces.

It was at this *cursillo* that I first met Felipe Ramos, a person who was to profoundly affect my life. Unlike most Guatemalans, he was blue-eyed, blond, with a mass of curly short

* *Good News for Modern Man* (American Bible Society: New York; 1966).

hair, of medium height, built like an athlete, supple as a cat. He was studying psychology at San Carlos University. His intelligence was so keen that it was almost a hindrance to him, because he could analyze a situation more quickly than he could identify with people *in* the situation. Yet the first thing that struck me about Felipe was his readiness to serve. When his squad was assigned to wash dishes, he was the first one there, and he stayed to make sure the job was finished. His attitude was in contrast to that of many of the other boys, who were often careless or tried to avoid work and difficult situations.

After breakfast one morning, when the others had left, he remained at the table talking to another boy. I went over and joined the conversation. He was saying that he couldn't understand how Christ on the Cross could have said, "Father, why have you abandoned me?" if He were truly God. I shared my thoughts on these words with him. They had caused me to wonder, also, and I had not been able to resolve the mystery to my satisfaction. We talked often after that.

Xavier and some of the other *cursillo* teachers distrusted Felipe. They felt his questions, especially those about Communism, to be too knowledgeable. In a subdued manner and, it seemed, with a certain subtlety, he had challenged some of their points of social doctrine, and they hadn't been able to answer him adequately. They pointed him out to me as a possible Communist infiltrator. But long hours of talk with Felipe convinced me that he had not given his allegiance to any particular group or to any definite social ideology. He was searching for a viable instrument to bring about social justice for Guatemala, and was prepared to dedicate himself completely to the betterment of social conditions.

I did not feel that Felipe had experienced any very real or deep religious awakening during the *cursillo*. In his intellectual grasp of theory, he worked more like a chess player. He seemed to find a valid rationale in Catholic social doctrine for revolutionary ideas he had already begun to form. The Biblical or ecclesiastical basis of the doctrine seemed neither to inspire nor to hinder him. In the intensity of my own breakthrough, I believed I was able to sense Christ's working even in Felipe Ramos's thinking. Why not? Why should I try to restrict Christ's patterns of work to my own ideas? Christ works even through those unaware of His presence.

Perhaps this was error. I don't think that I can see any more deeply into the mysteries of Christ now than then, certainly not for judging Felipe's motives anyway. I found that how well I knew him and other students depended not only on our common ideology but also on the closeness of our relationship, how deeply we counted upon one another for survival and for morale, the openness and meaningfulness of our interchanges. Such knowledge is not always measurable in rational terms; it has to be sensed, intuited. This was one of the major lessons the *cursillos* taught me.

Xavier and I, however, both saw one important shortcoming in the *cursillos*: While they were a superb instrument for motivating people, there was no effective group or activity into which the people could thereafter channel their new-found enthusiasm. It was not enough to have vague ideas about fighting both Communism and exploitative capitalism. We felt it would be better to build small discussion-action cells of dedicated Christians to help us maintain clarity of purpose and unity, and thought this would at the same time encourage the members to work within existing organizations, infusing them with Christian idealism.

We formed cells with *cursillistas* according to the university course they were taking. Some went to Landivar—the Catholic university—and others to San Carlos. Felipe, Titina, Rosa, and I all attended the College of Humanities at San Carlos and began to meet regularly.

One day, as we talked in our cell meeting about alternative ways of living and working, I happened to mention what had become a yearly event—taking a group of the girls from Monte María to spend a week in the mountains working with Indian peasants. Felipe perked up at this. "What can they do out there?" he wanted to know.

I told him about getting to know the poverty, illiteracy, and also the warmth and openness, of the Indians through personal contact.

"Do you know," Felipe asked, "of a priest out there who might want me to come work as an assistant?"

"For how long?"

"Indefinitely. And, look, Sister, I want to be useful, not a parasite. I'll do *any* kind of work. I don't care about pay. I want to learn first-hand and, if I can, to be of some real help."

At his urging, I spoke to Father John Breen, who listened and then said, "O.K., if you recommend him."

I hoped that the work with the priests in Huehuetenango would help lead Felipe in the direction of Christian social commitment as a way of action and that his work would also help the Indians. But when I went to the Maryknoll Fathers' Center House in Guatemala City to make arrangements for his transportation, one of the priests expressed his doubts: "You mean that Ramos is a university student and is willing to give up his studies for some time to go up to the hills to work?"

"Yes," I answered. "Why do you find it so strange?"

"Well, because giving up his studies shows a lack of self-interest. What does he expect to get out of this?"

"He just wants to work for people in a more direct way."

"He must be a Communist," the priest said. "Only Communists can be that dedicated."

I winced. Yet this showed exactly what the *cursillos* were doing—producing committed people who found it hard to see where and in what way they could give of themselves, and who, when they made the attempt, were suspected of being Communists.

In the spring of 1964, Xavier told me that he was leaving the Jesuit Order. He wanted to study economics and become involved in politics in his own country, Nicaragua, and felt that he could be a more effective Christian as a layman. Although we would miss Xavier, I felt it was a good decision and congratulated him. Some of the priests at the school resented his leaving and tried to discredit him, but the students had known him too well to listen, and we gave him a great send-off.

It was customary for the sisters to return to the States every ten years for a six-month refresher course at the motherhouse in Maryknoll, New York. My turn came in October 1964. I hated to leave Guatemala, but I was anxious to see my family again after ten long years. My sister and brothers were grown up, and, except for the youngest, were all married.

I spent the two weeks permitted us at home getting to know my family all over again. But it was too short a time to do much more than get superficially reacquainted.

At Maryknoll, forty-three of us came together, sisters from missions in Africa, Japan, South America. We studied the new thinking on theology, liturgy, and the Scriptures and took part in seminars on social psychology and in counseling.

Vatican II was in session. The Church seemed to be coming to life. One day we came into the classroom and saw on the blackboard, in the handwriting of the priest who was teaching us, "God does not exist." The words blazed out at us. Shocked, we looked at one another, not knowing what to say. In a few minutes, the priest came in and walked directly to the blackboard. Under the previous sentence, he wrote, "God occurs."

All the dynamic impressions of my first *cursillo* came flooding into my mind. I was coming more and more to realize that religion consisted, not of a collection of doctrines and church rituals, but of living with other people and sharing meaning and direction with them.

In the courses at Maryknoll there came to me an even stronger sense of dedication as a nun, but more—dedication as a *person*. We examined the old concepts of God, of service. We began to see that Christ never meant the Church to be a pyramid of responsibility and authority, as the hierarchy wants it to be. God's people need to see themselves as equally sharing responsibility, *sharing* a vision.

I returned to Guatemala eagerly after only three months. I had just received permission to teach religion in public schools and had to make the January opening of the schools. This would be quite different from teaching rich girls. I felt that girls from more modest circumstances might work more deeply into the life of Guatemala and be less isolated than the upperclass students at Monte María tended to be.

I found out that Felipe Ramos had been sent home from the mountains after six months. When I saw him, he refused to discuss it.

"I helped to get you accepted for work up there," I insisted. "Don't you think I have a right to know what happened?"

Felipe looked at me and smiled gravely. I sensed his deep disappointment.

"Sister, respect my decision not to talk about it. I left. I had always known that priests were human. I have nothing more to say."

It was only a year later that I came to understand the restraint Felipe had exercised. I learned that he had been approached sexually by a priest and that it was this he had refused to gossip about. My respect for him increased when I realized he had not even tried to defend his own reputation. When he had rejected the priest's advances, he had been kicked out on a vague accusation of being pro-Communist. Some of the Maryknollers knew the truth but out of concern for the priest's reputation had refused to defend Felipe.

XV

Padre,
We Need Land

The Priest The lime cooperative was growing. Soon
after the truck arrived in Cabricán, the trac-
tor was sent in. But its arrival was almost anticlimactic—the
Indians already seemed to be getting used to such events.

The *ladinos* watched these developments with apprehension. As they saw the Indians actually starting to work in a
collective way, they began to spread word that the two ve-
hicles were really mine, that I was going to manipulate the
Indians into paying for my truck and my tractor. Others
maintained that I must be a Communist. Although some Indians who lived farther away from town took these rumors
seriously, most of them knew better. They had been treated
too long with contempt as *indios* and *brutos* to believe everything the *ladinos* told them; they knew they were expected to
live like slaves, not as owners of trucks and tractors, that the
furious *ladinos* felt jealous and threatened by the new competition.

We soon realized that we'd have to work fast to teach some
Indians to drive the truck—our *ladino* driver clearly couldn't
hold out long against the pressure being brought to bear on
him to stop working for the co-op. The *ladinos* in San Carlos
Sija even offered him money to wreck the truck. Because of
this pressure we pushed the Indian apprentice drivers hard—
too hard, as it turned out, because mountain roads require
great skill and experience. On one occasion the driver, failing

to make a turn in time, drove the truck over an embankment, and it landed upside down. Sometime later, the tractor went over a small cliff. Repair bills were high, and so were the monthly payments.

Ladinos from San Carlos tried to force the truck off the road on three different occasions, and succeeded once. The Indians won damages for repairs, but only because it was I who pleaded the case before the judge—an Indian seldom wins in court in Guatemala, unless it is against other Indians.

Plantation managers told the Indians they would not buy from them because it was said that they mixed sand with their lime. I helped them draw up a statement defending the quality of the co-op's lime, and it was issued as a flyer and passed around by the members.

The whole experience had an incredible effect on the Indians. The men gained self-confidence and learned to talk to store owners and to plantation managers. They made trips all over the Pacific coast of Guatemala and to Guatemala City. It was expensive, and the risks were high, but they loved every minute of it. Watching these people respond, appreciating their vigor and their genuineness, I grew to love and respect them more each day.

The original group of twenty-four owners soon expanded to fifty, then to seventy and one hundred, as more and more people wanted to participate in the co-op. The National Catholic Welfare Conference of the U.S. Catholic bishops lent us another $6,000. We bought land on which we built a two-story factory for both processing and bagging the lime. It was the largest building in town. The land was held in Bishop Manresa's name, since as a cooperative we did not have *personería jurídica* ("juridical personality"), a legal prerequisite in Guatemala for an organization's owning property. We bought two more diesel trucks and sold the old GMC as soon as it was paid for; it wasn't big enough, we had to make extra trips, and gasoline is very expensive in Guatemala.

By this time the co-op was no longer a secret. It was known, to Maryknollers as well as others, that one of their priests was deeply involved in commercial undertakings with Indians. The cooperative trucks were moving about the country, driven by Indians, with "Parish Co-op Cabricán" painted on their sides. The success of this endeavor won the support of the U.S. bishops' relief organization. Bishop Manresa named me co-ordinator for the other cooperatives that were beginning to spring up in our diocese.

The co-op grew to include 110 members. Each member had to contribute Q.120 as his share. But since Indians almost never had cash, it was decided that a new member could discharge his obligation by 120 days' work in the limestone mine, at the ovens, in the factory, on the trucks, or in the marketing agencies that the co-op had established around the country. It should be noted that one dollar a day, the pay rate under this arrangement, represented a higher daily wage than any of them had ever earned in their lives.

We did not seem to be able to provide work for more than 110. Yet there were seven thousand people in Cabricán, another five thousand in neighboring Huitán, and two thousand in Rio Blanco, to the west—all living in near-desperate circumstances. When we would talk over the problem within the co-op, member after member would repeat, "If we are going to help everybody, Padre, we need more land. Land is the only answer. It is the only thing our people know how to work."

If 110 Indians could break the pattern, why not the others? I sent a telegram to President Ydígoras and was granted an appointment. I left for Guatemala City.

After waiting in the presidential palace for two hours, I was finally ushered in. Ydígoras, a kindly-looking old man, listened sympathetically as I told him of the people's problem—not enough land. I reminded him of a visit he had once made to Soloma, when he had called Father Breen and myself to his side, then berated the town officials for not doing as much for the people as we were doing. John and I had been embarrassed and angry at the president for antagonizing the officials. But now I recalled his words to him, and he nodded. "I will help you," he said.

I returned to Cabricán walking on air. The next day we called a meeting. "Don't worry," I assured the leaders, "*El Presidente* is going to give you more land. I spoke to him."

They all nodded their heads knowingly—they would not insult me by saying what they were thinking.

We waited for months, but nothing happened. Finally, I asked for another appointment. The president's secretary assured me that *El Presidente* was working on providing land for the Indians. Meanwhile, there were reports in the newspapers about Ydígoras giving out land to his friends. I became disillusioned with the kindly old man.

My brother Art was at that time successfully developing a cooperative for merchandising coffee in La Libertad, Huehuetenango. Art had joined Maryknoll four years after me and had come to Guatemala in 1961, when I was already in Cabricán. He had been attending Boston College Business School when he decided to enter the priesthood. Although he had never mentioned such intentions to anyone while growing up, his decision had come as no great surprise, since many of our friends and relatives had long thought he had more of a vocation than I did. Still, his announcement had caught our family off guard.

Just before his ordination, the Superior General of Maryknoll was in Guatemala and asked me where I imagined Art would be sent. Since it was his prerogative to make the assignments, I sensed that he was only toying with me. So I seized the opportunity to ask him why Maryknoll had the apparent policy of sending brothers, several pairs of whom were in the Order, to opposite ends of the globe. He declared that no such policy existed, and that he would send Art to Guatemala. And to the surprise of all Maryknollers in Guatemala, Art was in fact assigned there in June 1961.

Even so, we didn't get together very often, since our mis-

sions were five hours apart. Furthermore, after leaving Huehuetenango the way I had, I was in no hurry to return. Many
apocryphal stories had sprung up about the "cross incident,"
and I felt no obligation to continually correct them. This
despite the fact that Tex Gerbermann had stopped Art on the
road once to tell him that his brother was the only one who
had ever done a "decent job" in San Juan Ixcoy—Tex's way of
telling me he was sorry for what he had done.

After Art had started his cooperative in La Libertad, he
came to visit me in Cabricán. He knew we were looking for
land. He explained how a few plantation owners in his parish
were taking advantage of hundreds of poor families in the
area by using them as tenant farmers on their overextensive
properties. "In order to farm a miserable piece of ground,"
he told me, "our people have to work months on end for those
lousy bastards. I wish there was some way we could help them
find other lands."

Suddenly the same idea occurred to both of us: Why not
see if the two cooperatives could lease jointly a big piece of
flat land from a plantation on the Pacific coast? Our people's
main staple was corn, and they could never get enough of it.
Lands on the coast produced two harvests of corn a year, compared to one crop grown in the mountains. Since the Cabricán
cooperative trucks usually came back from the coast empty
after selling their lime, they could truck the corn back. The
tractor could be spared from the mines for a few months to
do the plowing and sowing.

The leaders of the two cooperatives were excited by the
prospects and pitched right in to map out the details. The
Cabricán co-op built two aluminum-and-steel silos to hold
thirty tons of corn each.

The results of the experiment, however, proved disappoint-
ing. The plantation owner's rent was excessive, and the farmers
ended up paying him about one-fourth the value of the crop,
and thus the corn cost more than ever.

We learned a key lesson from this experience: You can't

make ends meet as a tenant farmer, no matter how large the scale. The men reverted to their original judgment—we need more land, land of our own.

The bishop visited us one Sunday to administer confirmation to hundreds of our new converts. Communions had mounted into the thousands, and he was surprised and gratified. He had continued to receive complaints from the sisters over my not wearing a cassock, my not being present every day to celebrate Mass for them, and, most of all, my involvement in commercial undertakings of a nonspiritual nature. Now he was dumfounded over the crowds of people who came to receive the sacraments. At this time the parish had been open about four years.

"If this is the response you get from the cooperative," he told me, "then keep at it."

I didn't like that motivation. I had experienced more real trust and communion in sweating out problems and following through opportunities in the co-op than I had in the church. Risks and necessities had brought us a closeness that had become organic to our very survival, a living Christianity. But I could hardly explain this to the bishop.

I told him about my visit to the president. He informed me that Ydígoras had given him a small plantation on the Pacific coast and said that since he wasn't using it, the cooperative could work it.

A few days later, some of the co-op leaders and I went to the coast to look at the bishop's plantation. The men were excited when they saw it—the land looked good, and it wasn't far from the land they had rented with the co-op from La Libertad. But this time no payment would have to be made to the owner.

We drove back up to Xela to see the bishop and to settle the arrangements for using his land. But he told us he had changed his mind, that he needed the land to raise produce for the seminary. We were all very disappointed.

The men and I frequently talked long hours into the night.

My rectory was always open to them, and they would come, sit, and smoke. If it was late when we finished our discussion, they would sleep on the floor of the rectory or on a mattress, bundled up in blankets, if there weren't too many of them. Nights were cold at 8,700 feet above sea level. I would also go to their homes and spend nights with them, sometimes to talk, sometimes because someone was sick. I learned that Christ can be shared outside of the Mass. The face of Christ seemed to me in those days to have the features of a Maya Indian. But all that time, there sounded in my mind the same litany of anguish: "Padre, we need land."

When President Ydígoras was overthrown by the military, Colonel Enrique Peralta Azurdia took over. He adopted as his theme *Operación Honestidad*, to show the country he was going to clean up the corruption that had prevailed under Ydígoras. After more talk with the cooperative members, it was agreed that I would arrange for an appointment with the new president to determine whether he would give the people some land. I sent another telegram and once again was given an appointment.

Once again I waited in the presidential palace; once again I was ushered into the office of the president. This time, no sympathetic looks, no understanding nods, only an unblinking stare. I felt I was speaking to a brick wall. There were no interruptions, no questions, until I finished speaking.

Then Peralta Azurdia said: "You are an American. Your countrymen have more land in my country than they know what to do with. I am told they are selling some of it. Go ask if you can buy some land from them."

He was referring to the United Fruit Company. I had heard that they were selling land, but I knew that the price would be high and that the government, on the other hand, had lands to give away.

"But the land I ask for is not for me, Your Excellency, it is for my parishioners, your countrymen, and they have no money."

He waved me summarily away: "Go see the Compañía Agrícola." This was United Fruit's landowning subsidiary. I was discouraged, but at least there had been no song and dance, no false promises.

Then I heard that Peralta Azurdia's brother was a lawyer for United Fruit. I was told that he perhaps might be helpful, and so I went to see him: No, he was not a lawyer for United Fruit, nor would he ever be; yes, United Fruit was selling lands to Guatemalans, but only to its own company executives, "to keep the lands in the family." This was the company's way of trying to get around the antigringo feelings so prevalent in Guatemala, and directed especially at itself for its unpopular role of more than fifty years' duration.

United Fruit, or "The Company," as it is known in Guatemala, is famous for the exploitative terms—including near-total tax exemptions—of the contracts it negotiated early in this century with Guatemalan dictators, and has since refused to renegotiate. When President Arévalo tried to bring The Company to heel in the late forties, it was able, as sole owner of the country's railroad and shipping facilities, to close down the economy until he backed off. When a United Nations economic mission studied the Guatemalan economy in 1950 and accused United Fruit of charging the highest rail freights in the world and paying next to nothing in taxes, The Company, in wounded pride, pointed to its higher-than-average wages and worker benefits. When Arévalo's successor, Jacobo Arbenz, decided it wasn't right that a single foreign company should own more land than the total holdings of fifty percent of the nation's population, keeping, moreover, more than ninety percent of its holdings in reserve, he expropriated half the land, as well as that of other huge *latifundias*, and gave the acreage to a hundred thousand landless families. United Fruit screamed "Communism," and John Foster Dulles, who had been a senior partner with Sullivan and Cromwell, the law firm that represents The Company, asked his brother Allen for CIA help to train some Guatemalan rebels then living in Honduras and Nicaragua. As President Eisenhower reveals in his book *Mandate for Change*, the aid was provided, the invasion was successful, Arbenz was overthrown, and United Fruit was given back its lands. Yet The Company was more unpopular than ever.

Peralta Azurdia's brother doubted that The Company would sell to the people of Cabricán, since it refused to sell to its own workers. In 1958 United Fruit had lost an antitrust suit in New Orleans and had been ordered to sell forty percent of its assets to competitors. Since the 1954 overthrow of Arbenz, its lands had been the most vulnerable of these assets. When 2,500 Guatemalan workers for The Company heard that their employer was about to sell a substantial portion of its reserve lands, they tried to buy them. The Company, however refused to make the sale, maintaining that "another group of twelve employees" had spoken up first. When it became known that the twelve employees were all top company executives in Guatemala and that they would make a collective contract to sell all their bananas only to United Fruit, no one was fooled. The president's brother did not have much trouble convincing me that it would be a waste of time to expect help from the United Fruit Company.

Still, the cooperatives kept on expanding. Our own co-op bought two wheat threshers. Three credit unions, spin-offs from this first co-op, were formed. One of them, made up mostly of lime producers, managed to accumulate Q.3,000 in savings and had loaned over Q.8,000 in small amounts to its members by the time I left Cabricán in January 1966—astonishing amounts in their penny economy. I also took a hand in revitalizing several credit unions in other areas. More were established, and later they were joined in a confederation, the National Federation of Credit Unions, the country's first and only cooperative league. Bishop Manresa was very pleased.

But though expansion was the watchword, we were still reaching no more than a small percentage of the people. Only with more land could we begin to effect any substantial change. Because of this desperate need for land, some people were moving to the barrios of Guatemala City, or to the Pacific coast to work on the coffee and cotton plantations for a pittance or a small plot of land.

One day I read in the newspapers that INTA (the National Institute for Agrarian Transformation) was planning to give out land in the Zona Reina (also called Ixcán), a junglelike area northeast of Huehuetenango. I paid a visit to INTA headquarters in Guatemala City, and was informed that if government lands were to be distributed out there, the people of Cabricán would be the first to receive a share. I went back to the village and told this to the people—there was more nodding of heads.

But then someone suggested that we make a pilgrimage into the Zona Reina and publicize the trek and INTA's promise, and thus try to force their hand. The idea caught on quickly, and shortly thereafter, about twenty "pilgrims" were on their way. Among them were representatives from five villages; an engineer from INTA and a man from the Ministry of Agriculture; Father Bill Woods, a priest with similar social concerns; and myself. We did not ask for ecclesiastical permission—if and where and how the Indians in Cabricán should seek land did not seem to us a Church matter. The area we were exploring was in Huehuetenango diocese, but I saw no reason to let this prevent me from accompanying the people.

We set out early on a Monday morning. The round trip took a week, with camping at night along the way. It was a rough journey, mostly on foot, on narrow trails, across the range of the Cuchumatán mountains, and down into the jungle of Ixcán. There we met some settlers who knew members of our group. Farther along, we were told of a big *ladino* landowner from near the Mexican border who had been trying to claim land close to this first Indian settlement. The *ladino* had threatened the Indians and ordered them off the land, saying that they would be thrown off eventually anyway. They were ridden with anxiety, even though the backlands were almost uninhabited and inaccessible.

Our entrance into the Zona Reina was like passing from near-desert wilderness into the rich promised land, and there was both enthusiasm and apprehension among the Indians. However, as we were soon to find out, the representatives of the Lord were somehow not entirely ready for our people to settle over there.

We trekked back, with some help from pack-mules, and arrived between 9 and 10 the following Saturday night at Barillas, the furthest parish on our side of the mountains.

As we walked into Barillas, I found Father Woods, who had returned two days earlier, waiting for me with another priest, Father Edward Doheny. He had been sent to meet me by Bishop Gerbermann, whose diocese included the area we had traveled into. Doheny was noted for his apparent belief that he had won the war in Korea singlehandedly.

He said to me: "I've been named by Bishop Gerbermann to head up this land project. I've been taken out of my parish and assigned full-time to working out plans for settling Indians in Ixcán."

I was dog-tired, filthy, and wet, and I had fallen at least twice on the bad trails. I shook my head—this had to be a bad dream. We had discussed the new lands project with many priests in the area, but Eddy Doheny was the one man we had deliberately avoided. He was just too difficult to work with.

Earlier, some other priests who had been deeply concerned over the land question had sent me to Bishop Gerbermann to determine whether we could help the Indians get lands. He had looked at me, his face flushed, and had declared, "You're in danger of losing your soul! You're here to save souls, not to get into politics and money-making."

The next morning, however, he changed his mind. In the course of a meeting of all the priests on liturgical changes, some of us brought up the land question, and it produced a lot of active interest. Tex seemed to realize which way the wind was blowing. He immediately proposed to have me pulled out of my parish in Cabricán (both my Superior, Father Curtin, and Bishop Manresa would have had to agree to that) and to put me full-time on the land project.

"Hold on a minute," I said in dismay. "We've barely got started. We don't even know what is possible yet. I'm up to my ears in co-ops and credit unions, let alone my active parish work in Cabricán. I'll help, but I don't want to leave Cabricán just yet."

He hadn't been able to forgive me for that. And here, on this weary Saturday night, I met my answer from him in the form of Father Doheny. My eyes must have shown my anger and disgust.

Bill Woods said to me: "That's all right. Doheny can run the job from Guatemala City. Let him do it. We'll help." We spread out our maps to show Doheny where the Indians wanted to settle. "None of that," he said. "I was trained to read maps in the Army. Thousands of lives depended on my map-reading in Korea. You don't have to show me all that."

He believed what he said so deeply that you could never determine when he was telling the truth and when he was off on a flight of fantasy. Bill Woods had told me that Doheny hadn't gone to Korea until after the war was over.

"Eddy," I said, "you'd better handle this yourself. I think I'll kind of bow out."

"*Bow* out?" he exclaimed. "Buster, you've been *thrown* out!"

Father Bill chuckled. Later he said to me: "He'll fool around with it for six months or so. He won't go out into the jungle himself to check out the land. He'll foul up, and we'll pick up the pieces."

"Yes," I answered, "but what gets me is there are lands out there right now. The people need them desperately. Doheny's not going to do anything to get this moving. He was distrusted by the people in his own parish. He can hardly even speak Spanish. Why should these people—even the few who might make the move—go hungry another season on account of him and the bishop?"

I was disgusted. I explained to the people in Cabricán that Padre Eduardo would be in charge of the project.

"We'll see how it goes," I told them.

Then came a directive from Bishop Gerbermann: "The only people to receive new land are to be people who already live in our diocese."

"How can *he* decide that?" I fumed.

Doheny studied maps and made voluminous plans as the months went by, but, as predicted, he never visited the area. Instead he spent his time in government offices, trying to determine who owned what lands—to be sure, a very essential point. He instituted courses on agriculture in Huehuetenango. He was getting people excited over land, but still had acquired none.

Then I heard of undeveloped lands in the Petén region. This time we did not spread the word beyond the parish, among either priests or Indians. I talked in Guatemala City with officials of FYDEP, the government's Institute for Economic Development of the Department of El Petén. "No problem," they assured me. "We have land for your people." I didn't believe them. Then Colonel Samayoa, FYDEP's "coordinator of colonization," offered to take me up to look at the land. Five of us went with him by air. For the four Indians who came with me, this was the first plane ride of their lives. We flew to Flores, an hour from Guatemala City, then traveled by jeep for forty miles, then two more hours by dug-out canoe.

The land Colonel Samayoa showed us was on the edge of a beautiful lagoon, about one-half mile in diameter. The fish were literally jumping out of the water, and the gleam in the men's eyes was unmistakable. Though the texture of the soil looked to me as if it had a high clay content, in comparison to the barren hills of Cabricán the land seemed like the Garden of Eden.

The Indian leaders decided to start right away, and fifteen families agreed to begin a trial settlement. One difficulty arose almost immediately however: The Indians were terrified of flying, especially the women—it was alien to anything they had ever known. Many of them were not even accustomed to automobiles or trucks. It took much to convince them; the strongest argument was their need for the land. In the beginning, I went up on Mondays to help out, returning on Fridays to celebrate Mass and minister to the needs of Cabricán parish on weekends.

By the terms of the original agreement made by the Maryknoll Superior with the Spanish sisters, I was supposed to be in the parish every day to celebrate Mass for the nuns. Jim Curtin hadn't shown me the agreement, however, and I didn't feel bound by it. Furthermore, the nuns' excessive emphasis on communicating with Christ at Mass, in evident preference to seeing Him in our Indian parishioners, made me feel that they would be better off with fewer Masses. I had told them this on a number of occasions.

More families were overcoming their fears of flying and travel, and moving to the Petén region. But I still had not informed Bishop Manresa—squabbles over diocesan jurisdiction would not have enriched the land for crops. Nor had I informed the sisters. However, they were becoming steadily more resentful over what they felt was my neglect of parochial religious activities for economic projects. And the movement of whole families out of the parish could hardly be hidden from them for long.

One weekend, word came to the parish center that all the members of an Indian family were sick in bed. The nature of their sickness was known to their neighbors, who predicted that they would die. People came to the home to pray the rosary all night and to sing songs for the sick.

I was not prepared to discount their judgment—more than

once an Indian who appeared outwardly in good health had come to me and said, "Padre, I'm going to die." In a short time he would be dead.

Nonetheless, I felt the members of the stricken family might be saved by a treatment which included intravenous feeding most of the night. I asked the sisters if the girl assistants could spend the night in the home to see that the needles stayed in the veins.

"No," said their Superior. "It's against our rules."

"But not you. Only the girls."

"No."

"The people are *dying*."

The sisters finally said, "We'll make a special sacrifice. We'll go out ourselves, see the people, then come right back."

I drove two of the sisters to a place below the sick family's house. It was almost dark when we got there, and the house was up the hill by way of a narrow path.

I turned my jeep around while they were climbing the hill, and drove off. *Now they'll have to stay*, I told myself. *They can blame me for making them break their bloody rules.*

The next morning, I ran into one of the neighbors who had been staying up with the sick family. "Are the sisters still there?" I asked him.

"Oh, no. They went back."

"How are the people?"

"The mother and three children all died. The father is still alive."

Later I found out that the sisters had stayed with the family a few hours and had left. They had reached the convent about 2:30 a.m., after walking home in the night.

As soon as Mass was over, I went to see the sisters, who were waiting for me.

"You talk about Christian charity all the time, and then you leave two poor, defenseless sisters out among those people in the middle of the night."

I was wild.

"The mother died," I told them. "The three children died."

The sisters told the bishop that I was no longer a priest, that I was abandoning the ministry. I knew I had gone too far, the same mistake I had made in San Juan Ixcoy. This time I thought I could assuage the bishop's anger by admitting my mistake and offering to resign as pastor. In view of my success, both spiritually and socially (is there a difference?), I didn't think Bishop Manresa would accept my offer; but I had misjudged him—he did.

This time, however, the reaction of the people was far different from what it had been in San Juan Ixcoy. Some four hundred men went to protest to the bishop, but he was conveniently out of town. Two truckloads of men, seventy-five or eighty altogether, traveled all day to Huehuetenango to see Bishop Gerbermann. He listened sympathetically. Another group went to Guatemala City to see the archbishop. The governor of Quezaltenango, who had been impressed by my work in Cabricán, told the people he would intercede with Bishop Manresa for me.

The bishop, however, had already named my replacement. The new padre was worried that the people would take out their anger on him.

I explained to him about the thirty or so families out in the jungle colony in Petén.

Bishop Manresa was upset when he learned that I had helped to transplant whole families up into the jungle without his permission. He complained to Jim Curtin.

"Why didn't you get permission?" Curtin asked me.

"The people don't need to get permission from the Church to move from one town to another."

"*You* do," he observed pointedly.

"I only ministered to them."

He wouldn't accept this answer. "Bishop Manresa wants you out of his diocese," he told me. "I don't know if Bishop Gerbermann will have you back in Huehuetenango. I may have to send you to El Salvador."

My stay in Cabricán had terminated after six invaluable years, the most important and happiest years of my life in Maryknoll. I was heartbroken that they were coming to an end, and I wasn't sure I felt up to making a new beginning.

Gerbermann, it turned out, had been impressed by the Indians from Cabricán who had petitioned in my behalf. They had asked that I be reassigned to Cabricán, not understanding the workings of Church authority—that Quezaltenango was not within Gerbermann's domain. He did promise them, however, that if I came back to Huehuetenango, he would speak with the bishop of Petén, and arrange for me to visit periodically the people who had moved out there to the settlement we had named "Pope John XXIII Colony."

XVI

What Is Relevance?
What Is Chastity?

The Nun When I returned to Monte María from my
trip to the States, I joined the other sisters in
a deep evaluation of our work, and of our roles as nuns and
teachers. Vatican II was generating profound repercussions
throughout the Church, and our group was no exception.

For myself, all this was crucial. By this time, I had been at
Monte María longer than anyone else—for ten years. I was
responsible for much of the tone of Monte María, much of
its way of being and teaching. As the years passed, I had come
to see that many school practices were, if not excessive luxuries,
at least diversions without real meaning. For the graduation
ceremony, wearing white formals had become a painful ex-
pense for the few girls who attended the school on scholarship.
I felt my own responsibility in having helped to originate such
customs, and thought that such practices should be discon-
tinued.

I knew now that the Colegio itself represented an antithesis
to what we claimed to want to do. Attending our school had
become synonymous, not with a concern with Christian
brotherhood and social justice and love for the poor, but with
an exalted position in society. To most of the girls, dress and
fashion were more important than being aware of and relating
to their country's realities and problems. I also felt that some
of the teachers failed to emphasize the girls' social responsibilities. I myself, on the other hand, had even been accused of

being a Communist by a group of irate parents upset about my portrayal of Guatemalan poverty in my sociology class. In fulfilling the parents' desire for the teaching of English, the school had become North-Americanized by the use of that language and of U.S. textbooks and Stateside teaching methods. Among the sisters, attitudes began to polarize, as we constantly debated just how "relevant" Monte María actually was.

One night, at a weekly evaluation meeting, we were vehemently discussing the school's value, just before our daily period of silence. Suddenly our Superior looked around at us and said, "All right, enough of this. I say that Colegio Monte María *is* relevant."

My heart filled my throat. I had a burst of courage that amazed even me.

"If you'll excuse me," I said, "I think that I disagree with that evaluation. And I would like to be able to state my opinion in such a way so as not to let it stand as if we all agreed with you. I think there are people here who also don't agree that Monte María is relevant as it now stands. We feel that drastic changes have to be made. Would you consent to let us get together and write out our reasons, and present them to you. May we have permission to go ahead and talk, though it is already nine o'clock?"

I hardly dared believe that our silence period could be broken.

"Yes," she said.

"Those who are opposed to this final statement of relevancy," I asked, "would you please raise your hands?"

Seven of sixteen nuns raised their hands. We had our meeting right then and there, and wrote up our reasons. Our arguments were based on the Vatican Council's pronouncements on the Church in the Modern World. As a possible solution we proposed that Monte María be sold to the government for a price equaling our remaining debt, with the condition that the sisters remain as teachers on government pay. Under government administration we felt the school could be opened to girls of all social classes. However, this proposal was rejected by the Superior, and the disagreement caused friction among the nuns.

By this time the desperate poverty in Guatemala had become almost an obsession with me. We sisters, as I was only too well aware, were not really keeping our vows of poverty. In the public school I had begun teaching girls who were really without means and, trying to relate with them, to reach them as individuals, I would say to one or another of them, "Would you come to visit me, and we can talk?"

"Where, Sister?"

When I told them I lived at Monte María—the fanciest school in Guatemala—they would give me a second look and murmur, "Oh, Sister, I can't go there." They felt too ashamed, too conscious of their lower social standing, to be seen at the rich girls' school. I knew that Monte María had become a countersign of Christianity. It didn't signify brotherhood, but aloofness, superiority.

When I returned from the States, I asked Sister Mildred, who was then regional Superior and responsible for all the Maryknoll Sisters' missions in Central America, if I could have permission to live in a small house—not in the ramshackle barrios, but on their edge, where lower-middle-class people resided. I wanted to undergo a bit of the poverty that I had vowed years before.

Sister Mildred, however, saw too many difficulties. Which sisters could live there with me?—I couldn't be alone. How would we support ourselves? Still, she said she'd think about it.

In the winter of 1966 the Mother General of Maryknoll came to our convent in the course of a tour of all the Maryknoll Sisters' missions in Central and South America. Each sister was given a private interview with her—a friendly visit and an opportunity to air any personal difficulties. When my turn came, I expected it would be routine, just a friendly chat. I didn't want to raise any controversial topics. There were still too many kinks to iron out of my plans. But she must have already been informed of my participation in the discussions on the relevance of Monte María, for she asked me about my ideas on poverty. She wondered how I proposed to live this ideal more fully in my own life. I finally told her of my desire to reside in a small house, among the families of the girls I was teaching.

Her questioning became sharp: "Who is going to live there with you?"

"I am just suggesting this," I said. "I know that there are two sisters here who are very anxious to share such an experience."

"Well, how are you going to support yourselves? If you want to be poor, you cannot expect your expenses to be paid by Monte María."

I had worked out a tentative plan for us to get jobs. But nothing I said seemed to reach her. She told me I was being fanatical, that I was trying to make a show of myself, an insincere posturing of poverty. I should try to experience poverty like the other sisters right here at Monte María. It was cheaper to live together as a large group. If we were all in smaller, poorer houses, the big residence at Monte María would be wasted.

I was shaken. I had never really intended to talk to her directly about my plans, but had thought that, when they were fully worked out, I would ask the Regional Superior to approach the Mother General on my behalf. But now here I was, in face-to-face confrontation with her—and she was telling me flatly, no. I was disappointed. I had really hoped to be able to begin a new kind of existence, one that would not contradict my vows but might better help me fulfill them.

Also in 1966 we began experimenting with a change in our dress. There were only three of us at first—it happened to be the three who spoke Spanish fluently. We exchanged the long, severe nun's habit for a short skirt, blouse, and a small veil. The change was quite an experience for me, and I found a certain irony in it. When I first went to Guatemala, we sisters had worn civilian clothes, because habits had not been permitted by the Arbenz government. After that regime was overthrown, the archbishop wanted all religious to continue to wear lay clothes for a while, feeling that the sudden sight of so many nuns would be too provocative to the anticlericals. I rejoiced when, after three years, I was at last permitted to change into my nun's habit, which I regarded as an outward sign of my dedication. Now, in 1966, we found ourselves eager to put aside the habit. Everyone said, "Who can understand you? First you are dying to get into your habit, and now you're dying to get out of it." But times change, and now, I believed, it was time to stand with the people.

The first day I wore my new clothes to the public school where I taught, I felt very self-conscious. I had given my classes advance warning, and I was supposed to record people's reactions—whether they were happy to see us in regular clothes or whether they preferred to see us in our habits—and tell the rest of the sisters.

The reception was fantastic. All the girls lined up on both sides. Everyone was applauding, and all the other teachers were looking on, as if to say, "Well, she's emancipated now. And now she's really one of us."

Before, there had been the distance established by a special kind of respect. But now the girls would come up to me and put their arms around me or touch my arm or hold my hand.

I generally missed many of the regularly scheduled activities in the convent, since I had to leave at 6:30 a.m.—public school began at 7:30. I rode a school bus, because sisters were not then allowed to drive a car alone. Since Monte María was outside the city limits, I spent two to three hours daily commuting to school and back. I also had to walk back and forth to the two different public normal schools where I taught which were on opposite sides of the City. This was quite a workout every day.

The other nuns wouldn't see me around except in the evenings, and they would wonder what I was doing that took so much of my time. There were three sisters in the convent who were close to me and supported me, and tried to help the others understand my work. Apparently some of the nuns believed I was teaching outside because they had given me little support in my work at Monte María.

There were many convent rules and regulations that began, little by little, to be relaxed. Originally, we had been forbidden to drive a car, or even to go out alone. There was a rule against talking alone with a man, except to consult a priest, and for this the confessional was recommended. I was much relieved when many of these restrictions were modified—they had made my work difficult, since it required me to do many things that were technically against the rules; yet I tried to be obedient and was always careful to ask permission for anything exceptional I had to do.

I was teaching religion to two thousand girls in the two public high schools, one lesson a week for each group. Many of the classes were supposedly on the same lecture material from one day to the next; yet I would find that the subject matter had evolved into something very different in content and approach from Monday to Friday. I had to grow to stay in touch with my students' widening awareness.

After my experiences at the first *cursillo* and during my visit to Maryknoll, I did not try to teach the girls formal religion as such. I asked them to indicate to me what they really wanted to talk about. They were to list two or three of their main interests on pieces of paper, unsigned, and turn them in to me.

More than three-fourths of the girls asked such questions as, What is love? How can I prepare for marriage? How can I relate to my boyfriend? What can I do with my life? What should I not do? How can I learn to get along better at home? How can I get over being shy? Only four girls in the entire two thousand asked about God or Christ.

In one of the classes, we discussed the nature of physical love. I tried to explain how the joining together of a man's body and a woman's body is a beautiful and real interchange. I wanted to help rid their minds of the idea that sex is dirty, a painful necessity only to be tolerated. They had the notion that everything to do with sex was a sin—even intercourse between marriage partners.

I made it as beautiful as I could, as I imagined it must be. It was then, I think, that I truly began to understand myself how beautiful love is, and that this was the way God had made us. I found myself going back and rereading Genesis, trying to find the real meaning of it behind the literal one.

Woman from man's rib—we are the same flesh. The important think was what Adam exclaimed after he saw Eve: "Flesh of my flesh, bone of my bone." We're so different; we're not the same. Yet we are also the same.

For one class, I took records and played some songs as illustrations of the different degrees of love: first, plain physical love—no other purpose but pleasure; then, beginning to seek together, until you really get to the heights of love, on a very spiritual level. Yet not spiritual, either—we are not body *and* soul: we *are* human beings. Our body and our soul are enmeshed, interwoven, and you can't separate them.

This deep examination was affecting my own thinking about my vow of chastity. I wondered now if this vow did not place a distorted emphasis upon sex. I was lucky in being able to love myself, to trust myself, enough so that I could recognize and accept my feelings for another human being who happened to be a man, without feeling guilty. I believed that the ability to identify with a person whom one could both admire as an example and feel affinity with as a comrade, was necessary for full individual development. Such identification might or might not take on strong sexual overtones, and by this time I wasn't sure that it mattered if it did.

One day I talked with Father Claude Philips, a Maryknoller

recently arrived in Guatemala, whom I had found to be a sensitive man and in whom I confided. I asked him if it might in fact be the sexual prohibitions themselves, and the accompanying guilt, that drive people to the physical expression of a love which might otherwise serve only as an intense motivation to live and do joyfully. It sounded to me as if we were always apologizing for physical experience, finding reason to discount it; but I was trying to get beyond that, beyond blind compulsion at all in the matter of sex. My convictions were more affirmative than that.

He told me he felt we should be able to recognize the complex yet elemental quality of our capacities to relate with other human beings without feeling threatened with sin; that we should be able to see our relationships as opportunities to grow and give to each other, without getting obsessed over having or not having sexual intercourse. He expressed his belief that, if people could refuse to feel guilty over embraces and simple affection, they might not feel driven to look for sexual experience to express their thirst for love. Their fear of sin becomes, in itself, a sin in that they come to doubt what is most sacred—the reaching out to other human beings.

Still, I could see the logic behind my vow of chastity, which rested in giving my life to Christ as my most real, most personal, friend. I asked Father Claude if he hadn't found that few priests or nuns seem to get beyond the negative dimension of chastity. In avoiding every expression of love—virtuously—one often fails to risk himself in a loving exchange with others. Maybe this is why we so often seem "stiff" to people, even sad.

Then I said to him, "Why is it that when you are talking to someone you love, your words cannot really express it. You want your body to express it, too, because it carries the entirety of you. You'd like to embrace a person, kiss a person. Why can't I?"

But just at that moment someone came in and interrupted us. The conversation ended, and we left.

Later he told me, "That wasn't fair. The next time you talk to me so frankly, don't do it where we can be interrupted so suddenly."

I was sorry, I hadn't wanted to tease him—I hadn't been talking about him. Yet I was glad, if he had felt that way, that we had been interrupted. I had trusted this priest enough to raise these questions with him. But now, whom could I talk to with honesty about these things without seeming to suggest other intentions or without obligating him or myself?

XVII

El Presidente and John XXIII Colony

The Priest In January 1966 I returned to Huehuetenango, with mixed feelings, mostly negative.
I didn't like the idea of going back to work for Tex Gerbermann, even though he seemed to be welcoming me with open
arms. His accepting me now, I felt, was no more directed
toward helping me than his expelling me from San Juan Ixcoy
almost six years earlier. Most of the priests I had liked and
admired in Huehuetenango had been deprecated or demoted
by Tex since my departure, transferred from their parishes, or
even removed from the Huehuetenango mission altogether. I
knew it would be only a matter of time before I would again
be in his disfavor and in a straitjacket as far as meaningful
work was concerned. Then, too, I couldn't easily forget
Cabricán.

Tex told me he was happy to have me back and that we
should let bygones be bygones. He went on to say that Father
Curtin was assuming authority that didn't belong to him in
Huehuetenango, and that it would be necessary to show him
who was "boss" from time to time. I could help make the
point by making a success of the Petén project, which Curtin
opposed.

I wanted very much to work in Petén—but I wasn't about to
get caught in a power struggle between Curtin and Gerbermann, where the losers would certainly be me and the
colonizers.

At this same time we were in the midst of our election for a new Maryknoll Superior. Curtin's six-year term was just about over, and there was much speculation about the choice of his successor. My old classmate Father Denny Kraus and a few others, including myself, were backing Father John Breen for the job. A larger group was pushing Father George Sullivan, an older priest who had held a position of authority at Ossining and had only recently come to Guatemala. He was amiable enough, but he knew little about the country and could not speak Spanish. Most of his ideas were conservative, and he was supported by priests of similar orientation, who shied away from John Breen because of his progressive views and outspoken manner.

Sullivan did much harm to his own cause by spreading petty stories about Breen. Although some of the uncommitted priests were hesitant about John's qualifications, he eventually won because many simply didn't want Sullivan. I knew that if I could hold out against Gerbermann's plans for me until Curtin went out of office, the Petén project would have a much greater potential for success when Breen became Superior.

Tex offered me as well the job of coordinator of all Church-related social action programs in the Huehuetenango diocese. My feelings about this work were also ambivalent. I had had essentially the same job in Quezaltenango under Manresa and had found that I was often bucking the opposition or lack of interest of many priests. I also recognized the severe limitations under which these programs operated. It had taken me years to form Guatemala's first and only cooperative league, and although I had received much help from the government office of cooperatives, its powers were negligible. As its director often told me: "Since the days of Castillo Armas, the cooperative movement is considered communistic by the government leaders."

That epithet "communistic" had long since stopped bothering me. The term was used by everyone and anyone against things they didn't like. Any measure that represented change was "communistic," and those who spoke out for social justice were "Communists." How many times I had been accused of advocating Communism by the *ladinos* of Cabricán and neighboring San Carlos Sija! Four of the cooperative leaders of Cantel, another town where I helped establish a credit union, had been jailed for attending a supposedly Communist meeting—it had dealt only with cooperatives. All these men were simple Indians who had no concept whatsoever of any political philosophy.

Even my biggest confrontation with Bishop Manresa had come over "Communism." As indicated earlier, the Cabricán lime cooperative had bought a piece of land for a factory but had at first held it in the name of the bishop, since property could not then be legally owned in the cooperative's name. A year and a half passed before the government granted the cooperative the necessary "juridical personality," and in the meantime the members had built their lime factory. When government approval came through, I told Bishop Manresa it was time to sign over the land to the cooperative, according to the arrangement he had agreed to. "Oh, I couldn't do that," he told me. "That cooperative may some day go communistic, and it is better that its lands and factory be in my name so that I can control it." I was stunned, and I said so. There were a number of other priests present, since we had just finished a conference with him; but I didn't quiet down: "That land is theirs; they paid for it. The Church in Chile is even now giving her lands to the poor peasants, and here in Guatemala the Church steals lands that rightfully belong to them. If these people ever go Communist, God knows they'll have good reason to, with the kind of treatment they continually receive from their government and their Church!"

The bishop was speechless. The other priests just looked at me, horrified. When he finally got his breath back, Manresa virtually shouted at me: "I'm not stealing! Bring them in tomorrow, and I will sign the lands over to them. If they go communistic, it will be your fault!" With a wave of the hand, he dismissed me and stormed out. I thought that someday I'd try to find out what Communism was all about, since the fear of it could make otherwise sensible people utterly irrational. The next day the transfer of lands was made with hardly a word passing between us.

Now Tex was offering me the same kind of job in Huehue-tenango—but I hesitated to plunge into it as I had in Quezal-tenango. How far could I go with cooperatives, given the prejudiced attitude prevalent in both the Church and the government? The National Federation of Credit Unions was doing well now, because it was being operated by the Peace Corps and the Alliance for Progress. There could be no fears of any "Communist infiltration" now that the U.S. government was supervising its functioning. Perhaps, in fact, this was the Americans' motivation in taking such an interest in the federation. Still, that was all right with me, if money was going to be put into the project.

I had served as treasurer of the federation in its early days, since I spent $1,000 of funds I had received from friends in the States to get it off the ground. The Alliance for Progress people paid me back, bought some new jeeps, hired a few Guatemalan technicians, and brought in strongboxes for each credit union. Its "Torch of Freedom" emblem was now appearing on all the federation's literature and vehicles. They organized meetings and training sessions and let everyone know what Uncle Sam was doing for them. They stepped on Guatemalan toes with their blatant nationalism and propaganda and were condemned for it in the press. I decided to get out before the conflict got any deeper.

Other peasant organizations didn't fare as well. Since Castillo Armas had broken the back of the labor movement by killing most of its leaders, it had become very dangerous to try to start a labor union or a peasant league. The daily news-papers consistently reported the discovery of one or more bodies, at the foot of an embankment or floating in a river, usually in plantation country on the Pacific coast. Often the bodies would go unidentified, indicating that they had been poor peasants, or, if they were identified, often as not, they had been leaders of a peasant group or in the process of organizing one. Little sympathy was shown these "Communist agitators." The bishops had forbidden us to aid in the organizing of labor unions or peasant leagues, because these affected the national power structure. It was rumored that the army was responsible for the executions, and we would be "mixing in politics."

I knew more about these things than most of our priests, few of whom were involved in social projects. The majority did not speak Spanish very well, and so, few of them read the Guatemalan newspapers. Even fewer listened on the radio to anything other than Voice of America broadcasts. Only two or three followed the migrant workers among their parishioners down to the plantations and saw the living conditions and the treatment they received from their *patrones*. Only one priest had faced down the guns turned on him by army guards stationed to keep "Communist agitators" off the plantations, and questioned the owner's sincerity.

Many of us priests were welcomed into the homes of the plantation owners as friends, spending our days off at their beach properties or using the swimming pools on their plantations. We flew in their private planes and enjoyed the comfort and luxury of their houses. But we did not venture into the workers' quarters, nor did we speak to the workers—this would have been a breach of good manners, even if it did offend us that people from our parishes were treated worse. than animals. "But," we were told, "the people are used to this type of existence, expect it, would not know how to live any differently." Nonetheless, I stopped going to the plantations for vacations after what happened to Silverio.

Silverio had been recently discharged from the army, and

his military experience made him ask questions about the "guerrillas" and the "revolution" he had fought against. He had borrowed money from a *habilitador*, a money-lending representative of a plantation owner, and so was obliged to go to work on the plantation for a few months to pay off his debt. While there he caught malaria and, instead of asking his fellow workers to take up the slack for him, as is the custom, he sent his wife to the administrator to request an advance of twenty cents for medicine, *camoquín*, to cut the fever. But Silverio didn't receive the medicine. Instead, he, his wife, and two small children were put off the plantation without money. He couldn't borrow from fellow workers, since they were heavily in debt themselves. The four of them had to walk two and a half days and two nights to Cabricán, begging food along the way. When they made it to town, Silverio's wife came to the rectory to request that I administer the last sacraments to him. This I did, and Silverio died a few hours later, a victim of disease and exhaustion that twenty cents' worth of medicine would have cured.

I could not accept such an incident with resignation, because Silverio was not only a parish statistic, he was also my friend. He had a face and a name, and he knew my name and called me his friend.

Now that Gerbermann wanted me to coordinate social action programs in Huehuetenango, I recalled other such incidents; and I asked myself, how far would such a program go toward really alleviating these people's problems? Or was I just going to make another big splash as in Cabricán, where much publicity was generated by the Church over minimal aid given to an insignificant minority?

I finally accepted the job, simply because I had no better alternative—knowing quite well that the most I would be allowed to do would be to help initiate a few more cooperatives that would permit the Indians joining them to work twelve, fourteen, and sixteen hours a day instead of their usual ten in order to gain a few more pennies. Nothing would be allowed to develop that would affect the basic power structure of the country that gave the landowners the power of life and death over their landless Indian countrymen.

I spent the next few months visiting various parishes in Huehuetenango, building a corn silo in one, holding organizational meetings in a second, establishing veterinary clinics in a few more, and generally explaining the colonization project, as well as making regular visits to the settlers themselves.

I couldn't really get enthusiastic over the work, however, because I knew that nothing was going to go far under Gerbermann. I had higher hopes for Petén, because the Spanish bishop there, Monseñor Artazcos, was very concerned with the problems of his people, and he agreed with me that land was the basic need of the peasants.

Right after John Breen's election as Superior had been confirmed by the Council at Maryknoll, New York, I went to him and explained the colonization project. In his usual direct fashion, he told me that, if the project represented what I claimed for it, he would assign me to Petén permanently after making a formal agreement with Monseñor Artazcos.

Gerbermann came to me one day in Guatemala City while he was attending the National Bishops' Conference there and asked me if I had any formal plans for the colonization program. He was sponsoring a resolution in the conference to request some millions of dollars from the U.S. Agency for International Development, and he needed to name several different projects on which to base the request. It all sounded very vague, but I cooperated by drawing some plans up that very night. I was greatly surprised the next day when the newspapers announced that the Bishops' Conference was going to sponsor the settlement of five thousand families in San Juan Acul, the area selected by our four Indian leaders from Cabricán. I was not opposed to such public fanfare, because I felt it would provide a good lever to obtain help we might need in the future, either for Church approval or for funds. But I considered the motivation to be the bishops' desire to get some more undeserved publicity.

I went to San Juan Acul to live permanently with the Cabricán settlers in the spring of 1966. It was about this same time that Julio César Méndez Montenegro was elected to succeed Peralta Azurdia as president. He was thought to have "communistic tendencies" by many people, and the army was seriously threatening to annul the election. But the U.S. Embassy announced that it wished to see the election results respected, thus serving notice on the military to keep its hands off. The U.S. did not necessarily like Méndez Montenegro; but it had liked even less the military government that had been in power since Ydígoras's overthrow in 1963.

If Méndez Montenegro was the political heir of Arévalo and Arbenz, there was hope that things would begin to change. I was glad to be going to San Juan Acul to initiate a land distribution program just when such a man was taking power.

San Juan Acul was both a fortunate and an ironic selection for our beginning. It was fortunate because of the tremendous amount of fish and game the people caught that not only tided them over until their first corn crop came in, but also put pounds on their skinny frames; our new home was also the site of six tin-and-concrete houses, outfitted with electrical wiring and water pipes, that we used to good advantage. The irony lay in the fact that these dwellings had been built to house Cuban trainees for the Bay of Pigs invasion.

The base had been one of the focal points for a controversy that raged during the Ydígoras regime. Ydígoras had fallen out of favor of the United States Government just after coming to power in 1958 because, he writes in his autobiography, he refused to 'pay the bill incurred by his assassinated predecessor, Castillo Armas, for the CIA-sponsored invasion that put the latter in power. Credits for the Ydígoras government dried up in the United States and Europe.

In 1959 the CIA began looking for bases for training Cuban exiles to overthrow Castro. Ydígoras offered Guatemala for the purpose. Credit eased immediately and old debts were forgotten. Globemasters began to land in Helvetia, a huge plantation owned by Ydígoras's crony, Roberto Alejos, and PBY's were touching down on the lagoon at San Juan Acul.

Ydígoras was accused of aiding the U.S. against Cuba just as Honduras had aided the CIA against Guatemala in 1954. Ydígoras denied the stories altogether as long as possible, then maintained that the U.S. advisers were there only to train the Guatemalan army in counterinsurgency tactics. He invited the OAS to inspect the new installations, which it refused to do. The president, in turn, accused Cuba of intending to invade Guatemala and called for the country to prepare itself—a typical Ydígoras smokescreen. When the base at San Juan Acul was discovered by some chicle-gatherers passing through the forest, Ydígoras claimed the trainees were invaders from Cuba and would be hunted down by his army.

Some elements in the army resented what Ydígoras was doing, either out of sympathy for Castro or merely out of opposition to U.S. interference. A revolt of young army officers occurred in November 1960, designed to stop the invasion plans. The revolt was unsuccessful, and some of the officers fled into the mountains of northeastern Guatemala. They were received sympathetically by the peasants in the area, who encouraged them to continue their insurgency, promising to aid the officers if the latter would give them lands whenever they came to power.

Over the years I had learned more about the 1954 overthrow of Arbenz and about his successor, Castillo Armas. Arbenz had been accused of promoting Communism; yet he had won the election overwhelmingly in 1951, getting more than fifty percent of the vote against eight rivals. John Foster Dulles had called the Guatemalan Congress a "Communist controlled legislature"; yet only four of its fifty-six members had been

*

Marxists. Dulles had also described the land-reform law that gave lands to 100,000 peasant families a "communistically contrived law."* Arbenz had made the mistake of expropriating United Fruit Company lands, as well as some holdings belonging to wealthy and powerful Guatemalan nationals.

The story of his overthrow is history, even the fact that Eisenhower, in an address on June 10, 1963, actually bragged about U.S. sponsorship for that overthrow. Also history is Castillo Armas's brutal suppression of labor and peasant organizations, and Ydígoras's rape of the national treasury once he began getting U.S. aid. When Peralta Azurdia took over in 1963, he named his government *Operación Honestidad* to show the nation that he would not sell his country to foreign interests as had Ydígoras. Peralta Azurdia ruled with an iron fist, maintaining he would stamp out all corruption and eradicate all "Communism." In the northeast, the revolutionary movement was growing among the peasants, led by two young officers who had been trained in counterinsurgency tactics by the U.S., and who had also participated in the 1960 revolt. The movement became stronger during Peralta Azurdia's rule. His efforts at suppression proved counterproductive, but he was determined to refuse U.S. control of the counterinsurgency campaign.

During those days I often heard American officials complain because Peralta Azurdia was refusing generous offers of U.S. military and economic assistance. He claimed Guatemala could handle its own internal affairs and stated he would not allow his country to become another Dominican Republic. I remembered my own visit with him and his tone of voice when he referred to my "countrymen" of the United Fruit Company. Thus it was that the embassy was not only happy to see Méndez Montenegro win the 1966 election but also blocked Peralta's attempt to retain control.

Gerbermann told me that right after his election Méndez

---

* *John Foster Dulles: radio and TV address on June 30, 1954, reported in Department of State Publication No. 5556, August 1954, p. 31.*

Montenegro had gone to Archbishop Mario Casariego to ask for Church support for his regime and that he was guaranteed it if he would get married in the Church. Méndez complied a week later in the archbishop's private chapel, and Tex said we'd have his backing for the land distribution program.

I wondered if Méndez would crack down on exploitative financial interests, and was puzzled by the U.S. ambassador's endorsement. I soon found out that in exchange for U.S. backing against Peralta Azurdia, Méndez Montenegro had agreed to accept U.S. military aid and advisers to suppress the peasant revolution that was gaining strength in the northeastern departments. As soon as he took over, on July 1, 1966, the aid began to pour in, and the revolutionaries suffered defeat after defeat. U.S. Colonel John Webber, who became the counterinsurgency expert for the new government, publicly defended his use of terrorism in the northeast with the statement: "That's the way this country is. The Communists are using everything they have, including terror. And it must be met."*

Ambassador John Gordon Mein's pronouncements on American activity in Guatemala were no more sophisticated than those of his military attaché. When he presented the country's army and air force with the latest communication equipment, grenade launchers, aerial surveillance techniques, and jet-powered helicopters, the ambassador stated: "These articles, especially the helicopters, are not easy to obtain at this time, since they are being utilized by our forces in defense of the cause of liberty in other parts of the world. But liberty must be defended wherever it is threatened, and that liberty is now being threatened in Guatemala."†

When the newspapers carried a story that one thousand Green Berets were in the country, the ambassador maintained that there were only thirty-four. The dispute was over the

---

* Time, January 26, 1968, p. 23.
† El Imparcial (Guatemala City), November 10, 1967. Ambassador Mein was assassinated in August 1968 by FAR (Rebel Armed Forces) guerrillas.

exact number, confusing the real issue: There would be as many Green Berets in the country as were needed to suppress the peasant revolt and maintain the status quo.

I hadn't really expected anything different from the ambassador or the government he represented—he had already stated publicly that he would pay a one-way fare to Cuba for a Maryknoll priest who had expressed approval of Castro's expropriation of exploitative U.S. financial interests. But I *had* hoped that Julio César Méndez Montenegro was truly the revolutionary he claimed to be. Now here he was, allowing the Green Berets into his country, to direct and participate in operations that had already included killing every male peasant in a village of Rio Hondo*—over a hundred—and those suspected of aiding the guerrillas in countless other villages. The president's offer of amnesty for all guerrillas while continuing the policies of his predecessors was a farce. I knew then that the kind of help we would get from him for our resettlement program would be a mere token at best.

About this time, we heard that the new president was coming to visit our cooperative settlement, as well as some others established by FYDEP's Colonel Samayoa farther down the river. Méndez Montenegro came, but stopped only at our own and at one other, the best of the FYDEP settlements—though all of these were in a rather sorry state, since the government had given them practically no help.

Much to the surprise of everyone, the Indian farmer who was president of our colony made an impassioned plea to the elected leader of his nation. He besought the president to see to it that the colonizers were given legal ownership of the land they had cultivated.

El Presidente responded with apparent sincerity: "If my government is to be remembered for anything, it will be remembered for the help that we have given to the poor." He

* El Gráfico *(Guatemala City), March 8, 1966.*

promised to see to it that the peasants who had built Colonia
Juan XXIII were given titles to their land.

A few weeks later, the president did in fact propose to the
Guatemalan Congress a law that would enable him to grant
titles to the families of the colonized jungle area. However, the
consensus in Congress was that, "We should wait to see how
the people have *developed* the land." Congress refused to give
the colonizers title to a single acre of the lands they had so
painfully claimed from the jungle.*

Some of the Indian co-op members declared that the people
should fight if anyone tried to take their lands. Some said we
should abandon the colony, while others believed the colonizers should live there as long as they could.

I was not the peasants' *patrón* or their landlord or their
elected leader. I wanted to teach them not to have to depend
on me. I had shown the men how to navigate the river, to
maintain the outboard engine on the boat, to run the gasoline
saw, and to replace the packing on the water pump. They
were not my children, though they called me "Father." Still,
I had helped open the way for them, had surely helped organize and guide them into their present situation. I had to
face with them the dilemma, moral and material, of the new
problems confronting them.

Should these people take up machetes to defend the lands
they had cleared to support their lives and their families?
Would it be wrong for the hungry Indians of the northwest,
of Huehuetenango, Quezaltenango, San Marcos, and the ad-
joining mountain areas, or those already fighting in the northeast, to fight to repossess lands lost four hundred years ago
when the Spanish came and took them away?

For Ramón Aguilar, the question grew out of the very
essence of his life: "This year from two acres I'll get six

---

* In August 1969, Congress finally passed the law, but it was drawn up so as
to effectively deny the peasants any real opportunity to obtain land grants there,
reserving most of the lands for large landowners with "sufficient capital."

thousand pounds of grain. Back in Quezaltenango, I had one acre and in a good year I got 750 pounds."

That land had been deserted, overgrown with vines, since the time of the Maya. But the Indians of the colony would be setting themselves up for slaughter if they should ever choose to fight. They couldn't defend themselves with machetes against a government force supplied with U.S. arms, advisers, and even napalm. Yet they felt it was better to die defending their land than not to fight and be kicked off and forced to return to a life of bare subsistence in the Quezaltenango hills or to plantations where the landowners could "suck their blood"—*chupando nuestra sangre* was the phrase they used to describe how the landowners treated them.

Such dilemmas were beginning to disturb my notions of what it meant to be a Christian, let alone a priest.

XVIII

The Crater of
the Volcano

The Nun When I returned from the States in January
1965, Father Jalón invited three or four of
the more active *cursillo* teachers and myself to attend a meeting in Medellín, Colombia. Father Aguirre and Father Jalón
had extended the *cursillos* from Venezuela to all of Central
America and Colombia. Now they were organizing an international training session for *cursillo* teachers where course content could be revised and brought up to date, and the *cursillo*
spirit could be embodied in a consolidated international
movement.

My Superior agreed to the trip, so I called a meeting of the
nine students who had been actively assisting as *cursillo* teachers and "commanders." Three of them were to go with me:
Titina, Julio, and María Elisa. Titina really embodied the
spirit of the *cursillos*. She was a tall and beautiful brunette
who was studying psychology at San Carlos University. Joyful,
eager to give her friendship, she was always available for work
and ready to do anything to help out. Her optimism was to
save us many times from giving up. She was respected by
everyone for her lucid presentation of the *cursillo* conferences
and for her intelligent participation in the discussions.

After Xavier had left, I hadn't been able to find another
student Jesuit or priest to work with us on the *cursillos*. It was
necessary that a man teach some of the classes, because the
male students needed an older man to relate to. I asked a

young Maryknoller, Father Joe Kelly, who was stationed in a parish in Guatemala City, if he would help us. He had a special gift for dealing with young people. But when I told the *cursillo* team that he had agreed to work with us, they were very skeptical. "He can't understand Spanish very well," they told me. "And we doubt that he, as a gringo, could teach university students about social problems in their own country."

"Why don't we give him a chance?" I said. "He doesn't have to teach those classes. He can take some of the ones on Christ and the faith."

We returned from Colombia with renewed enthusiasm and met with the other six *cursillistas* at the house of one of them, Rudy, to share new ideas. Titina told them about meeting Gustavo López, a Colombian student who had been our "commander" at Medellín. He had described how he had organized his classmates during vacation for volunteer literacy work in some of the more remote sections of Colombia. He had also told us about his sociology teacher, Father Camilo Torres, who had joined Colombian guerrilla forces and been killed in an ambush laid by the army. I mentioned that there was a good possibility that Gustavo would come and spend a month with us to help with *cursillos* and share his experiences.

Julio, thin and wiry, with dark curly hair and big black eyes, spoke quickly, his words tumbling out: "We should begin regular meetings, weekly at least, and not wait a month before vacation to plan the *cursillos*. Let's begin other activities, too."

"Do you have any ideas on what they could be?" asked Rudy. He was the oldest, rather stocky, with green eyes and brown wavy hair. He was a good teacher, spoke gravely, and his maturity had gained him the nickname "Papá."

"We don't have to decide today," said Julio. "That's the very subject for our next meeting. But if we want to preserve our spirit, we have to get together more often."

Titina agreed: "We can begin by studying together. There are many points in the *cursillo* classes that we should explore further."

"All right," I said. "I suggest that we rent a house where we can hold our meetings, sponsor occasional lectures, and keep the books and equipment we have begun to collect." I had accumulated dishes, pots and pans, and other kitchen utensils, as well as cots that had been donated to us.

Rudy was very practical. "What about paying the rent?" he asked. Before anyone else had a suggestion, he added, "I don't see why we can't each contribute a monthly payment. I think I could manage to give Q.5 a month."

Some offered Q.2, others promised more. Ana María, still in high school, a black-haired clown who could work inexhaustibly, said, "I volunteer to help Sister Marian Peter find the house."

With that we closed the meeting. Outside, Father Joe spoke to me: "I think I can get Q.100 a month from Maryknoll to pay for some of the expenses. Don't tell the students how much it is; let them feel the responsibility of financing it themselves. I like their spirit."

He made good his promise and spoke to Father Jim Curtin, his Superior; and we began receiving a monthly check.

Up to now we had never worried about finances. For *cursillos* we charged participants Q.5 for the week, and it was a mystery to us how we managed to feed the group, allow those who couldn't pay to attend for free, and still have a bit left over. Of course, the team didn't require pay for its work; the assistant cooks were volunteers; we fed the students simple food, some of which was donated; and we usually managed to borrow a school that was unoccupied because of vacation.

Ana María and I got together after school every day and began house-hunting. We found a perfect one right downtown, easily accessible, with a hall large enough to seat fifty people.

For our first meeting we sat in a circle on the floor, gloriously happy in *our* bare house. It was named Centro de Capacitación Social (Center for Social Formation), CEDECAS for short. We explored every corner and wondered who would give us some old furniture. The kitchen suggested an idea: How about serving noon lunches at cost for those students who lived far out of town? It would be a service and give us contact with more people.

I told the girls at the public schools about the lunch service, while the students passed the word around at the university. I hired a cook, and we began the prodigious task of preparing low-cost meals for an undetermined number of students.

Soon, most of the diners were the *cursillistas* themselves, eager to take advantage of the customary two-hour lunch break to get together to converse, to plan, to play ping-pong, to be together. Our student center became a real gathering-place, seldom empty, filled with music and activity.

When Father Jalón invited us to a training *cursillo* in Nicaragua during Holy Week, the whole group, now numbering twenty-one, made plans to go. Father Joe drove a carry-all, I borrowed a minibus from Monte María, and Roberto, the one boy in the group who owned a car, took his red station wagon.

When our caravan arrived in Managua, however, we were surprised not to be welcomed with a typically warm Nicaraguan reception. It turned out that the university students had clashed with their *cursillo* priest-director, leaving him with only a few young high school students. We were dismayed to realize that the program, which we had expected to be a challenging series of classes, hadn't even been planned. Father Joe and I tried to make the best of things by sitting down with Father Jalón and the Nicaraguan Jesuit to outline the three days of classes and activities. Five of the boys in the group took off in Roberto's Falcon to explore the small town near Managua where we were lodged.

When we were ready to begin the *cursillo*, the five boys were nowhere to be found. Father Joe and I went out separately to look for them.

As I drove around a curve in the road, my headlights picked out a hitchhiker. I was startled; he looked just like Julio. Then Titina, who was accompanying me, shouted, "It's Julio!" We stopped, he staggered in, and we tried to decipher his incoherent, drunken mumblings.

Titina gasped, "They had an accident."

I drove on, and we found four dazed young men looking at the red car—its headlights smashed and radiator broken.

"Rudy! What happened?"

"I didn't realize that the taillight on the truck wasn't moving. I tried to swerve but misjudged the distance," he said.

I was furious. They had tried to soothe their disappointment over the unplanned *cursillo* with some of Nicaragua's famous rum. But this wasn't to be the darkest moment of the week. Two days later, Igor and Carlos didn't show up for the afternoon class. Father Joe found them talking earnestly in the village pub, a row of empty beer bottles neatly lined up across the table, a glazed look in their eyes.

Father Jalón spoke to me the evening before we were due to head back for home: "You've been writing me about the team in Guatemala and how well they were working. But this bunch of drunks is terrible. You have two girls worth something, Titina and María Elisa. Your best bet is to dump the rest of the group and start all over."

"But, Father," I pleaded, "you can't deny that Carlos, Rudy, and Juan José are very good teachers."

"Intelligence is worthless without moral integrity." He didn't have to tell me that—still, I tried to stand up for them. My cutting words to Julio and Carlos had made clear my own utter disgust at their behavior; but the boys knew that I felt the lack of cooperation on the part of the Nicaraguan university students was a partial explanation for the way they'd been acting.

We returned to Guatemala and a week later had one of our most soul-searching meetings. Weakness and immaturity were admitted, and we recognized that mutual respect had been wounded. But the love that had grown between us somehow not only survived the disappointments but seemed to bind us more closely together.

The "Days of Action" we held twice a month on Sundays served further to consolidate the group. The *cursillistas* took turns, in groups of six, preparing and directing the day's events. We would invite about forty high school students from private and public schools for a day of talks on social questions, and on their responsibility to remedy Guatemala's grave social injustices. The bus ride out to the small country house we borrowed for the Days of Action, a picnic lunch, games, and a Mass actively participated in—all helped the students from competing schools to get acquainted and break down barriers. The *cursillistas* would sometimes find the discussions boring as some of the less experienced students repeated simplistic arguments, but they were elated with their responsible involvement in meaningful activity.

In June, after six months of working with us, Father Kelly's increased parish duties prevented him from helping us any longer. The boys wondered if the Nicaraguan episode hadn't discouraged him. They were more than ever determined to prove to themselves that they were capable and responsible individuals.

They often brought copies of the FAR (Fuerzas Armadas Rebeldes) guerrilla newspaper to CEDECAS. This publication was clandestinely distributed by them and other students, who would find copies piled in the men's rooms at the university. I was curious to know something about the guerrilla movement, which had begun in 1960. The daily papers carried incomplete accounts of sporadic clashes between the army and the guerrilla units operating along the highway to Puerto Barrios, on the Atlantic coast.

I asked a U.S. Army colonel whose daughter had been one of my students at Monte María to come one evening to tell the sisters about his activities in Colombia. In Guatemala, his job was to train both U.S. and Guatemalan rangers in counter-insurgency techniques and to direct field actions against the guerrillas. He brought charts and slides that he used in his classes at the Instituto Polytécnico, Guatemala's military academy, and gave us an illustrated lecture on an ambush he had directed against the guerrillas. He told us that the two principal guerrilla leaders, Yon Sosa and Luis Turcios, had been Guatemalan army officers trained at Fort Gulick, Panama, and Fort Benning, Georgia. They were leading the guerrilla forces in skirmishes with the army along the highway to the Atlantic near United Fruit Company lands. He was sure that if they continued these tactics instead of going deep into the jungle, they would be defeated in a matter of months.

The FAR newspaper explained that many peasants had joined the organization to fight for lands which they had received during the presidency of Arbenz and which had been reclaimed by Castillo Armas. Gradually I realized that the guerrillas were fighting for the rights of the peasants. But I was determined to find a way to apply Christian social doctrine and obtain those rights for the peasants without using violence.

Late one afternoon I was working alone in the kitchen at the Student Center—the students had left for their evening classes at the university—when I heard someone come in. I turned around and was surprised to see Felipe Ramos, whom I hadn't met in months. He had taken a job and gone back to the university, where he was active with a drama club. He was amazed at how the student center had developed; somehow he had never expected the *cursillistas* to be dedicated enough to accomplish so much. After that, Felipe dropped in frequently, though always unexpectedly. Since he was practicing for a part in Bertolt Brecht's drama *Mother Courage*, we discussed the play and Brecht's other works. He read me revolutionary poems by Luis Felipe, a Spaniard. We discussed philosophy, argued about evolution, and wondered if the military dictator, Enrique Peralta Azurdia, would permit elections in 1966 as he had promised.

One day early in the spring, Felipe saddened me with the news that he was going to work with the FAR. I knew he had many friends who were members; I knew he thought the

FAR had more answers to social problems than the *cursillos*; but I told him I hated to see him get involved in guerrilla violence.

"Tell me," he retorted, "who is being violent when insecticides are sprayed in a cotton field where the peasants are working and are thus poisoned? And who are the violent ones when bulldozers raze a village where people have lived for twenty years?"

I told him, "I know the peasants are constantly hurt, but that doesn't give the guerrillas the right to blow up Esso gasoline deposits."

"All right, how do you propose to exert pressure on the government to pass and implement legislation in favor of Guatemala's poor? They're eighty percent of the population, you know, and they've got an average income of no more than Q.100 a year."

"There are legal means to demand social justice."

"Fine," he answered. "You find and work with legal means, and I will become a pin to prick this insensitive and sadistic oligarchy that rapes our people."

"Felipe, take care. Will you come to see me still?"

"When I have free moments, I may drop in. I'm going to be very busy."

He had given up his car, his studies, even his job, which had been his first and only income; his time was no longer his own. I couldn't help contrasting his utter dedication to an ideal with that of so many CEDECAS students who, though they tried to be Christians, still had many excuses to be selfish with their time, their energy, their possessions.

Some of the girls at INCA, one of the public normal schools, begged me to take them on a hike. I thought a long trip with just girls would be risky, that we needed a man to come along. I knew Felipe would be the most knowledgeable, dependable, and helpful man I could ask. He agreed delightedly and asked if he could bring a friend. Since he couldn't anticipate his free times, he told me to be ready to go on short notice.

One Friday evening Felipe introduced me to his friend Juan de Dios—a man in his middle twenties, thin, with deep-set, penetrating eyes—and told me that Juan would also be coming along on our camping trip. As we were starting out a short time later, Juan said he wanted to buy some steaks. I was surprised at this man, whom we had just met, putting down his money for steaks for all of us.

Felipe, Juan de Dios, seven girls, and myself piled in a jeep and headed for the volcano called Agua. But before we left the City, Juan de Dios also bought a machete and a three-cornered file. I watched him as he lovingly honed the cutting edge of that machete with the file. It took us two hours to get to the town at the foot of the volcano; it took him just as long to sharpen the edge of his machete.

In the town under the volcano Juan de Dios borrowed a *mecapal*, a two-inch-wide leather band used by the Indians to carry their loads. This was surprising: I could tell he was educated, and educated people just don't use *mecapals*. First, he tied all our supplies into a compact bundle, then he attached the ropes dangling from the *mecapal*. He stooped down, adjusted the leather band over his forehead, and came up into a bowing position. The band dug into his forehead, taut with the weight of the supplies resting on his back. He carried the load deftly—this obviously wasn't the first time he had used a *mecapal*.

On hikes up to Agua, a guide is necessary, and he usually helps carry the supplies. Just about this time, an Indian guide showed up. He was too polite to make any remark about our friend and his *mecapal*. Juan de Dios greeted the Indian in a brotherly way. He clearly had respect for an Indian as a man—a rare experience for an Indian in Guatemala.

Only a man in excellent physical condition could have hauled a load with a *mecapal* up a hill as my new friend did.

As we walked up the steep path in the dark, we laughed and joked, and encouraged each other. One of the girls was very stout. Sweating and grunting and sobbing, she had been ready to give up at a particularly steep section of the path, when Juan de Dios, load and all, scrambled up this steep section, then stopped, and with just the right words coaxed the fat girl up to where he stood.

All of us were bushed when we reached a level spot on the crater floor. We had hiked from 10 on Friday night until 4 on Saturday morning. Juan de Dios eased his burden to the ground, then straightened up. He and Felipe got busy building a fire and putting on coffee to boil. They brought out the cups, and we were more warmed by their spontaneously hosting us than we were even by the hot coffee. But the girls had had it, coffee or not—they went to sleep almost at once.

I was too wide awake, and so were Juan and Felipe. We looked at the sleeping girls, who for months had coaxed me to make this hike with them. For myself, it wasn't just a hike, but kind of a folk pilgrimage to Agua. Since I had first seen Agua of the perfect cone, on my arrival in Guatemala twelve years before, it had become a symbol to me of this adopted country of mine. The volcano gets its name, which means "water," from the fact that its crater once held a lake. An earthquake in 1600 sprang a leak in the crater wall, and the water rushed down and drowned the headquarters of the Spanish conquerors of Guatemala.

We walked up to the rim of the crater into the dawn. Felipe then reintroduced me to his friend—Juan de Dios's true name was Luis Turcios. I gasped, suddenly realizing that I had spent eight hours with Guatemala's feared guerrilla leader. But I had experienced him as a person before I knew he was Turcios.

The army and the police wanted Turcios dead or alive. The oligarchs knew Turcios, especially the rich men he had kidnapped and held for ransom, his way of collecting "taxes"—rich people in Guatemala scorn to pay the official taxes; the United Fruit Company had labeled Turcios "a Red who must be stopped"; the CIA knew Turcios—the gringos were out to get him. But the Turcios I knew was a man relaxing among friends on a twenty-four-hour vacation from being one of the most hunted individuals in Guatemala.

The miracle of the sun just before dawn was ours. We were high enough to see both the Pacific Ocean and the Caribbean Sea; Guatemala was spread out at our feet.

Turcios told me how once he had wanted to be a Christian Brother; but the false piety he had witnessed in the novitiate had disgusted him. His teachers couldn't explain to him what life was all about.

I was a sister, and I knew what he meant. This surprised Turcios, and he wondered about me. My students discussed what they wanted to talk about—not God. He was just another worldly Thing to them; nor was it Christ—they had seen too many effeminate Christs on holy cards. What they wanted to talk of was boys and dates. And I said I believed that God is Love and that, if we say we love God and hate our brother, we are liars.

Turcios liked the flavor of all this. He said he felt a sense of kinship with me when he found out I knew and was concerned about the wages earned by the fathers of my students at the public schools. He smiled, but was angry, too. I learned much about Turcios's attitudes when he spoke about his guerrilla activities—his compassion, his sense of humor, his complete commitment to a relentless struggle against the oligarchy. He told me how it felt to be a hunted animal, and I wondered how he could withstand the constant tension. Turcios also spoke of his ideals; he was ready to lay down his life in defense of the poor man's right to be a human being and to live in human dignity. His altruism was not based on any thought of reward in a future existence.

I wish I remembered more about Turcios. I do remember his deftness in cooking the steaks for the girls and the way he stoked the fire. When a group of boy hikers came by, curious about meeting girl hikers, his eyes shot back and forth all the time, wary of strangers.

I remember the way he had the girls talking about themselves, how fast his friendship with the Indian guide grew. The girls never guessed he was Turcios—to them he was just a friend of their teacher's.

I returned to my girls' school late on Saturday night. The white sheets had never seemed more inviting. Here I was as well off as the richest girl in Guatemala, with more than enough to eat, with all the comforts of home. But I couldn't get to sleep. What was Turcios doing at that moment? I was uncomfortable as I compared my quite limited sacrifices as a sister with his life given to the poor at immeasurable risk, with even a price on his head. I was anxious concerning the reactions of the people in my home, the nunnery, who would be unable to understand if I told them I had just spent twenty-four hours with Luis Turcios.

When I saw Carlos and Titina come bounding into the Student Center one afternoon, I could tell they were up to something. Carlos was twenty, but his boyish face, topped by a mop of blond curly hair, made him look younger. He had a keen intellect and, in fact, was to become our "thinker." He had just transferred from Landívar, the Catholic university, to San Carlos, where there was more student activity and political involvement.

"We have it!" they called out, "A name for our house."

"You know how we've been wondering what to call it—Centro de Capacitación Social is just too unwieldy—and now Carlos and I just found the perfect name," Titina said, all in one breath.

"The Crater," Carlos announced solemnly. "Isn't it perfect? Our emblem is an erupting volcano. Well, this is the crater from which burning lava will flow!"

Then he grew intense as he described how we would bring justice and love to all of Guatemala. As he spoke, I was remembering standing on the crater of Agua with Turcios. But I didn't dare mention this to anyone—it was too risky, and I felt the experience had been given me in trust.

· · ·

Sister Gail Jerome had worked for three years in a small mining town deep in the jungles of Nicaragua before she was assigned to Monte María in June 1966. Here she found herself teaching the daughters of the elite, and I could tell she resented such a drastic change. Almost immediately, we found we were kindred souls, and she began to help us at the Crater with the Days of Action.

Gail and I realized that it was necessary for the students to have contact with the Indian people, the peasants whom they talked about so much in the classes on social problems, if they were to achieve a real sense of social concern. Guatemala City is a modern metropolis—centuries ahead of the primitive, simple life of the countryside. The students had the facts and figures on the inhuman working conditions on the plantations and were becoming more and more determined to do something. But their knowledge was purely theoretical and abstract. They had had no direct contact with the impoverished classes of their country.

At a CEDECAS meeting I suggested we plan some volunteer work in the rural areas during vacation. Juan José thought this was unnecessary. He was an excellent orator and could convince any audience that it was their moral duty to do something about the lack of housing, the illiteracy, the hunger in Guatemala. But winning an oratorical contest in Mexico City had worked havoc with his sense of humility. No one could convince *him* of anything.

Manuel, a medical student who had become one of the most faithful collaborators on the Days of Action, wanted to work among the Indians. In his middle twenties, he came from a lower-middle-class family and had himself experienced much hardship due to lack of funds. He began convincing fellow medical students to accompany him.

I wrote to Father Denny Kraus at La Libertad, his new parish, to ask him if he would be interested in working out a plan for ten volunteers willing to give four to six weeks of their vacation. Father Denny wrote back an enthusiastic welcome, and his organizational ability was clearly evident in his proposed plan for a vaccination and literacy campaign. He mentioned that Father Bill Woods might also be interested.

Early one morning in August I went to the Maryknoll Fathers' Center House in Guatemala City to talk by radio to both Father Kraus and Father Woods.

There were seven or eight radio transmitters scattered throughout the various Guatemalan missions, and 8 a.m. was the scheduled hour for radio communications. The radio shack was empty, but I finally found a priest whom I hadn't met, eating breakfast.

"Would it be possible for you to operate the radio for me, Father?" I asked.

"Sure, Sister," he answered. "I'm Tom Melville, what's your name?"

So this was Father Melville, whom I had heard so much about from Father Denny. I was very interested in finding out more about his work in Petén.

After talking by radio to Fathers Denny and Bill, we walked to the door, as I answered his questions about the Crater and the students' volunteer work.

"I had no idea there were so many persons here in Guatemala City really interested in doing something about the plight of the peasants," he told me. "I think, myself, that the guerrillas are the only ones who have the answer."

I stopped and looked up at him. He had just voiced a growing conviction of my own that I hadn't dared as yet to admit to myself. We talked for a few more minutes before I had to rush off to class. I knew I would have to see a lot more of him.

XIX

Conflicting Currents
of Thought

The Priest In the latter half of 1966 the Petén program began picking up steam, not so much as a result of my efforts, but rather because many Guatemalan officials began to say that resettlement of landless Indians in the Petén jungles was the answer to Guatemala's social ills. I was more critical of its potential now that we had a sense of the Méndez Montenegro administration. Even so, I gave the project all I had. If resettlement was not the answer, I had to ask myself if any answer existed.

The U. S. bishops' National Catholic Welfare Conference, the same organization that had lent the Cabricán cooperative $6,000, now donated the cost of a new water pump and a twenty-five-kilowatt diesel-powered generator to supply all our electrical needs. Father Cy Schlarman, a dynamo from the Peoria, Illinois, diocese, heard about the project and got us a secondhand D-6 Caterpillar bulldozer for land-clearing and a dozen used John Deere tractors for plowing. John Breen gave us $5,000 from Maryknoll, and three lay missioners came from Spain to teach in the palm-thatched school and to attend to the dispensary. One of them, María Luisa Palau, had been in Cabricán. She had been expelled by the sisters and sent back to Spain, but had now returned to Guatemala for at least four years more.

My brother Art, stationed in San Antonio Huista, Huehuetenango, sent a group of his parishioners, fifteen families in all, to settle with us. Even the Guatemalan air force cooperated by flying the new settlers from Guatemala City to Flores, Petén, for only the cost of the fuel.

I was making numerous visits to Guatemala City to make arrangements for the three lay missioners and the incoming equipment. I had obtained my pilot's license in order to fly myself back and forth. We had cleared a landing strip at San Juan Acul, and Denny Kraus and I had made payments on a Cessna-150. I could fly to Guatemala City from Petén in fifty minutes, whereas it took all day to go by boat and jeep to Flores and wait for a cargo flight to the capital.

One day when I was sitting in the Maryknoll Center House in Guatemala City, a Maryknoll sister asked me to contact Fathers Denny Kraus and Bill Woods by radio. I obliged her and was surprised to hear her talk with them about sending Guatemalan university students into the mountains to instruct Indians in social action programs. I was somewhat taken aback, because, as a close friend of Denny and Bill, I'd thought I knew all about what they were doing in the field of social action. I was also surprised to find out that Guatemalans from the capital were that interested in the problems of the peasants in the mountains. And what was most unexpected was the fact that a Maryknoll sister from Monte María would be involved in such a project.

I had come to view Monte María as a countersacrament, an emblem of what Christianity was not—teaching the little rich daughters of the country's oppressive oligarchy. I had stopped going there years before, even though it was only three miles or so from our Center House. Thus I avoided the nickname "Convent Joe," often pinned on priests who visited the sisters frequently, and who, it seemed to me, were in search of their masculinity through long drawn-out bull sessions that allowed them to relate to women without being threatened by the experience.

When Sister Marian Peter had finished making her arrangements over the radio, I questioned her about her work. Her knowledge of the actual situation in the country, her desire to work for the poor, the intensity of her dedication—all impressed me. She smiled like a pixy, and the light that shone in her eyes indicated a happy disposition that would be difficult to discourage.

"Would your students be willing to go to Petén?" I asked her.

"They are not my students," she replied, "but if you invited them, I'm sure they'd be glad to cooperate in teaching the people of Petén anything you or they feel would be useful to them."

I was struck by the way she spoke. There was no mistaking the tremendous respect she had for the students she was working with as well as for the colonizers with whom I was involved. When I said good-by to her, I knew I would see her again. Her views on Guatemala and its problems came closer to my own than those of any other person I had met. I wanted to share some of her insights.

On my next visit to the capital, I went to see Sister Marian Peter at Monte María. I asked her if she and any other sisters would meet with some of the priests who had shown concern for social problems. Her response was immediate: "I was thinking of getting in touch with you to ask you the very same question."

When John Breen became Superior, he started to update our work. Vatican II had shaken up the complacency of the Maryknoll Society, and everyone was engaged in re-evaluation, both personal and institutional. John offered to pay the bill for any of us who wanted to attend, in any part of the Americas, a Church-run program of studies in the latest theological developments, as stimulated and fostered by Vatican II. He also started a series of meetings in which, every few months, all the priests, brothers, and sisters in a given area would discuss the practical application of the Council documents and new Maryknoll statements to the actual situation in Guatemala. However, there was a split within the mission between progressives and conservatives, and the meetings degenerated into futile intellectual exercises. My suggestion to Sister Marian Peter had the aim of providing a substitute for these meetings—with the difference that our gatherings would involve only those priests, brothers, and sisters who agreed that the Church's past performance in Guatemala was inadequate and who wanted to see some radical changes.

So it was that in late 1966 some ten of us began to seek ways of translating our vision more directly into practice. We discussed poverty and its place in the Gospels and its relation to our lives. We decided that we in fact were not touched by poverty in our own personal lives but only preached it to others.

During one of these meetings, I rather impetuously declared, "I am going to marry an Indian girl and raise a family and see what it's like to have hungry kids look me in the face and ask for their meals. Then I'll dare one of you well-fed gringos to come around and tell me and my family to have patience, that God loves us, that everything will be all right in Heaven."

I was angry because our discussions of poverty and misery seemed to me to be purely academic exercises. We were trying to relate to these people as teachers, as inspirers, as leaders, as Christians, while their lives and sufferings were so foreign to us that we might as well have been watching them in a motion picture.

After that meeting, Sister Marian Peter came up to me and said, "You don't have to marry an Indian girl to do that. Marry me, and we'll find out together what it means to be peasants."

She laughed lightly, then became embarrassed, while we both stood there looking at each other. Then she turned and walked away.

Actually, her proposal was not so bold as it might sound. We had discussed the barriers we had erected around ourselves to "preserve" ourselves for God and from each other. The sisters were in the process of getting rid of their long, somber habits. I myself had stopped wearing my Roman collar years before. We had also decided to drop our official titles and go by our Christian names: I had become Tom, Sister Marian Peter became Marjorie, and there were also Gail and Mimi and Charlie and Jim and Blase and others.

We discussed celibacy, how it was tearing the priesthood apart, how the Church had rolled all Ten Commandments into one—Thou shalt not commit adultery—and forgotten the obligations of love. Birth control was a burning issue, and we knew it could not be solved intelligently by men living within the hothouse subculture of the Vatican, who were afraid to develop a theology of sexuality because of what it might do to their own precarious psychosexual balance.

When Marjorie said to me, "Marry me, and we'll find out together what it means to be peasants," she said it in the same vein that I had used in speaking of marrying an Indian girl. I was not talking about an actual person I expected to marry, but only vaguely suggesting the kind of thing that had to be done to bring more realism to our lives, to get us out of our ivory towers.

She had taken me by surprise, and I let her go. I knew she was the outstanding nun in Guatemala. She was in the midst of everything, always doing and being and thinking. In the meetings, she often expressed my own thoughts. Then when I spoke, I would see her nodding her head in agreement and smiling at me. I realized that I was very fond of her and she of me, but we had never acknowledged it between ourselves.

Yet, even as I tried to brush off her suggestion as having no concrete meaning, it occured to me that perhaps it would not be a bad idea after all—ultimately, it might be the only way to bring my life into line with those to whom I was sent to teach the mysteries of life and love.

She avoided me for a few meetings after that, and I didn't speak to her, since I hadn't figured out whether I should throw cold water on her first statement, ignore it completely, or somehow follow it up.

The revolutionary activity in the northeast and the daily appearance of dead bodies in the countryside were subjects of intense discussion. Is there such a thing as Christian revolution? Does a Christian have any role in revolutionary times? Does he ignore revolution or condemn it or aid it? Do foreigners in Guatemala, particularly Americans—since our government was helping to suppress the revolutionary movement—have any role to play in Guatemala's revolution? These were all questions we confronted without reaching any definite conclusions.

Marjorie was the most vociferous in proclaiming that we had an obligation to become involved, that we were not foreigners, and that only by participating at some level could we hope to bring to bear on events the moral principles we preached. I agreed with her, because I was convinced that the U.S. counterrevolutionary role on behalf of the oligarchy gave us an obligation to support the peasants.

It became known to some of us that Marjorie had met some of the guerrilla leaders through her work with university students, and I was afraid she would get involved over her head. I mentioned this to Charlie Reilly, another priest who knew of Marjorie's contacts, and he suggested that I go with her to meet them and try to find out their real intentions. He was even more distrustful of them than I was.

Still, I was wary. I knew that any meeting with the guerrillas would produce a debate and I realized that I wasn't yet sure of my own position or my own solutions, and was inclined to be grateful to the guerillas for their struggle. I was not certain I trusted myself to speak with them. I knew I didn't trust Marjorie to talk with them alone.

Shortly after Charlie Reilly made his suggestion, I asked Marjorie point-blank how involved she was with the guerrillas. She told me she was helping them in small ways, such as driving them around Guatemala City.

I was upset by her response, and told her to get into my

jeep. I drove out of the City, up into the mountains, and across the pass toward the Salvadorian border.

I felt she was ruining all her previous work.

"Margie, they're just using you as a front. You're romantic. You're tired of being a teacher. You've forgotten your commitment." I just blurted it out. Was I afraid her involvement would commit me before I was ready?

She came right back at me: "No, Tom, I'm not just a front for them. I'm beginning to realize for the first time that I am able to do many good things, not because I am a nun, but in spite of it. I'm not ashamed of what I'm doing."

"They're using you."

"Is it so terrible to be used? For something good?"

"But, goddamn it, you know what the papers are full of. The bodies keep showing up."

"Yes. And you know who they are. Bodies mostly of innocent people. People who spoke up. Their relatives. It's mostly the work of the police and the army."

"I know. And you'll end up that way, too. Suppose you get really involved with them, and see them shoot down people. You know they will. You'll come back crying—with nowhere to go, no one to turn to. You'll be cut off from the Church. You won't be able to influence the students. Now when you're beginning to get somewhere with them, you'll blow it all and run off like a stupid adventuress with a bunch of desperadoes playing Robin Hood." I knew, even as I spoke to her, that I did not believe all I was saying.

"No, they're good people. They're doing what has to be done. Nobody else is going to do it. I'm sorry you feel this way, Tom. I felt that way once, too, when Felipe Ramos told me he was going with them. But it's necessary, and I'm going to help them and work with them as well as I can."

Damn! I thought I had found one individual in Guatemala with wisdom and courage together—one human being in the Church whom I could fully trust. But now, she was ruining it.

She was proving to her students, to the priests and sisters who trusted her, and to me that she didn't have the patience to work inside the Church to bring the Spirit of Christ to life.

She must have read my thoughts, for she said, "Christ is almost dead in the Church, and you know it better than I do. Besides, you told me you thought we all might have to work with the guerrillas someday."

"Marjorie, I'm afraid for you. When I said that, I was angry and desperate. I know you think you're sincere. But I'm convinced that when you tie yourself up with those people, you'll be crucifying Christ all over again."

"You know who's crucifying Christ nowadays!" She began to cry.

"But those guerrillas are Communists! They don't care for your dignity or your liberty. They're just using you. You and your idiotic nun-front. You're a dupe for Communists and terrorists!" I was startled by my own language and by the depth of my feeling. Why was I talking this way to her when I myself was seeking a way somehow, somewhere, to help in this revolution? I had begun to realize that its ends were just; and, if its means were not always so, as the newspapers claimed, then that was my fault for not participating and showing them a better way, if I had one. Why was I bandying about the very term—"Communists"—that had been hurled at me and at other dedicated people so many times? What was I actually trying to say? I knew what it was, and yet I would not admit it to myself: I was desperately in love with Marjorie, and the agony of seeing her walk this road alone, this very dangerous road, was distorting my vision.

Meanwhile, Marjorie was in the jeep, but she was not in the same world with me. I didn't know how to reach her any more—I had driven her into herself with my shouting.

I was thinking to myself that I could never see her again. I had the colony to worry about, people who depended on me— two hundred and fifty Indians, rebuilding their lives in the undeveloped jungle mud. I couldn't desert them. I wanted to help 25,000 Indians to settle in the Petén, and then 250,000, and then 2,500,000. But I couldn't do that and play revolutionary with Marjorie at the same time.

Just what was it about those people that had captured her mind? She wasn't a fool; she knew the risks she was taking. I was fighting a million currents of thought and emotion.

She was so small, yet I could tell that she wasn't afraid. Had she fallen in love with one of them? With Turcios or César Montes? I hated myself for thinking like that. I was just jealous, I thought, and stupid. An American Catholic missionary sister working with Communist revolutionaries. Sister Marian Peter and Comrade César Montes. I was in love with her, and I couldn't hide it from myself any longer.

I drove her to the student center, El Crater, and let her out of the jeep, not knowing how to say good-by. She stood on the sidewalk and looked at me in what seemed a pleading way, as if to say, "I'm going to continue to help them. I hope you will meet with them, talk with them, at least before you make any more judgments."

I smiled wanly and drove off.

The next day, I was back at San Juan Acul. The peace and quiet were broken only by the cries of the *sarahuates*, the big black monkeys whose meat the people refused to touch—"Padre, they look too much like human beings"—and by the periodic crash of another felled tree making room for yet a few more stalks of corn. I had time to think through a maze of questions, aided by the earthy wisdom of men whose horizons had never extended beyond their own small plots of ground. I was gaining a grip on my indignation at the Church's indifference to the problems of life and its near-obsession with the niceties of belief; I was concerned with the difference between Communists—actual party members—and "communists"—Marxists, socialists, and Christian Socialists, and also my feelings toward Marjorie. Other things were falling into place, too.

Gerbermann had offered me Doheny's job, since he hadn't gotten the Ixcán land project going and the situation was becoming embarrassing with regard to the people whose hopes had been kindled. When Tex told me, "I'll put you in charge of Doheny's project, too," the tune sounded exactly the same as when he'd told me he was giving me a second chance by sending me to Cabricán, six years earlier.

I was hesitant to take over Doheny's work. As for arranging to bring to Petén people who had originally hoped to go to Ixcán, all right. Under pressure, Doheny had made one trip, the only one during that entire year, to the far side of the Cuchumatanes. A Texan had donated $10,000 for an airplane for that project, and Doheny had sent some men to build an airstrip. He finally settled a few families, but there were no titles to the land. In Petén, we had no titles either; but at least we were sure that the lands belonged to the government, because no titles had ever been issued for that area. There was no such guarantee for Ixcán.

Shortly after I had been offered his job, Doheny went to live in the jungle of Ixcán. He stayed a week, came back enthusiastic, and talked up the project. I was glad; if something finally was to get going there that would help provide new lands for the Indians, so much the better.

Meanwhile, the newspapers were carrying a story about a big dispute between Guatemala and Mexico. It seemed that on the Usumacinta River, which formed part of the boundary between the two countries, Mexico was building hydroelectric dams that might cause waters to back up and flood the Petén region. The Guatemalan government publicly declared that the reason it had consented so readily to the settling of these lands was in order to strengthen Guatemala's case, if actual flooding occurred. The president of Guatemala met with the president of Mexico, who denied any danger of flooding.

The Indians believed, and I agreed, that any arrangement the government made with Mexico would fail to take their interests into account. Nothing in the history of Guatemala's treatment of her Indian people could lead anyone to believe otherwise. When the news story first broke, Father Doheny said, "See? That's the way Melville works. No plans. *I* make plans, Melville doesn't."

He was right in one sense: I had not made plans that would effectively protect the people against manipulation by their own government. I was now convinced that radical new approaches had to be taken. The Indians were exploited by the Church, the landowners, the army, the government—on different levels, of course, but exploited nonetheless.

A few weeks after my jeep ride with Marjorie, I returned to Guatemala City, but didn't try to reach her. However, I ran into another sister who had seen Margie.

"Why don't you call her?" she asked. "Why don't you see her?"

I couldn't determine how much the sister knew about what was between me and Margie. I headed for El Crater.

Marjorie walked in—she had cut her hair. When she had removed her nun's veil some time earlier, I asked her to let her hair grow long, like the Indian girls, and she agreed. When I saw that she had cut her hair, I figured she was angry with me.

"You've cut your hair?"

Actually she looked prettier with her hair cut. Still, it bothered me to see it.

She stood and looked at me. I floundered on: "You know, I think you look nicer with your hair cut than with it long."

She smiled shyly.

"You cut it just to spite me," I accused her in jest.

"No, not to spite you. I cut it because there was no reason any more not to cut it."

I plunged on: "Our meetings are getting to be all theory. I think we ought to forget them. Attendance has fallen off, anyway. Do you think you could introduce me to some of your friends?"

She was overjoyed, though she tried not to show it. By then, I think we both knew we were in love with one another.

The next day she told me that Felipe Ramos had arranged a meeting at Monte María, and some of the Catholic students from El Crater who also wanted to meet the guerrillas would be there as well.

When I arrived at the school, Margie was already there with one university student. There were two young men and a young woman whom I presumed to be revolutionaries. I later learned that one of them was César Montes, or "Flaco" ("skinny"), as he was called; the name of the other man was Nestor Valle. I never learned who the young woman was.

Everyone shook hands; but it was clear at once that something unusual was going on. Ordinarily, Latins take many pains introducing themselves. North American brusqueness and efficiency seem cold and offensive to them. They may take half an hour simply for ending a visit or a meeting; they will touch you, a friendly grasp of your arm, or an *abrazo*. But here no names were given—only handshakes, with a terse *Mucho gusto de conocerlo* ("Very happy to meet you").

César Montes's hair was dyed red in a long crewcut, and he had shaven off his mustache. (The police later penetrated his disguise.)

When one of the men asked me what work I was doing, I felt a little on the defensive. I suppose I had expected to be congratulated—I thought I was risking a lot even meeting with them.

I replied simply, "Land reform."

The questioner pushed on: "Do you really thing the Guatemalan government will ever allow many people to move into large colonies, or land reform areas, especially if it would deprive the plantations of their slave labor?"

"I hadn't thought of that too much," I answered. "Anyway, I feel I have to help as many as I can. Two hundred and fifty peasants have already moved to Petén. I hope soon to bring in one thousand, maybe five thousand, and who knows how many more."

"That's all very well, very Christian," he told me. "But at the same time, those few are receiving something the thousands and thousands of others can't touch. If your few fail, it will be said it is because they are Indians. Meanwhile, for allowing it, for lending a few planes now and then to take people to the new land, the government will claim the credit. When we accuse them of exploiting the Indians for the plantation owners, the officials will say, 'Oh, but look at how we helped the Indians in Petén!' "

"Then," I put in, "you don't want any Indians to be helped just to make your claim of governmental tyranny seem consistent?"

"Nonsense. You know what a tyranny the government is. Don't play that game. What we are trying to say is that your work is giving the government an insurance policy. Don't you have to balance that off, what you are doing and what you are accomplishing with a minimum number of people, against the evil that is continually perpetrated against the great majority of slave laborers who remain behind and whom the government will never allow to participate in land reform? Don't you ever feel that you are spreading a film of seeming goodness over a terrible evil, making it appear that the government is really interested in helping the Indians? They've already publicized the work in Petén widely, small as it is, as if it were all their doing. Does that make you proud of your work?"

"I don't care what they say as long as they don't interfere."

"What's to stop them from interfering when you have done the job and made them look good? In a sense, aren't you *fronting* for the government in its policy of supporting the enslavement of the Indians?"

Thus it went, back and forth. As I came slowly off the defensive, I began to be impressed by their sincerity, their real feeling for the people. They conceded that if the government ever allowed enough people to go up to the jungle to build colonies, there would be no need for revolutionaries. But past governmental actions gave no indication that such a policy could honestly be hoped for.

Then, ironically, they congratulated me for what I was doing. The problem of my work and its meaning was like a two-edged machete: It was important to educate as many people as possible to the potentialities of land reform without building in them a false illusion that it was about to, or ever would easily, benefit them. The revolutionaries, in fact, saw their own work as essentially one of education and considered themselves "armed teachers": "If the government left us alone to teach the people, we wouldn't need guns. But the landowners will never allow the government to educate the peasants to their rights. We have to do it."

The more we talked, the more I realized that what these guerrillas were telling me were things I was already convinced of; I could not deny that our positions were in fact identical.

When *they* took over, they said, they would need people like Margie: "We will need people who understand the Indians and their faith."

I asked them, "How can we tell that you won't oppress the people even more than they're oppressed now?"

"Well, those of us who are leaders now will surely die in the struggle anyway. We believe, though, that once people learn to fight for their rights, it will be virtually impossible to impose on them a more oppressive system."

Nestor Valle, one of those who spoke that day, is already dead. I have heard that the government also claims to have killed César Montes. But I already knew that over the years more than four thousand students, labor leaders, and peasants had been assassinated for speaking up.

Later, when Marjorie and I talked alone, she asked me what I thought.

I said: "I no longer doubt their sincerity. If they're using anybody, they're using themselves."

Even so, I didn't completely agree with the revolutionaries. Later on, I had at least two severe arguments with one of them, who had the gall to quote Scripture to me.

I spoke to him coldly: "Look, let's just talk about this in human terms, political terms. Don't you start quoting the Gospel to me—you don't even believe in Christ. You're just using Christ to win points against me."

Calmly, he answered me: "I accept Christ as a historical human being. I accept the Gospels as a record of what he said. Don't try to justify your position by claiming the message of Christ for your personal property. He belongs to every human, Christian or no."

I had trouble with my own conception of Christ. I call myself "Christian"—what does that mean? Why should I be upset that this guerrilla regarded Christ as a great human being? Could I accept Christ on those terms?

For me, Christ had meant celibacy, and reading the Psalms of the breviary every day. The bishop was His voice: "Do it. Don't do it. Do this, don't do that."

Being challenged by a Communist guerrilla to talk about Christ, not as the Son of God, but as a man, to take what he said at its own face value, threatened me. What did these secular men know of the real Christ?

My own troubles with the hierarchy didn't help me resist the revolutionary approach. My deepening awareness of the actual role of the Church discredited breviary-reading as a living connection with Christ.

My admiration for the revolutionaries was slowly growing. They got to me by their direct questions, questions that had churned in my gut but that I had tried to keep out of my consciousness.

My personal misgivings about the Church increased at the same time. I began to ask myself: What will the land program in Petén lead to? How far will it be allowed to go? Is it worth the publicity the government and the Church are getting out of it?

About this time, as if designed to confirm the warnings of the guerrillas, Colonel Oliverio Casasola, governmental director of the land distribution program, gave a speech in Guatemala City, a kind of "State of the Union" message on land reform.

The newspapers published his statement:

Let's speak more plainly. The aim is not to populate Petén at any price and thus contaminate from its beginnings an enterprise that must remain absolutely healthy in order to generate health throughout the country.

An example: The illiteracy rate in Petén was once one of the lowest in Guatemala and in Central America, but in recent years it has risen to twenty-two percent. The cause? Kekchie Indian immigration to the municipality of San Luis, due to the economic and agricultural disaster in Alta Verapaz. . . . It is important to note that, of the 2,849 migrants to Petén, 1,908 were Indians and 941 non-Indians, an equation of retrogression, since whatever sympathy the Indians' problems may inspire in us, they are not the human element that Petén needs to make progress. . . .*

I shouldn't have been surprised. This was not a new policy or a new attitude. The Indians represent fifty-six percent of Guatemala's population, and they and the twenty-eight percent of the population listed as poor "white" (*ladino*) together own only sixteen percent of the country's privately held lands, and most of this on mountainsides. With two percent of the people owning seventy-two percent of the total private holdings in Guatemala, there was really no reason for me to believe that Petén was suddenly to become the portion of the disinherited.

It was a song I had heard more than once. Its usual lyrics went something like this: "Our Indians are all very colorful, lovely, simple people, but they have no education and no capital, and they don't know how to work. We must not give

* El Imparcial, *October 5, 1967.*

them any large landholdings or allow them to have very much power."

A few years earlier, some twenty-five priests, including myself, had met to discuss the socioeconomic problems of the people in their parishes. The report that emerged from our conference pointed up two basic areas in which the people needed help:

1. *Migration:* In order to survive, Indian men often have to work on plantations during certain months of the year. This causes splitting up of the families. Mothers and children are left to watch the corn crop and to endure alone while the husbands are gone for months on end.

2. *Lack of land:* The peasants have to migrate because they don't own enough land on which to grow food for themselves. Indians are kept virtually landless and thus are forced to work on plantations at wages ranging from ten to eighty cents a day. Eggs sell at sixty cents a dozen. Meat is high. Peasants grow beans and corn and coffee for themselves on their miserable mountain plots.

When plantation managers have found themselves short of migrant workers, the army has been known to herd men onto trucks and deliver them to the plantations. If the Indians were to strike and refuse to serve as migrant workers under existing conditions, they would be in trouble not only with plantation owners, but also with the government and the army.

The areas represented by the priests participating in this meeting provided, we calculated, seventy-five percent of all the migrant laborers in the country. We wanted to serve as a buffer between the landowners, the government, and the army on one side and the peasants themselves on the other.

Our report was submitted to the bishops of the four dioceses in which we worked. A week later, we were advised that we were mixing in politics, when our real job was to preach the

Gospel. If we were sincere, we would preach to the land-owners, and they, on hearing the message of charity and justice and peace, would put it into practice in their own good time.

By the bishops' orders, then, the life-and-death struggle of our parishioners to find sustenance for their families was to be no concern of ours. I wondered what Christ would have thought about this interpretation of His Gospel.

In the fall of 1967 a number of Maryknoll priests and nuns, including Marjorie, my brother Art, and myself, went to San Salvador to attend the International Convention of Latin American Sociologists. There were perhaps 150 sociologists and as many observers from related fields, from every country in Latin America. The conference was dedicated to the memory of the martyred Colombian priest Father Camilo Torres, who had been killed by government troops while fighting with the guerrillas in his country.

The conference workshops covered many subjects, but the one that especially interested me was land reform. I was surprised to find that most of the workshop participants saw revolution as the only answer to Latin America's main problem, the unjust distribution of land. At first, I thought they were talking about revolution only in the sense of social reform; but, before long, it became evident that they understood that the people of Latin America would have to overthrow governments by force if they were ever to replace the present feudalistic social and political structures with regimes that would allow them to live decent human lives.

A few weeks later, I was in Guatemala City, having returned from the Petén region, where the leaders of Pope John XXIII Colony were continuing their dialogue on how to hold onto the lands they were clearing and how to obtain more land for their landless brothers back in the mountains. I went to see Marjorie, and we discussed the meeting in San Salvador, the fact that so many outstanding social scientists were openly professing revolution as the only answer. I was still afraid of the personal implications of such an idea and I struggled with it in terms of the "right" time, the right place, the right way. We talked about Fidel Castro's Cuba and what he had done to help the poverty-stricken masses in his country despite economic, political, and even military attempts of the United States to destroy him and his revolution. Margie told me that she had learned that the Papal Nuncio in Cuba was in favor of what Castro was doing and had referred to him as "politically a Marxist and ethically a Christian." For myself, though I acknowledged Castro's achievements in the fields of health and education, I wondered about the human price that some of the people had had to pay for these advances. But I finally agreed that since I hadn't taken part in the Cubans' struggle for justice, I had no right to complain about the results—and this would apply to Guatemala also.

Mexico perhaps offered better guidance than Cuba as to what could happen in Guatemala, since the cultural/class conflict there was similar. Mexico's revolution had caused a million deaths, yet most of the peasants today are as badly off as when Zapata first decided that no more lands would be stolen from them. We agreed that the only way to insure a successful revolution in Guatemala would be through participation by enough people who were concerned that the Mexican experience not be repeated.

Two things were now prodding me on toward action. First, my awareness that as a priest I had served too often as a pacifier to the people in their terrible need. Didn't I really want to see the peasants stand on their own feet? I began to surprise many Indians by telling them that I wouldn't be happy until they started disagreeing with me and questioning me and making their own decisions.

The second thing pushing at me was the U.S.'s military assistance to the Guatemalan government. I could not quietly accept a policy that destroyed any hope of real betterment of these people's lives. Powerful interest groups in Washington were influencing or making decisions in terms of what was good for the United States without understanding or concern for the Guatemalan people. It was not uncommon to hear aspiring diplomats who could hardly speak Spanish expound on Guatemala's problems. I once heard an AID man defend his inability to speak Spanish with the remark, "We are down here to help them, not them us. It's their job to learn English—they're the askers, not us. Why should we learn Spanish?"

I spoke of my steadily deepening convictions to my fellow priests. Some responded positively, but most refused to think about revolution because their parishes didn't seem to be directly affected. Most thought it natural to maintain their ties with the American community in Guatemala. Then again, there was the matter of their own psychological security: Questioning the Church was one thing, questioning the United States government another.

About this time, Marjorie informed me that my brother Art had tried to go to Cuba to get an idea of the Cuban people's feelings about their revolution. I had not realized that he felt so strongly. I knew that he had been full of anguish when the president of one of his parish cooperatives had been murdered, and I had even tried to help by seeing the judge in Huehuetenango to find out if something could be done about the murder. People in the parish charged that the culprits were the local mayor and a large landowner; they even produced witnesses to the crime. Nothing came of it.

Art's planned trip had run into snags, and he hadn't gone. I was glad, because I felt such an action would have undermined his own future effectiveness.

I wanted to see Art right away. I left Guatemala City and drove to Huehuetenango, and the following day continued on to San Antonio Huista. It was raining hard, and I was stuck several times in the mud on the way. Art was not home, he had gone to Jacaltenango, two hours away by horse. It was still raining, and I couldn't follow the trails because the mud was too deep. When I reached Jacaltenango, four hours later, a meeting was going on. Everyone was surprised to see me, soaked to the skin. I sat in on the meeting and said nothing.

After supper Art and I went to his room. I asked him about his plan to go to Cuba. He didn't look surprised. He said, "I knew you'd find out sooner or later, but I didn't tell you because I didn't want to compromise you."

If Art wasn't surprised that I had found out about his trip, neither was I surprised to hear about his ideas and feelings. We didn't communicate with each other very often in Guatemala and went our separate ways, yet the roads were always remarkably parallel.

We talked until 4 a.m. He told me of an upcoming meeting in Escuintla with the Christian students of the university, some priests and sisters, some peasant leaders, and Felipe Ramos. I related my own talk with César Montes and Nestor Valle a few weeks previously and expressed my interest in attending this new meeting, whose theme was to be Christian Revolution.

XX

A New Life Breaks Through

The Nun It was October 1, a Sunday morning, and I
was at the convent drying the breakfast
dishes when I heard a car come into the driveway. Somehow I
knew it was Felipe. "Someone in the parlor to see you," one
of the sisters called out. I found Felipe sitting on the couch,
his elbows on his knees, his hands clenched.

"You look as if you just lost your best friend," I exclaimed.
He looked up at me, surprised. "I did," he said. "Luis
Turcios was burned to death at 1 a.m. this morning. He was
driving too fast. His car somehow turned over and caught fire.
He was trapped. I was waiting for him, and he never came."

I couldn't speak. We just sat together, silently remembering.
Then I asked, "What now?"

"I don't know," he said. "But I must go, there are many
things I have to do right away, and I can hardly move, I'm so
numb."

Not more than two hours after he had finally left, I was
called again to the parlor—it was Father Tom Melville, whom
I had been expecting. How relieved I was to be able to share
my grief at Luis's death with someone I now knew sympathized with the guerrillas.

But we also had something very much alive to share—he
had an idea. "And so have I," I said to him. When he told
me his plan, I could hardly believe my ears: We had had the

very same one. How often this was to happen to us from then on!

Our plan was to arrange regular meetings with a small group of priests and nuns who shared our concerns and attitudes. I knew that three of the sisters, Gail, Jeanne, and Rose Guadalupe, felt much as I did. He said he would ask four priests who could plausibly travel to Guatemala City every two weeks or so. We felt that, together, there must be something we could do instead of just bemoaning social conditions, the Church's policies, and the attitudes of most of the missioners.

At the first meeting, we discussed the question of poverty. Missioners preached to people that God loves the poor, while they lived comfortably, and the rectories and convents were usually the most luxurious buildings in town. All of us decided to try to live in as simple and austere a way as we could. At a later meeting we resolved always to speak Spanish whenever a Guatemalan was within earshot—so often we inadvertently but rudely excluded them from our conversations.

If we were to break down the barriers between us and the people, it was necessary, we felt, to begin to accomplish this among ourselves. And so the titles of "Father" and "Sister" were dropped. Now I became just—Margie. These meetings seemed to help us grow closer to the people we had come to serve.

Maryknollers were supposed to make an eight-day retreat once a year. It was a time to pray, to get away from regular routine duties, to meditate. You were expected to look into yourself, to evaluate what you were actually doing and how well you were doing it. Usually we went on retreat in our own convent, but there we always had reminders at hand to make us anxious about our daily work.

I wanted to be free during my vacation to work in the countryside; so when I heard about a retreat being given in Huehuetenango for some American sisters who had a hospital there, I asked permission to make my retreat with them in September, and it was granted.

I took with me a document from the Vatican Council, *The Church in the Modern World*. I went through it very thoroughly, constantly asking myself what I could do to make the Church relevant in Guatemala. What kept going through my mind was: *Guatemala is in revolution. It's happening and it is being fought against. Where do I stand in all this? We American missionaries are aloof from events. We should be part of them, we have to be Christians first and Americans second. How should I relate to this?*

I wanted to visit the guerrillas' encampment in the mountains of the Sierra de las Minas, to see what they were like and whether I should work with them or not. But a difficulty here was that I would have to be honest about where I wanted to go; yet by asking permission, I would put my Superior in the position of being responsible for me.

I read a book on the life of Father Lebbe, a Belgian missionary to China in the thirties, who was one of my heroes while I was still in the novitiate. He had adopted Chinese dress and worked with Chinese guerrillas. A co-worker of his, Father Cotta, an Egyptian, had been stationed as chaplain in our novitiate. I read an article written by two Australian Catholics who had taught at Peking University, about the role of the Church in China, which corroborated my feelings that in Guatemala the Church was also remaining aloof from the needs of people.

To quote a few paragraphs:

There is no need to add that they [Christian evangelists in China] came from corrupt societies where Christianity was very powerful—that is to say, very corrupt.

These were the societies Marx studied. It was natural enough that the Chinese, never slow to sense hypocrisy and insult, should have reacted in the same way as Marx.

The result is a violently anti-Christian China, which is not as disastrous as it sounds. Anti-Christianity is not always anti-Christ. A society can have Christian features without knowing Christ. Certainly a pagan society can be more Christian than one which has betrayed Christ.

In other words a rejection of a pseudo-Christianity is not necessarily a rejection of Christ himself.

For there is another Christianity, and a much harder one to kill. It took centuries of capitalism to cripple it in the West.

It is a subtle, classless, pervasive spirit. Its essence is Christ's message, which can be spelled out in words of one syllable. If man is to have faith in God, he must have faith in man; he must first have hope for man, or he can have no hope for God; and if he wants to love God, he must first love man.

Unless this is accepted as the key to Christianity, the Incarnation is meaningless. . . .*

After the retreat I returned to work at the Crater and continued my teaching—though with many of my questions still unanswered. But I was calm. I knew that opportunities to contribute to the search for justice would flow naturally from my work and from my interchange with many friends, that answers would come in their own good time, and that I would have many valid alternatives from among which to choose.

With the help of Sister Maureen Bernadette, a team from the Crater gave a Day of Action in Huehuetenango city in late September. Sister Bernadette taught in the public high school and was able to recruit a group of fifty for the Day. This was our first experience outside of Guatemala City, and we found that many of the young people in Huehuetenango, mostly *ladinos*, were very enthusiastic about engaging in work like ours. They formed a group which they called *Chispa* ("spark"), since they saw it as a spark from the Crater that they hoped would set other places ablaze.

* *Neale and Deirdre Hunter: "Christian China," in* Soundings: Occasional Notes on Christianity and International Service (*Council of International Lay Associations: Washington, D.C.; 1966*).

Meanwhile, the Jesuits at Landívar University asked some of the boys from the Crater if they would arrange food and lodging for peasant leaders. The university was then initiating a new program for so-called *promotores sociales,* financed by AID, in which groups of peasants would come for six-week courses on community development and social action; AID would pay the Crater for feeding and housing them. The Jesuits liked our spirit and felt that the students at the Crater would provide the "promoters-in-training" with good social contacts in the City.

The plan was made to order for us. We could now have our own *cursillo* house furnished for fifty people; and since only six courses were planned during the whole year, it would be free for our own use for several weeks. We could make enough profit to provide the small income we needed. We preferred to finance ourselves and be independent rather than count on Maryknoll's Q.100 a month. We borrowed some money, rented and furnished an old farmhouse, and hired three maintenance personnel. It became the "Big Crater," and we inaugurated it with two vacation *cursillos* and then opened its doors to the *promotores sociales* in January 1967.

Felipe came to see me one day at the Crater. He had to leave soon for the guerrilla base of operations in the mountains of the Sierra de las Minas. He had been Luis Turcios's bodyguard in the City, and now he was to accompany César Montes, the new leader.

He told me, "I don't want to leave any evidence that would endanger my family. I want to make it clear that I have left home completely. How would it be if I gave you all my books? Would you keep them for me?"

I said, "Sure." I didn't want him to see how worried I was about him.

One night, during the rehearsal of a play we were doing to raise money for the Crater, I looked out from the stage and saw Felipe, sitting quietly. He motioned to me, and I went over to him. I was always nervous when he showed up, because

I never knew who might be following him, or if we might be caught. Yet I enjoyed seeing him.

He said, "I have the books for you. They're in the car outside."

I went out to the car with him, and saw a fellow in the front seat. We nodded to each other.

Getting these books from him meant that he would soon be leaving, and I felt sad that I might never see him again. But I knew that this was his commitment.

As we stood by the trunk of my car, I asked, "Who is that in the car?"

"César Montes."

"Oh, man!" I said sharply, "what are you doing?" The risk was fearful. As chief of the FAR, Montes was the object of an intensive search.

Montes had been a teacher and then begun to study law. Later, he quit his studies to join the guerrillas. He was in his middle twenties, rather short, and the way he held himself and looked and spoke manifested his intensity.

Felipe asked, then, "Do you want to come over and meet him?"

I said, "Sure."

Just then eight policemen passed by, looking at the three of us. This was late at night. In those days, anybody who seemed at all unusual was liable to be searched or watched.

César Montes, without moving his head, followed them with his eyes.

Finally, he said, "There's no problem. They'll leave us alone." He was very cool.

Then I said to Felipe, "Will we see you again?"

"Who knows?" he said.

That was it—the end of all our long talks about poetry and history and politics. I stood there as they drove away, and when I went home, I carefully unpacked his books and put them on my shelf. They were chiefly on psychology and pedagogy.

A few days later, Felipe telephoned me. It was November 2, All Souls' Day. In the countryside, it is celebrated with a Feast of the Dead, and the poor take food to leave at the gravesites. In the city, people take wreaths and flowers.

Felipe said, "We want to go visit Luis Turcios's grave before we leave."

I told him, "You're nuts. The grave will be watched."

He said, "We'll be there just for a moment. And César wants to go, too. Will you come with us?"

I thought to myself, *I'm either with them, or I'm not. If I'm with them, I'll do this. If I'm not with them, I'll say "No" right now and have done with it.*

I said, "Yes, I will. What time will you pick me up?"

We drove to the cemetery in a small, white, very powerful Alfa Romeo. I wore a skirt and blouse, but my small veil identified me as a nun. We parked along a side street. There were many people milling about.

The three of us walked into the cemetery.

Felipe said, "It's over in that direction. Let's walk slowly."

They had me walk between them, using me to distract attention from themselves. Guerrillas would not be expected to be seen with a nun. I knew that, and I thought it was a good idea.

We walked along and saw a man sitting on a gravestone, next to Luis Turcios's grave. He was carefully looking at everyone who passed by.

Felipe said quietly, "*El es una oreja* [he's an 'ear']. He's there to see who visits Turcios's grave. So don't stop now."

We stopped at the grave on the other side of Turcios's plot. We stood a moment with our heads bowed. Then I blessed myself.

César had been baptized a Catholic and then as a young man had joined the Mormons.

"Now," he had told me, "to be frank, I don't believe in either religion."

We turned and walked away.

César said, "Keep your cool, and walk slowly."

Felipe said to César, "A jeepful of secret police just passed by."

César: "Did they recognize us?"

Felipe: "I'm not sure."

The secret police walked by us into the cemetery.

Felipe murmured to me, "I think they're getting ready to turn around and come back after us. You be ready to jump aside if anything happens, and fall flat on the ground. Now walk evenly and quickly."

He expected that he and César might be shot. We moved a little faster. Automatically, I got on the outside.

"Jump aside, nothing," I said to him softly. "If I can help you to escape, I will."

We approached the car. I said, "Do we dare go to the car?"

Felipe affirmed, "Yes, we have to. It's our only chance."

We went on. Felipe opened the car door quickly and we got in. He started off rather deliberately at first. But as soon as we were out of sight of the cemetery, we began to race through the streets, in and out. We drove up to a housing project, and Felipe stopped the car. We relaxed. Felipe got out for a moment to relieve himself—I guess the excitement had been too much for him. I stayed with César Montes.

César was very sad. He had admired Turcios very much.

He kept saying, "I'm not made to be the leader of this movement. I don't know if I can follow in Luis's footsteps."

I tried to encourage him: "He trusted you so much, you were his top lieutenant. You planned all the field activities. Everybody looks up to you. You can do it, and you have to do it. Luis Turcios would expect you to."

Just then, a car drove by, very slowly. The three occupants looked at us, stopped up ahead, then drove off. Felipe had come back quickly. We continued to feel we were being watched. César and Felipe were in fact being looked for all over the City.

Two days later, Gail and I were staying overnight at the Big

Crater, making last-minute preparations for the *cursillo*, when Felipe called.

"Hey. We're stuck. We have no place to stay tonight."

I said, "Come on over. I think you'll be safe."

I didn't dream then that a month later the Big Crater would be searched by twenty soldiers, who broke down fences and looked into every corner and cranny, while a helicopter hovered above. Because of our activities with the peasants, the house downtown had already been visited by the secret police, and we often caught glimpses of men watching us from parked cars.

When Felipe and César arrived, I handed them pillows and sleeping bags, and gave them a room. As we talked, they crawled into their sleeping bags on the floor. Each one placed a gun within easy reach, along with a flashlight. The song *Guantanamera* was playing softly on the radio.

César said, "Listen. This is one of my favorites. Listen to the next verse. . . ."

With the poor of this earth, I have cast my lot. . . .

"That's my life. That's why I'm doing this. My father is an old man, yet he has given me his blessing. He said, 'Son, go ahead, do what you have to do.' "

I said, "That's my life, too. Yet why are our lives so different?"

He laughed. "Well, if you ever want to come up to the mountains with us, you're welcome."

Felipe said, "No. Not yet." He worried about the risks. Yet I think he would have been glad for me to have gone.

A few days later, Gail and I went to the northwest mountain country to work on the literacy program, and Felipe and César returned to the northeast Sierra.

The November–December vacation was a whirlwind of work for all the *cursillistas*. Titina, Rudy, and Juan José took charge of preparing, recruiting, and giving two *cursillos* in

Guatemala City and one in Huehuetenango. Manuel, María Elisa, Gail, and I organized and supervised two teams for vaccination and literacy programs in La Libertad with Father Denny Kraus. Three medical students, each with two girl assistants, traveled to twenty villages, giving diphtheria–tetanus–whooping cough vaccinations to more than two thousand children. In order to be effective, the vaccination had to be repeated three times, with twenty-day lapses. Hence, they made the rounds in October, November, and December. They got to know many of the people through these triple visits, and came to appreciate their urgent and basic medical needs.

Another ten students lived in four small, isolated villages for six weeks. They slept on the floor, ate beans and tortillas with the villagers, and taught two or three literacy classes a day. They began asking questions: Why are the parcels of land held by these people so small that they cannot raise enough corn and beans to subsist on, while many wealthy landowners have large tracts of land they don't even cultivate? Why are these people denied the opportunity to get even an elementary education?

Meanwhile, Gustavo López, the *cursillista* we had met in Colombia, came to Guatemala at our invitation. He stayed with Carlos, and they spent the vacation helping with *cursillos* and working one week with us at La Libertad. Carlos's discussions with Gustavo gave him many ideas on how the understanding gained in *cursillos* could be channeled into programs of action.

The meeting in Colombia had not started a unified international movement. The directors of *cursillos* in each country were left to work independently, and most were content to give *cursillos*. Carlos and Gustavo agreed with me that we had to go further. We had to bring Christian social doctrine to life.

A new crisis arose in 1967 and precipitated a new stage in the development of the Crater. We had not had a priest as director or adviser for a long time, and some felt we needed the paternal authority of a priest. Others felt that I was a satisfactory adviser and that our free-spirited, democratic organization should be given permanence. I could understand the reasons for the conflict over my position. On the one hand, I was a woman, a nun, and a *Norteamericana*; on the other hand, I was a hard worker, and dedicated to the students and to our work. Finally, at a meeting there was a hot debate, and the underlying clash between Juan José and myself became evident.

He wanted to look for a priest-director and to continue to study and give *cursillos*. I wanted them to elect a director from among themselves, to let me be a member of the council with veto powers, and, besides giving *cursillos*, to try to practice what we taught.

Carlos was overwhelmingly elected director, and Juan José and two of his friends left. We made plans to recruit more *cursillistas*, but we tightened the membership regulations. Number one was "no drinking." Alcohol had continued to plague us sporadically, and Julio was finally asked to leave because of it. Maturity came painfully, but the new year promised good things.

Manuel, María Elisa, and the other students had returned from La Libertad with an enthusiasm that was contagious. Sister Maureen Bernadette wanted us to cooperate further with Chispa. Our Days of Action were thus transformed into weekends of leadership-training in the rural area. We began going nearly every week, in groups of six or eight, to villages in Huehuetenango. The men in the classes were catechists and other local leaders gathered by the Maryknoll priest in each village. The classes were on such questions as: *What does it mean to be a man? What is work? What is social justice?* The students taught one class on the great civilization of the Mayan Indians. They encouraged the Indians to be proud of this heritage, to throw off their ingrained feelings of inferiority. We taught them that their oppression was not a punishment from God for the sins of their forebears, but was an evil created by men which could be corrected.

During the day there were several discussion periods, and here the students had as much to learn as the peasant leaders, if not more. They found that expressions such as "revolution" and "agrarian reform" had a different connotation among country people—were, in fact, feared. For most of those who had worked for reform during the Arbenz regime had afterward been killed, their homes burned, their families turned out into the street.

The students also found that the most animated discussions were those where the men spoke in the Indian languages. We would sit next to a young man and ask him to translate for us, so that we could participate.

These trips were demanding. The students had to skip class at the university on Fridays, since the journey took a full day each way. This meant longer hours of study during the week. Yet they were more than ever determined to become good professionals and thus be of more service to their people. Most of our forty members were participating two or three times a month in Days of Action.

Father John Breen gave me Q.1,000 for the Crater, and we filled our long-lasting need for a jeep and a typewriter. We bought Father Denny's Toyota for Q.800 in order to make the trips to Huehuetenango easier.

Most of the villages were quite remote, and the priests usually had to ride horseback to reach them. The Indians used mules to carry very heavy loads, but they themselves almost always walked.

When we started working in the mountains, we decided that we, too, would walk, because we wanted to be a part of the people. This had an interesting side-effect. Some of the priests came to understand that riding horses identified them with an elite, and they began walking, too. The Indians also saw that we wanted to become closer to them, and that we were trying to make things less difficult for them. They would no longer have to send horses for us, which had involved much effort.

At the Crater we decided that the best application of Christian social doctrine within our means would be the organization of migrant workers into peasant leagues, since this was apolitical. The students began researching the subject, and it became one of the topics of our study sessions. One day Carlos, Rudy, and I went to visit the office of the Federación de Organizaciones Campesinas (Federation of Peasant Organizations) to offer the services of the Crater and to ask for training.

We were invited to a training course being held in Puerto San José, on the Pacific coast. The three of us spent a day learning how to organize a peasant league. Most of the participants were illiterate peasant leaders from the southern coast, and the course content had to be painstakingly reviewed so that they could memorize the many legal details. (Although eighty percent of the prospective league members had to be able to read and write in order to have a union legally registered —a prerequisite specifically established to discourage the peasants from organizing—a sympathetic examiner might let them pass if they could sign their names.)

At the Crater we continued studying and attending lectures on union organizing given under the auspices of the Christian Democrats. Rudy began to work with them in the formation of peasant leagues; Carlos was invited to give classes to peasant leaders in Quiché, a department whose population was more than ninety percent Indian. Both Carlos and Titina taught classes for the *promotores sociales* at Landívar. But, as we discovered later, two lectures given by Rudy and Carlos at the Military Academy in which they outspokenly condemned existing social conditions made them suspect, and their names were put on the secret police's list of possible subversives.

In March, Pope Paul published his encyclical *Progress of Peoples*. I brought copies over to the Crater, and we began studying it. A key statement: "Development is the new word for peace." The section on private property we found especially powerful:

Private property does not constitute for anyone an absolute and unconditional right. No one is justified in keeping for his exclusive use what he does not need, when others lack necessities.

This applied unequivocally to the unjust possession of land by Guatemala's oligarchy.

Father Blase Bonpane, a Maryknoller, came to work with us at the Crater that same month. He was an ex-marine, tall, graying, in his late thirties—a gentle man. He had been Superior of the Maryknoll Fathers' Rocky Mountain Region. Before coming to Guatemala, he had earned his master's degree in Latin American studies at Georgetown University. He had a historical perspective on social conflict in Latin America that none of the other priests possessed—his master's thesis had been on Fidel Castro's relationship to the Catholic Church. Father Tom Melville invited him to our meetings, together with Fathers Jim O'Brien and Charlie Reilly.

At first, the students at the Crater doubted that he could do much to help because of his poor Spanish; but they soon learned to appreciate him for his readiness to help them in many small ways. Father Breen had assigned Father Bonpane to work with university students. But at the Crater, the students felt they were under no authority except their own. I was a member of the group; Blase could be also if he wanted to fit into its pattern. Theirs was *not* a "Maryknoll" student group. Still, since he was a man—and a priest— some felt he would or could take charge of the Crater. Yet, from longer experience there, I had a much better grasp of what was going on. Blase was considerate, eager to work, but diffident about imposing his own way. At times it must have been a terrible strain for him. Involved in a totally new, even dangerous situation that demanded quick response to an ever-shifting course of events, he must sometimes have wondered what was happening.

Blase and I had one important disagreement. He was always

getting involved in giving out powdered milk and other such remedial activities, whereas I insisted we must go to the roots of the problem. While arguing with him, however, I would remember many of my own projects at Monte María and elsewhere. "I guess you'll just have to go through all this," I told him.

He worked hard. I consulted with him about the guerrillas and whether I should help them, but I began to wonder about his attitude. He seemed to admire them very much, yet at the same time he cautioned me, "Don't go near those people."

Shortly after coming to work at the Crater, he remarked to two American free-lance reporters that I had said I planned to work in the mountains with revolutionaries. I was furious.

"They will broadcast the word all over," I told him angrily. "If I weren't actually thinking about it, it wouldn't be so dangerous. But now it'll be nearly impossible, because I may be watched. You just can't say things like that."

"I'm sorry," said Blase, "but, look, publicity is good. This can't hurt you and people have to learn what the struggle is about."

"Haven't you ever heard about the right-wing secret organizations—like the White Hand?" I asked him. "They're out to kill any would-be revolutionaries." Then, sarcastically, I added, "Thanks a lot."

I walked away disgusted, yet somehow I couldn't really blame Blase. He seemed not to understand that honesty doesn't mean a literal approach to reality. To be really honest, we have to recognize circumstances; else, in the name of honesty, we commit murder.

Then, in June 1967, tragedy struck. We had agreed to have a Day of Action in a village in Huehuetenango, but some students had exams, and I couldn't go either. At a meeting, I told the group, "We have a commitment, so somebody has to go. Whoever you decide on should go." I left and did not hear what they decided.

I came early to the Crater that Friday morning.

The telephone rang. "This is Tono, Guayo's brother. Do you have any idea where Gustavo is?"

I hesitated. I didn't know if Gustavo had been one of those who had finally gone. I also didn't want to give out any unnecessary information—we had begun to be called "Communists," and the right-wing terrorist organizations were very active.

I answered, "No, why do you want to know?"

When he spoke again, his voice was strained. "I—we—just received word this morning that my brother Guayo was killed in an automobile accident. I—wanted to know if Gustavo had gone with him."

I couldn't answer Tono; I felt a horrible paralysis. I said to myself, *I knew this would have to happen sometime. We've been doing too much traveling to get off untouched. An accident . . . or some encounter with the secret police . . . or something . . .*

I didn't know what to do, whom to turn to. I telephoned Juan, as I knew he had planned to stay home, and he was calm and dependable. But he had gone to the store, so I left word. He was back at the Crater in about fifteen minutes.

There was a core group at the Crater who worked in deep mutual confidence, who understood the risks involved and yet were willing to give themselves completely. The other students, on the edge of things, weren't included in such plans as organizing unions because we felt we had to make sure we could trust them.

I told Juan that Guayo had been killed, and that I didn't know who else had gone with him and if they were all right or not.

Rudy's father then called me: "Tell Rudy I want him at home at once when he comes in." At that moment, I didn't know if his son were alive or not, and I didn't know what to say. "All right, I'll tell him," I said simply.

I asked Juan to go with me to look for them. I had borrowed Father Breen's car for the weekend. Juan had to drive,

I was too upset. When we arrived at the scene of the accident, fifty miles out of the city, the only sign of it was broken glass. We drove to the police station, where we were told an autopsy was being performed at the cemetery. (The law in Guatemala requires an autopsy in the case of accidental death.) The accident had occurred at about 4 a.m. The car had been totally wrecked.

We didn't know what to expect when we got to the cemetery. As we came in, Guayo's father walked over to us. He said, "Sister, he's in there with his mother."

We went into the one-room building. Guayo was lying on a stone slab. The blood had seeped through his shirt and trousers. I could see the black stitching on his neck where they had opened him up for the autopsy. His face was just recognizable. His mother was leaning over him, weeping, praying to God to take her son to Him. Guayo had been a remarkably energetic and committed worker among the Indians. He was very thin and short; his nickname was "Spider."

His father said, "The ambulance is coming. We've made arrangements with the funeral home. But I'm very worried about the other boys. They've been taken to the hospital in the town nearby, Sister. Why don't you go to see them?"

As I turned to leave, he touched my arm. This was rare— for a man to touch a nun—but I understood the urgency of his gesture.

"Sister . . ." he hesitated, then looked at me directly. "Guayo was so intent on working with the peasants, and this was so much a part of his life. . . . You see, I knew that sooner or later something was going to happen—that people would want revenge."

I hadn't expected this. There was no accusation in his face or in his voice, no bitterness toward us.

Juan and I drove to the town, about half an hour away, where the hospital was. It was ancient, and no one seemed to know about the boys. We walked through halls, across patios, and finally we found them. The first student I saw was Rudy, but I could hardly recognize him. His lower jaw had been broken in three places, and he had lost some of his upper teeth. He was conscious, but could not talk. Near him lay Luis, also hurt badly and unable to talk. Gustavo could speak. He told me about the accident.

They had left at 3 a.m. to get to Huehuetenango by daybreak and thus have two full days of work. Guayo was to take a bus for Quiché at the crossroads. Guayo drove the jeep in the rain, and the others slept. Gustavo didn't know exactly what had happened, but the jeep had crashed head-on into a local bus. Either Guayo had fallen asleep, or possibly the bus had skidded because of the wet highway.

I had trouble reconciling myself to the boys' suffering. The accident shook me to the core. Now, with actual casualties, it was inescapably clear that we were not, if we had ever thought so, inviolable heroes, we were not playing games. We had to be prepared to risk our lives.

A few days before, I had met the trainer from the Christian Democratic course on organizing peasant leagues. He had told me that three of the men who attended the class with us had been tortured and killed. Their crime was trying to organize their people.

The activities of the right-wing secret terrorist groups, the White Hand, the CADEG, and the NOA, increased. They had announced, "Paint a black cross on the door of any house where you know a Communist lives, and we will kill him." The next day black crosses did appear on a few doors. More and more people were disappearing from their homes; every day it would be announced that bodies were awaiting identification. In Gualán, in the department of Zacapa in the northeast, where we gave some Days of Action, the people told us that they didn't fish in the river any more—all that their nets trapped was human bodies.

One evening a Monte María teacher and her husband had just gone to bed and turned out the lights when there was a pounding on the door. The husband, Jorge Macías, got up to answer it, and several men pushed past him into the living room. "You're coming with us," they said. The men went into his room with him while he dressed. They hurried him out of the door. His wife rushed to the window. All she saw was two cars, without license plates or any other markings, driving off.

For eight days she combed the police stations, hospitals, and military bases for some trace of her husband. Finally she received a phone call from the office of the criminal court. Some garments were described to her. Were they possibly her husband's? She thought so. If she wanted to identify his body, she would have to go to Zacapa, one hundred and forty miles away, and ask to have the body disinterred. She went there and watched as a straw mat was removed from his naked body. It was so disfigured from torture that she had asked to see his teeth, and the graveyard caretaker had opened his mouth with a stick.

It was the secret police who had abducted him. He was César Montes's brother, and they thought he might know something, although he had been completely aloof from the revolutionary movement, and César had never been near him or his home. It was just another commonplace example of reprisals.

Many knew that the terrorist groups were in fact government-sponsored, though few dared say so publicly. Then Carlos wrote a manifesto against extremists, in which he accused the government of not only condoning but also sponsoring terrorist tactics. The council at the Crater approved it; we published it. It was distributed one evening at the Law, Medical, and Humanities schools of San Carlos University. It issued the challenge:

> Think, then, oligarchs, militarists, and reactionaries, that even
> if you sustain the status quo for a few more years, you will leave
> a legacy to your children—a bloody country, an abortion of
> violence . . . socioeconomic structures do not change with
> bayonets; they change with effective agrarian reform which

248

gives the land to those who work it; with reform of industry which permits the worker a life of dignity.

The declaration went on to state that we at CEDECAS found among the left-wing groups sincerity and a valid goal, but that the right-wing groups, which served as a secret arm of the oligarchy and the army, were murdering people who dared oppose them by working to better social conditions. We deplored the institutionalized violence in the country. The publication of the declaration caused quite a stir among the oligarchy.

The archbishop sent for me. But I was away, and Father Blase and Father Jalón, who happened to be in town, went to see him without me. When I returned, Father Blase assured me that the matter was settled.

Somewhat nettled, I said sarcastically, "I'm much obliged, Reverend Father." Actually, they well may have done me a favor, for I would probably have become excited enough to say things that were better unsaid.

On the following Thursday, we called a meeting at the Crater. Blase informed us that the archbishop had said that we were under his direction and that we should not speak out as in the declaration. We blew up. We quoted Gospel at Blase: "You pharisees, whitened sepulchers . . ."; we quoted *Progress of Peoples*.

The students said, "We are lay people working on our own. The archbishop has nothing to say about our activities. We are not a Church group." I thoroughly agreed with the students. I didn't see why we needed to check with the archbishop before making statements. Poor Blase was caught right in the middle.

"You can speak to the archbishop if you want," I told him, "but all he can do is have my Superior take me out of this work. If he does, the Crater can and will function perfectly well without me."

I said this to Blase, yet I knew that more than ever I felt

a sense of oneness with the students at the Crater. Recently we had gone to a house in the country for a day of quiet and reassessment, reviewing our aims and tactics, reading the Gospels, meditating on our role as Christians, and smoothing out our personal relationships. The highlight had been a Mass celebrated by Blase. We stood around a table; *abrazos* were the "kiss of peace" greeting, and we shared Holy Communion. After the Mass, a small group of us stood talking. The question of my position as a nun came up.

"I no longer feel that vows of poverty, chastity, and obedience are the essentials of religious life," I told them. "We just kid ourselves about being poor. Chastity seems to negate love, and I see love as the power of life. Obedience shouldn't be the object of a vow; it is a normal necessity for any smooth-working organization."

"Then what keeps you a nun?" asked Rudy.

"I have come to see community, the unity of people who love and respect each other, as the needed bond to accomplish the work of a Christian."

"And we have become your community, Sister?" asked Rudy.

"Yes, you really have," I answered. But the realization jolted me. Yes, it was true—these students were my community. *But then,* I wondered to myself, *what does it mean to be a nun?* I wasn't sure.

In May, I got a phone call. It was Felipe.

"I'm back in town."

"You're alive!"

"Yes. We're back. César is with me."

"Can I see you?"

"Yes."

"Right now? I'll come in the car and pick you up."

It was evening, but I got permission to go out, and Gail came with me. (In retrospect, I really don't know how I managed all those permissions.) We picked up both of them and drove them back to the convent. We talked for a long time.

"How'd you like to go with us to Cuba?" César asked me.

"Of course, I'd love to visit Cuba. But I couldn't get permission. I couldn't come back, and I'm involved in so much here. I don't have the right to desert it all."

"Then," he said, "come up to the mountains and work with us. You can help with our literacy programs for the peasants."

"I'm not so sure I want to go right now," I told him. "We're working well at the Crater. We're just beginning to help organize labor. I would like to follow this through."

I told César about *Progress of Peoples*, and he wanted to read it. Sister Gail got a copy for him, and we discussed parts of it—the causes of social conflicts, which are clearly spelled out; the evil of the economic deprivation of large segments of the population, and the resulting emotional and psychological deprivation. We wholeheartedly agreed with the statement that "avarice is the most evident form of moral underdevelopment."

Later, I came across a write-up of an interview with César Montes that took place in the summer of 1967. César quoted the encyclical, and I knew that this had come out of our conversation, as he had taken the encyclical with him.

Although I had Gail to confide in, I couldn't help feeling nervous about my talks with César. It was risky, given the tense atmosphere in the city. And the other nuns would certainly not understand.

I remember a conversation I tried to have with Sister Mildred, my Superior, in November 1966. She was busy at her desk, but she was used to my running in, full of enthusiasm about some new idea. She glanced up at me rather absentmindedly, and continued her work.

"You know about the guerrillas in this country, and that there's a revolution going on," I said. "I just wanted you to know that I've talked to some of them. And I've been very interested in what they have to say."

"Yes, dear," she said. "Oh, yes. That's fine, dear."

She wasn't listening. I was upset, but felt that I had told

her, and if she wasn't interested, it wasn't my fault. I did a lot of thinking and reading and praying. Harvey Cox's book *God's Revolution and Man's Responsibility* and Teilhard de Chardin's *Building the Earth* encouraged me in my determination to be instrumental, so far as I could, in changing Guatemala. I thought often of a key passage in Pope Paul's encyclical:

> The world is sick. Its illness consists not only in the unproductive monopolization of resources by a small number of men, but even more so in the lack of brotherhood among individuals and peoples.

It suggested the need for men to engage in dialogue. I heard that Jesuit scholars were holding dialogues with Roger Garaudy of the French Communist Party. And so I proceeded.

My trust in Tom was growing. We saw each other often on his trips to Guatemala City on colonization business. He questioned me on everything I said; he wouldn't let me get away with anything. If I said the structure of Guatemala needed changing, he would ask: "Why?" and "How?" Yet I knew he was looking for the answers to these questions himself.

In April, Carlos, Manuel, and I went with Tom to his jungle colony to have a Day of Action with the men of the cooperative. Tom was very pleased with Carlos's presentation. The younger man had the knack of expressing complex and profound ideas in simple terms, and his sense of brotherhood with the peasants was evident.

It was becoming clearer and clearer to me that Tom was also a brother to the Indians. When I saw him touch a man's head in blessing, as was the custom, and then bow in turn to receive the man's blessing, I thought, *Here is a missioner, a Christian among the people, not the father over them.*

There was a similar kind of brotherhood between Felipe

and a tall peasant, a field lieutenant of the FAR, called Zacarías. He was in town one day on business, and I went with Felipe to drive him to the train station. When Felipe told him I was a nun, and sympathetic to their work, he looked at me with great interest.

"How good it is," he said, "that the Church is beginning to understand what it means to be a peasant."

On the way back to the Crater, Felipe said, "You can't say you are a brother to a peasant until you sit on the ground next to him, as dirty and as tired as he is, tell him an idea or a plan, then have him say to you, 'No, brother, that's not the way it is. Listen to me.' *Then* you can say you are his brother."

It became increasingly difficult to work quietly. Some of the students' parents opposed their work. Titina's mother and father were particularly distressed—they didn't approve of her frequent trips to the villages, and were afraid her health might suffer. And, too, they didn't like her going alone, or with two or three boys, even though she was twenty-two years old. She was interning at a hospital as part of her work toward a degree in psychology. Her parents spread many rumors about our involvement in "dangerous" activities. The students came under surveillance from the secret police, and on one occasion the Crater was searched.

Some Maryknoll priests, especially Father Jim Curtin and those working in Guatemala City with the archbishop, became suspicious of our work in labor-organizing and claimed we were a "Communist-inspired" group. More than once in my presence the Crater was referred to as subversive. We received letters from some of the priests in Huehuetenango saying only, "Please don't return to my village." The students would wonder how a Guatemalan village could "belong" to a priest. But we respected their requests—we had enough work with those who welcomed the students. Father Denny Kraus and Father Art Melville were particularly interested in their work, and other priests also gave the students the adult guidance and cooperation they needed. Father Tom often came to the

Crater and shared his insight, understanding, and love of the Indian people with us.

Bishop Gerbermann began to hear of the accusations that we were Communists and called me one day to ask about it. I told him that the leadership-training sessions for the peasants were open and that anyone who wanted could come to hear what we were saying and teaching.

None of the students at the Crater knew that I had talked to guerrillas—this seemed safer for them and for myself. One day Carlos was talking with several of us: "I think a friend at the university might get me the chance to talk with one of the guerrillas."

"Oh?" I said, feigning ignorance. "That might be interesting." I was aching to tell them, but I didn't feel I had the right to get them involved. What they were doing in the literacy program required enough risk as it was.

When I had a chance to talk to Carlos alone, he told me he wanted to speak to César Montes.

"I know César Montes," I told him. "He's in town now. In fact, if you want to—I hadn't wanted to get you involved— you could see him. He told me he wants to meet you, he read your declaration. Are you interested?"

He was thrilled: "*Seguro* (of course)!"

The arrangements were made, and we drove to the meeting place agreed on. Another car drove up. The driver was Nestor Valle, whom I had met at Felipe's house, and he told us, "I'll drive this car. You two get in the other one."

Then he added, "If you don't mind, for your own safety, would you close your eyes so that you don't know where we're going."

What we didn't know couldn't be tortured out of us, should we later be interrogated. We closed our eyes and sat low in the car. He drove down some dirt streets and finally into a garage.

"All right. You may open your eyes now."

We went into the house and met César. Carlos had read

Marx and Lenin, and he explained his objections to the revolutionary position, particularly his conviction that the use of arms only breeds more violence. At the same time, he declared, he was open to other approaches. César asked Carlos whether we planned to help defend the peasants we were organizing, or were we going to let them all get killed. Carlos had no answer.

Later on, Carlos met with Felipe, and the two argued about all kinds of intellectual ideas and differences. After a month or more, Carlos invited Felipe to work with us. I was pleased when César agreed to let him come. Felipe began going to Huehuetenango for the Days of Action.

Carlos then told me he was planning to go to Cuba. He had often talked about how much he wanted to see Cuba, and now César had agreed to make the arrangements. This was an enormous decision—if his visit were discovered, he would be a marked man. We agreed to tell Titina, Rudy, and Carlos's best friend, so that someone would know where he was, should anything happen to me while he was gone.

In August, César and Carlos were set to leave for Cuba, and I offered to drive them out of the country. I borrowed Blase's car, without explaining why. Since I didn't want to drive back to Guatemala City alone after delivering them to the Mexican border, I asked Titina to go with me. She was one of the few students at the Crater who had come to realize the full extent of our danger. Several of her university friends had become guerrillas.

Titina and I picked up the three who were to make the trip—César, a girl companion, and Carlos. A car with an FAR girl and Carlos's friend would follow us. We left about 8 P.M. and drove all night. A few miles before we reached the border, the other car turned around and went back to Guatemala City.

The others had all their papers in order. I had no visa, however, and the border guard didn't want me to cross.

"I just want to drive these people to the next town," I explained. We were let through.

César was afraid that he might be recognized, even though he had dyed his hair bright red. He was pretending to be eloping to Mexico with the girl. They acted like lovers, and even while we were stopped at the border, kept their faces hidden as they kissed and nuzzled each other.

We went on to the next town and left the three of them at the bus. Titina and I had breakfast, and then went back to Guatemala City. Going and coming, I had driven an almost uninterrupted stretch of twenty-four hours. I was very tired, yet ever since the wreck in which Guayo was killed, I preferred to drive myself.

César had left Felipe with us, saying to me, "Sometimes Felipe gets too drastic, gets ahead of himself. He's brilliant, but he doesn't always lay the groundwork for what he sees needs to be done. You keep him in tow. Don't let him go too far."

We worked extensively in September and October with peasant leaders. The students had talked with Father Art Melville, and he agreed to work with them even if it meant helping the peasants defend themselves. One of our more successful projects had been the legal establishment of a land cooperative in a small town. Official authorization for the cooperative meant that the town's communal lands could now be used by all the villagers instead of being reserved, as they had been, for one large landowner. When the law student organizing it received the official approval, he sent a telegram to the co-op president. But the telegraph operator informed the mayor instead. The mayor and the landowner killed the cooperative president. It proved impossible to get the police to take action.

It was at this time that some of us at the Crater decided it was urgent to call a meeting with a number of the students, some peasants, and a few priests, to decide: "Where do we go from here?"

XXI

Escuintla to Expulsion

The Priest The meeting to decide our course of action was to be held in an unoccupied farmhouse near the town of Escuintla during the first week of November 1967. Before the meeting, I discussed our plans with the two outstanding leaders of the colonization project at San Juan Acul, explaining our idea of a Christian revolutionary movement. They were neither surprised nor frightened. They themselves had talked many times of what they would do when the *latifundistas*, the large plantation owners, appeared with titles to their cleared lands. I had been preaching at Mass for several months about the obligation of a Christian to stand up physically against the oppression and injustice of prevailing political and social institutions. Now that we were to have a meeting on the meaning of a revolution, Tomás and Jesús were unusually quiet, pondering the implications of such a momentous decision.

Tomás was the older of the two, in his early or middle forties, the father of seven small children. He did all his errands at a jogging clip, and he laughed easily and often. When I would go to the town of Flores on a shopping trip, he was always the first at the river's edge when I returned, to help unload the boat.

Jesús was perhaps twenty-four years old. He was enormously respected for such a young man. He had taught himself to read and write, add, subtract, multiply, and divide, and had never spent a day in school. His store of knowledge never ceased to amaze me. Jesús would listen to both the Voice of America and Radio Havana on his transistor radio, and later would ask me questions about the war in Vietnam and other world problems. He bought a little map in Guatemala City, and when a country or city was mentioned on the radio, he would search for it on the map. He was five feet nine, taller than most Indians, with extremely broad shoulders and chest. He was the best hunter in the colony and often brought home more game than his family could eat—which he would then share with his neighbors.

Thomás, Jesús, and I met in my hut every second or third night until the Escuintla meeting to discuss the points that should be considered there.

The Nun The students and I continued our weekend visits to the villages, where we taught the peasants. When we spoke of human dignity, of the value of each individual, we could see the men stand taller, lift their heads, and look us straight in the eye. Our conversation was cautious; but when we suggested they discuss what they considered their most serious problem, they invariably said, "Land, we need more land. There's a lot of uncultivated land around. We want to do something about it."

Late one night, eight of us were squeezed into the jeep, returning from a visit to Father Art Melville's parish of San Antonio. The jeep was so crowded that whenever Tono negotiated one of the sharp curves on the dirt road, we hardly shifted our positions, but just softly rolled as a body from side to side.

The drive to Guatemala City was a long one—about eight hours. I thought we should have left a lot earlier, but the conversation had been good. Father Art and Felipe had had a long argument, with the rest of us interjecting ideas. Since I couldn't sleep in the lurching jeep, I went over the questions which had come up and which would have to be discussed at Escuintla the next weekend. When would we have to go into hiding in order to keep teaching the peasants? Would this be considered a new guerrilla front? And if it were, would we identify it as "Christian"?

"Definitely," Art had insisted.

"If we do," said Felipe, "we'll be just as sectarian as the FAR is accused of being. More so, since they don't call themselves Communist or even Marxist, and they welcome all those who agree with their goals."

"But the majority of the peasants identify themselves as Catholics. They have been taught to fear Communists as if they were devils," replied Art, and most of us had agreed with him.

We also had to consider the need to help the peasant leaders defend themselves. It seemed unjust for us to talk to the peasants about organizing unions and cooperatives that would meaningfully affect the country's power structure and then let them get killed as if they were mechanical ducks at a fair. They had no one to turn to for protection. The national police and the army defended the privileges of the rich. The peasants had—and still have—no choice but to arm themselves for their own defense.

This had become even clearer to us when one of the boys from the Crater, who was teaching literacy in a village, was picked up by the army. Several masked men had come one night to the hut where he was sleeping and had marched him away. The catechist in whose house this occurred went immediately to San Antonio to tell Father Art.

Art rushed to the army post about two hours away and found the boy there. There were no charges against him, and the officer in command explained it was just a matter of "routine questioning." He had no answer when Art asked why the soldiers had been masked. Art's intervention probably saved the boy's life. Such incidents were forcing us to consider what alternatives lay open to us.

About a dozen people were expected at the meeting. The students who had been working in Quiché with Father Luis Gurriarán said he was in sympathy with us, and he was invited. He had been expelled from Guatemala about three years before by the Peralta Azurdia government because of his success in developing cooperatives in the Quiché area. Many of the Indian leaders of the movement had been jailed at that time. Father Luis had recently been re-admitted to Guatemala by President Méndez Montenegro, after Archbishop Casariego assured the government that he would keep Luis on a tight leash. We thought that the experience must have radicalized Luis, and we were eager for his contribution to our meeting.

Tom wanted two or three peasant leaders from different areas to give their points of view. We decided that three students could represent their fellow Crater members. Art had surprised and pleased us by saying that Sister Paula, from his parish, would accompany him.

We also invited Father Alejandro Del Corro, a Jesuit from Ivan Illich's Intercultural Center in Cuernavaca, Mexico, who had conducted extensive research into violence in Guatemala. He had done similar studies on Colombia and Venezuela; and on a previous visit to Guatemala, he had visited a *cursillo* and shared his thoughts on the "Revolution of the Poor," which he saw beginning in many parts of Latin America.

I felt that the meeting would clarify the best route for us to follow in the months ahead. As we drove into Guatemala City, dawn was breaking. Agua and Fuego were sharply outlined against the mauve sky.

The Priest The Escuintla meeting was arranged to see what we, as individuals and as a group, could do to bring about a meaningful revolution. We would talk about concrete plans. We kept the meeting secret because we knew the Guatemalans involved might be either jailed or murdered if they were exposed, while the rest of us might be expelled from the country.

Tomás accompanied me from San Juan Acul to Escuintla. We had decided that only one man should be absent from the colony for the planned four or five days of the meeting, so as not to awaken suspicions among those who had begun to wonder about our frequent nightly get-togethers. I would have preferred to have had Jesús along because of his greater understanding and knowledge, but I respected the two men's decision. By this time they were already discussing with eight other settlers the matters we touched on in our own sessions.

The meeting at Escuintla lasted three days. We came up with a "manifesto" based on Pope Paul's encyclical *Progress of Peoples*, and on the Gospels. However, we intended not to publish it until we were ready to move.

We were determined to maintain our Christian identity and independence and not to join with the armies of César Montes or Marco Antonio Yon Sosa. We could relate to each other and respect each other without working under the same banner, and it was important not to give the government and the Church any excuse for denying our Christian identity and purpose. We would arm ourselves and the peasants when the time came, but our immediate plans were for organizing a base among the peasant leaders and preparing ourselves physically and psychologically.

The Nun During one session, Felipe Ramos spoke of an incident that deeply upset us. He said that the guerrillas had picked up a young American who had been asking questions about the FAR in the Sierra de las Minas, where they were operating. He had been in contact with an American photographer in Zacapa, the capital city of the department of the same name. Under questioning by Luis Turcios, he readily admitted his name, Hornberger, and said he had been a U.S. Green Beret in Vietnam, from which he had just returned. He was an expert, he claimed, in automatic weapons and was willing to teach the guerrillas. His story didn't hold together; and he was embarrassed by the discovery of a nylon cord wrapped around his waist, claiming it was to strangle any would-be attacker. His extensive knowledge of the terrain startled his captors. Turcios asked Felipe to continue talking to him. Felipe told us that Hornberger showed no signs of fear and actually seemed to be savoring his experience. He knew who the guerrillas were, and their mode of operation, but was ignorant about their political and social beliefs, nor was he interested in these. The American became angry when Felipe questioned him on his own views and ideas, and refused to answer. After an all-night session with Hornberger, Felipe was convinced he was an infiltrator who intended either to assassinate Turcios or to reveal the guerrilla locations and contacts to the photographer in Zacapa city, who in turn was probably an agent of the army.

The guerrillas decided they had no choice: It was impossible to take the Green Beret (his identity was confirmed afterwards in the newspapers) into the hills with them; but to let him go would mean certain death for many people. Hornberger and Moran, the photographer, were both executed, and their bodies buried in shallow graves in the Sierra. We were stunned by the starkness of Felipe's explanation. But when he demanded to know what we would have done, we suddenly realized we were not playing games; this was war. I was nauseated and could only hope that I myself would never face such a decision.

We dealt with other practical questions. Some of the university students and several of the Indians were to begin looking for possible areas of operation in the mountains or jungle.

The only other nun present was Sister Paula, and her courage, certainty, and determination calmed my fears of the danger and suffering I anticipated. She told me that a conversation with a peasant leader had helped her make her decision. He had asked her what the obligation of the Good Samaritan would have been if he had been riding a slightly faster mule. When she had asked what he meant, he had explained that if the Good Samaritan had arrived half an hour earlier, he might have found the thieves and murderers beating up the man from Jericho. Should the Samaritan have waited until the job was done so that he could then practice his charity on the half-dead victim? Or should he have shaken his head with a few "Tsk, tsk's" and told both sides to love each other? Or should he have tried to rescue the man before he was badly hurt? She knew that by "rescue" he meant "fight."

She also told me that Sister Cathy Sagan, her companion in San Antonio, had asked to go with us when we went into the mountains.

The Priest When would we move to the mountains? Father Gurriarán was convinced that we would do so very shortly and that we would never be able to walk the streets of Guatemala City again. Art said that we would be in the mountains with our own guerrilla movement in a month and a half—by Christmas. After much discussion, he revised his estimate to spring, 1968. I thought it wouldn't be for years, since I thought it would take that long to prepare the people adequately.

We decided it was impractical to talk about dates, since these depended on the peasants, not on us. However, we would be ready to move to the mountains as soon as any sign of danger appeared, so as not to jeopardize the lives of people who were working with us on nonrevolutionary projects. I myself didn't put much stock in the possibility of such a danger at that time.

After the meeting, we were each to begin sounding out the peasant leaders on their feelings concerning a Christian revolution based on an organization of self-defense, to reoccupy the lands that had been stolen from them by generations of white men. The risks for the peasants were extremely high— yet I was amazed by the positive response of those with whom I raised the subject. Almost the only question they had was: "I won't go to Hell, Padre? We can fight for our lands, and God will not be angry?"

Often, there was no need for me to even bring up the subject. Once the two leaders of a co-op in Huehuetenango told me a local landowner had threatened them with murder unless they dissolved their co-op. I asked them what they were going to do.

They answered, "I guess we will have to die for our people. If they kill us, they kill us, but we are going to keep on working."

I asked them why, instead of dying, they didn't *live* for their people. There was no divine law against fighting back, and in fact, they had a moral obligation to their children and to their people to protect themselves. They were overjoyed that someone in the Church should tell them it was permissible for them to fight for their rights.

At the end of the Escuintla meeting, Tomás came to me and wept. He told me he knew he was going to be killed, but if there was to be any future for his seven children, he had to join the revolution. I realized that his tears were half in sorrow over the idea of leaving his family alone, and half in joy that we were now embarking on a course that contained a spark of hope for the future of his people. Tomás, a great man and leader, has been missing now for over a year. Like six thousand others of his countrymen, he has almost certainly been killed by the army, and indirectly by United States Green Berets who train Guatemalan soldiers in counterinsurgency, with no knowledge of the tremendous injustices that have led the people to fight.*

* Editorials in the newspapers during '66 and '67 put the death toll at approximately one hundred per week over a period of eighteen months. The Christian Democratic candidate in the recent elections gave a figure of six thousand dead during the four-year term (1966–70) of the outgoing regime.

The Nun

After the meeting, the general activities of the Crater continued. Forty-five students volunteered to live in villages around Quiché and Huehuetenango and give literacy classes during their six weeks of school vacation in November and December. Word of the Indians' favorable response the previous year at La Libertad had gone around, and interest was widespread.

We planned a week-long *cursillo* of training and preparation for the volunteers, some of whom were public high school students of mine who had had no teaching experience. A few saw themselves as "saviors" of their people; they had the attitude that they were sacrificing their vacation to help the "poor people." At the *cursillo*, they were told that if they were going to do anything for these people, they must respect them. They had to be ready to listen and learn. Their values were going to be changed.

The method used to teach the peasants to read was Paulo Freire's *concientización* ("awakening of consciousness") technique. This system is based on principles of social justice and has been used successfully in some areas of Brazil and Chile. The Indians learned: "You are a man. You have great value. Your value does not come from what you own or from your education. It comes from being a man—a human. The land is good. The land is yours. Work together to improve your life. Union gives strength."

Father Blase supervised the group in Quiché. He was committed to what we were doing, though at this time he did not realize how far we had gone in planning for the peasants' defense by organizing a cadre of leaders. He had arranged for Caritas to donate surplus food to supplement the host-villages' meager supplies so that the student team would not be a burden for the people.

Despite the problems he had occasionally caused us, Father Blase's comprehension of the local situation far outstripped that of men who had been in Guatemala much longer than he. Working with the Guatemalan university students in the capital, he had developed an understanding of political currents that were remote to the mountain priests; and he was blessed with a capacity for sensitive and committed response to human suffering. He promised that if it were ever necessary, he would return to the States and explain the realities of the situation in Guatemala.

The Priest At about this time, Father John Breen asked me if my brother Art was sympathetic to the guerrilla movement. I said yes, just as I and many others were, and that we ought to discuss it in the open. He agreed, but asked if Art had any particular plans. I told him that I did not know and that he should talk to Art himself. He took my statement at face value.

John was suspicious precisely because Art had suddenly become very quiet and stopped talking revolution. By being open about my feelings, I thought I could both allay any suspicions concerning myself and heighten Maryknoll's awareness of what was going on in the country. I didn't like the idea of concealing the truth of our plans from John, especially since I thought he might possibly understand what we were doing. But I could not afford such a gamble.

The Nun Tom and I had another question to face. We had known one another for over a year and had finally recognized that we loved each other and wanted to share our lives. After long agonizing about the effect of our marriage on our parents, Maryknoll, and our companions in the struggle for social justice, we decided that we had to be true to our own convictions. So we began to make plans to marry and to live and work among the Indians, though we were still quite uncertain as to when and how. There were few opportunities for us to see each other, and when we did, it was under conditions that were far from tranquil.

Father Charlie Reilly, a recent arrival in Guatemala who was working with the Huehuetenango student group Chispa, began to sense that we were involved in more than a literacy campaign. He asked many questions that seemed, however, to stem more from curiosity than from genuine interest. Even though I liked and respected him, I considered it unsafe and unfair, both to him and to us, to tell him of our plans.

Charlie was very intelligent and sensitive to the needs of the people, but he believed we should work only within the existing structures to resolve the country's social problems. We had more than one heated argument on this point. I held that it was Guatemala's power structure that had virtually enslaved eighty percent of the population and that no power bloc would willingly subvert its own foundations. Although Charlie could accept my reasoning, he could not accept what I then said was the only path left to follow to achieve social justice. I dared not continue the argument with him.

He began telling people that Art, Tom, and I were up to something fishy. To calm his suspicions, Tom and I decided to share our plans for marriage with him. We told him we felt Maryknoll was going nowhere and that the hierarchy would not allow us to participate in effective programs to aid the people. We could not give our lives to an organization whose main purpose was to perpetuate itself. He was sympathetic, and even congratulated us. Only later did I realize that he still thought we were planning to do more than marry.

The Priest

Art was not happy about our proposed marriage—he said people would accuse us of joining the revolution only because we wanted to get married. I considered this argument irrelevant, since if we only wanted to marry, we could obviously do it more easily in California or Michigan than in the jungles of Guatemala. Even so, I realized we probably *would* be giving ammunition to those who would attack our revolutionary activities. Nevertheless, I told Art that our marriage would help serve notice that it is time the Catholic hierarchy began treating sex as a good and healthy part of human nature and married people as first-class members of the Church; that marriage and any problems related to it would never be understood as long as celibacy was equated with priesthood. Art agreed, but said we should fight one battle at a time.

Father John Breen visited the land project at San Juan Acul. He was enthusiastic and decided to give us a monthly allowance for our Spanish lay missionaries. He had already sent us a Maryknoll brother, Augustine Hogan, a proficient mechanic and carpenter. The archdiocese of Los Angeles, California, had provided us with a lay missionary pilot and a Cessna-180 for ferrying purposes.

Brother Gus Hogan and I soon became good friends. He was a completely unaffected man who obviously enjoyed teaching the Indians. The people took him to their hearts right away, and the laughter that boomed around the colony was often provoked by one of Gus's jokes.

One day, out of a clear blue sky, Gus suggested that some-one should teach the peasants the meaning of a Christian Revolution—"a new Crusade to recapture the Holy Land," he called it. I didn't answer right away; but when I saw he was serious, I told him about our meeting in Escuintla. He became apprehensive—he understood the implications immediately. A few days later, in an offhand manner, he told me he would help indirectly if he could, but that he would not go into the jungle and personally participate in armed battles. It was not that he had any difficulty over the morality of using a gun in revolutionary self-defense. The problem for him was the same as for the rest of us: emotional and psychological. Our backgrounds hadn't prepared us for taking part in an armed conflict, and we were much inclined to tell ourselves that our job was on the fringes of the struggle.

Brother Gus's offer of help was timely. Immediately after Escuintla a dozen university students had met and decided that new techniques of defense had to be worked out. The revolutionary movement was taking a beating in the northeast, because the recently installed government of Méndez Montenegro had begun to use terroristic methods against peasant supporters of the guerrillas. Marjorie told the students that in a talk at Monte María, a U.S. colonel had said that the jungles offered better refuge than the mountain areas. Therefore, we decided to operate from a jungle base and not get caught, as the FAR had, in the mountains. The students thought of Petén, but since Father Gurriarán had suggested that we begin in Quiché, where he had "thousands of Indians organized," I discouraged them. Petén was nearly one hundred miles away as the crow flies—across jungle, swamps, and rivers.

Nevertheless, the students decided to investigate the region and try to find staging areas for military actions and hiding places for caches of food and weapons. They planned to cut their way through the jungle with machetes. I knew they wouldn't get very far, but decided to let them find out for themselves. Brother Gus offered to drop three of them some distance down the river from San Juan Acul. His cooperation was important, because he often made supply trips in the boats and would not awaken any suspicions among the settlers, only about ten of whom were prepared to join us at that time.

On the way downriver, a boat with a Peace Corps volunteer at the helm and a dark-complexioned Latin standing up in the bow with a rifle in his hands approached Gus. A Guatemalan would normally not approach with his gun in a threatening position, and Gus and the students were apprehensive. The Latin looked them over without saying a word, then continued on.

Brother Gus put the students off on the river bank, and they disappeared into the underbrush. When I told Tomás about them, he and some of the other peasants went out to look for them, then began taking them food every four or five days. After about a month in the jungle, the students had gone no more than six kilometers. They were beginning to recognize the futility of their attempt to cut their way through.

By this time I was beginning to see the wisdom of Art's timetable. It was impossible to go much longer without being discovered—too many people were now talking about the revolution, and excitement was building up among the peasants. Yet we still had the problem of determining where we could operate and who would lead us. Only Felipe Ramos had had any military or guerrilla experience, and he alone was not enough. It occurred to me that Blase, as an ex-marine and an expert in small arms, might serve the struggle better in the guerrilla vanguard than by explaining it in the States. Yet I felt we couldn't take the chance that our message would be misunderstood by the U.S. public.

The Nun

I wrote a letter addressed to Sister Mildred, the Regional Superior, saying that I wanted to be married and that Tom and I would like to be missionaries living among the people. I didn't know when I would give her the letter, since I realized she could only answer that I would have to leave Maryknoll and get an official dispensation from my vows.

Father John Breen was the priest I most trusted and often consulted. I wanted to show him my letter first, since I had spoken to him of my doubts about being a nun. He had long known, as well, of my concern with social problems and of my sympathy for the guerrillas. I had promised to tell him of any plans I made. I intended to tell him when I would be leaving but not until things were definite.

Tom also wrote a letter to Father Breen. However, we

decided to wait until a few hours before he was due to leave on a trip to South America before we gave him the letters. Then he would be unable to act on them immediately, and we would gain a few more weeks of much-needed time.

Two days before John was to leave, Tom's mother arrived unexpectedly in Guatemala. She was worried, because for over a year he had been writing her about his change in outlook, his growing conviction that giving old answers to new problems was a blind man's way to play at life. Her coming made him happy, because he knew it would be easier to explain the need for revolution both in the Church and in the civil society if she saw for herself what was going on in Guatemala.

The Priest Our problem was that we regarded our marriage as an integral part of our revolutionary plans. Seeing the Church as the moral bulwark of the unjust social and political status quo, we felt that it had to be transformed before even the hope of change in the civil society could be entertained. If celibacy kept us from understanding the people and their problems, celibacy had to go. But when should Margie and I marry in order to get our message across clearly to the Church? If we waited until after we had moved to the jungle with the guerrilla front, would the accusations that Art feared be more likely? If we married before we went to the jungle, Church authorities would persuade the government to expel us from Guatemala in a way that would not make the Church face the celibacy issue squarely. By telling John Breen of our marriage plans just before his long trip to South America, we hoped to start the interchange of ideas without giving him time to act decisively on our proposal. It was a dilemma to which no answer was really right.

We expected him to ask us to leave Guatemala, and we intended to resist by appealing to Maryknoll and then to the Vatican. We also hoped to gain a few months' time to help the students and the peasants to prepare themselves, diverting talk and attention from their activities to ourselves. After this we would leave the country. We would be married, perhaps in the States, and later move back to Guatemala, ready to continue the struggle.

The morning John was due to leave, Marjorie was to tell him of our plans to marry. I would see him afterwards. But when I met him at breakfast, he told me his trip was off. I knew at once that something important must have come up, because he had been going to a meeting he himself had planned—a meeting of all Maryknoll Superiors in Latin America, at which they were to discuss the future of the Society in Central and South America. I told Marjorie to wait until we found out what had happened. That evening we found out.

Art, Marjorie, and I were in my mother's hotel room. Art had agreed to help us explain our marriage plans to Mom, because she would be more apt to listen to him as a relatively disinterested party. Then Sister Paula came in and announced that Father John Breen, Father Charlie Reilly, and Father Rudy Kneuer, John's first counselor, were downstairs and wanted to speak with the three of us.

Downstairs in the restaurant John started right in: "Don't try to deny anything. You had a meeting in Escuintla recently, and you talked about revolution and guerrilla warfare." He named the date and ticked off the names of most of the people present, but claimed not to know the rest. Then he added, "There are university students in Petén right now trying to cut a road through to Quiché."

It was obvious that someone who had been at our meeting had told him everything. When we admitted it, he said, "I'm glad you didn't try to deceive me. I've spoken to the American ambassador, and he wants you on the flight to New York tomorrow. We have reservations for the three of you and for your mother."

At this, Art exploded. His voice was steady and controlled but filled with emotion: "My mother is almost seventy years old, she has come down here to see us and to have a vacation. If you think we are going to let you railroad her out with us, you have another thought coming."

John started to protest: "But the ambassador . . ."

Art's voice was like a hoarse whisper: "I don't give a good damn what the ambassador wants. If need be, I'll resign from Maryknoll right now. But our mother is not leaving until her week is up. Then we'll all go."

Marjorie and I had said nothing, but John knew that Art spoke for us as well. He realized that if we were forced to leave Guatemala the next day, it would be only in chains. He finally shrugged and agreed.

The Nun My first thought was for the safety of the students whose names had or might have been revealed. Though only three had attended our session, other committed students had attended a second meeting at Escuintla, where they were told of our plans. We had no idea who had divulged our secrets, but it was essential that we discover his identity. In listing the names of the people at the meeting, Father John had left out the names of two priests, Sister Paula, and one peasant leader. We thought it had to be one of these four. We decided that we would confront each one without revealing that our meeting had been exposed.

Then parts of the puzzle began to fall into place. I went to the airport to say good-by to one of my public school students who was going on a trip. As I walked into the terminal, I saw Father Luis Gurriarán. He seemed as startled as I was and his greeting was guarded and cold, not the warm and smiling welcome I had grown used to.

He stepped away from his group when I signaled him that I wanted to talk to him alone. He told me that the peasants had responded negatively to his queries about arming for self-defense. He didn't seem surprised at this, although he had previously told us there were thousands ready to join the struggle and he, of all the participants at the Escuintla meeting, had been the most assured and enthusiastic about what we were doing. He had been in the City a week, he said, "to take care of some business," yet he had not tried to see any of us.

I said good-by, knowing I would never see him again.

Before I left the terminal, a young man came over to speak to me. I knew him only slightly but recognized him as a friend of Julio's who worked at the Office of Internal Security.

"What are you involved in?" he asked. "Have you formed a new political party or something? This morning I saw a list of names of students from the Crater that was being sent over to the secret police for investigation."

I tried to be nonchalant and told him, "I knew that Carlos and Rudy had their names on a list because of some talks they gave, but I wasn't aware of anything like this. Can you remember who was on it?"

I wasn't surprised at any of the names he recited. They had all attended one or both of the Escuintla meetings.

I looked for Tom right away. He reported that he had spoken to the other priest whom John had not named. He told Tom that before the Escuintla meeting, Gurriarán had expressed doubts to him as to the advisability of a guerrilla movement—something he had never given us an inkling of—and had mentioned that he was going to tell the head of the Christian Democrats. Underestimating the implications of Gurriarán's statement, the priest had failed to warn us. Later we found out that after the Escuintla conference, Gurriarán had gone to see Father Jim Curtin, who by that time was working in Guatemala City with the Bishops' Secretariat. News of our meeting had spread quickly. Our intentions had been distorted and enlarged upon in the tension-filled atmosphere of Guatemala City, where a rumor can sometimes be as effective as a military coup. Father Breen and the ambassador had seen no choice but to expel us.

I talked with each of the students involved. They could either stay and hide, or leave and regroup outside the country. Nine of them were so committed to continuing the struggle that they decided to leave and organize outside the country rather than go into hiding individually. Titina and I planned code names and meeting places in Mexico. I obtained a false passport for one boy, and another went to advise the three who were exploring the jungle.

The Priest Our last week in Guatemala was a frantic one. We realized that if the American ambassador knew, then so must the Ministry of the Interior—and that would mean imprisonment or death for many students and peasants as soon as we were out of the country. We knew they would wait until then to avoid making an international incident of the affair. John had assured us that we had no need to worry, that the person who had informed him had promised not to tell anyone else, nor would the ambassador. While John had always shown himself quite innocent about Guatemalan political realities, I hadn't been prepared for the full extent of his guilelessness. I should have known better.

For example, despite the evidence, he wouldn't admit that his secretary's husband worked with the Guatemalan secret police. I had always thought it odd that a woman of her high social standing should work as a secretary to the Maryknoll Superior. Her husband, Major Fred Woerner of the U.S. Army, was in charge of the "pacification" program in the Zacapa area. When I noticed that the license plate of his car began with "P42," the same initial three letters as on the secret police cars, we had a friend in the police records office check out the number: The plate *was* listed as belonging to a secret police vehicle. But when I told John, he scoffed at the idea.

Now he had the credulity to tell us, "Even if the Guatemalan government should find out about the other people's involvement, I personally guarantee their safety."

Art took Mom up to see his parish in Huehuetenango, and, since we were not prepared for any holding action in the countryside, I drew Q.2,300 from my account in the bank and flew up to Petén. Some of this money was mine, the rest had been donated by John to the land resettlement project. I gave the ten settlers involved in our revolutionary plans Q.1,500 to get to Mexico. Most of them were familiar with the southern states of Mexico; once there, we would reunite and plan our return to Guatemala. I also left some money with Gus Hogan to pay for transportation to Huehuetenango or Quezaltenango of any noninvolved Indians who wished to leave because of our departure. I was sure there would be much disillusionment, once Gus announced to them that I and some of their best leaders were gone for good.

Then I took my turn escorting my mother around while Art went to warn *his* people. I asked John Breen to buy our plane tickets via Mexico so that we could deplane there. He insisted that his obligation was to see that we went to the States—after that we were no longer his responsibility. He would buy tickets for New York City via Miami, where we could get off and use the remainder of our tickets to fly to Mexico. I thought that the U.S. government would pick up our passports at Miami and we would then be unable to return. But John checked with the American ambassador without divulging our plans and assured us that our passports would not be touched at Miami. I respected John and trusted him, despite what had happened.

On Tuesday, December 19, 1967, my mother left Guatemala. She was heartbroken. She knew I was going to get married and even accepted some of my arguments for doing so. But she also knew that something else was wrong, although we hadn't gone into the details of our plans. She didn't cry—but she looked at us as if she would never see us again.

On December 21, Art, Marjorie, and I left. Father Breen came to the airport to see us off. He was most friendly, but told us he was glad we were leaving, for the preceding week had been a strain and he needed a long rest. We looked at him incredulously. "John," I said to him, "you may not realize it, but your problems are just beginning."

A photographer began taking our pictures. When Art and I asked him what it was about, a big burly man stepped behind him and the photographer claimed he was taking everyone's picture.

John swore: "They told me they wouldn't make a fuss." We were amused at his innocence. As we began boarding the plane, the photographer took more pictures of us.

It wasn't much of a good-by, but then there was no need for one. We planned to come back, and John didn't seem to have any doubt that we would.

XXII

Mexico: Quo Vadis?

Tom On the flight to Miami, my feelings oscillated from nostalgia at leaving it all behind to a fierce hope that I would return. From Miami, we flew to Texas and from there, took different buses to Mexico City.

Slowly and carefully, we began making contacts with the university students. We didn't know if we were being followed, and we did not want to be identified as a Guatemalan group. We had only $300 among the twelve of us, but fortunately the cost of living in Mexico is quite low. We lived in twos and threes all over Mexico City. Every group kept its address a secret, but we would arrange times and places to meet one another, with alternate hours and locations in case anything happened. However, we felt we should meet all together at least once. It seemed unwise to do this in Mexico City, so we decided to have a picnic at the ruins of the ancient city of Teotihuacán.

We gathered there on January 7, 1968—Art's thirty-fifth birthday. The towering ruins were overwhelming, and we tried to imagine the people who had built this city over one thousand years ago.

Felipe Ramos, who could wax poetic at the drop of a hat, likened the ancient monuments to the modern monument that would also require sweat and blood to build—the Revolution –effected by free men believing in their right to work for themselves, to preserve their own cultural heritage, and to build a future.

I added, "The new monument, if it is not to become a dead ruin like so many other idealistic movements, has to stay free from dogma and remain in motion—built on the interchange of ideas and the trust of aware and dedicated individuals." More than once I had heard revolutionaries in Guatemala condemn the Soviet Union for having sacrificed their revolution in the name of a suffocating bureaucracy whose self-perpetuation had become more important than serving the people. They hated the Russian government even more than that of the United States. I felt their criticism was just as applicable to the Catholic Church's bureaucracy and dogmatism.

We sat in a circle on the platform of one of the pyramids and renewed our commitment to the peasant people of Guatemala. There would be difficult days ahead. We had to wait for word from the peasant leaders who had gone into hiding, and we had to find a source of funds. Our immediate plans included studying U.S. Army counterinsurgency manuals and writing manifestoes to be published in Guatemala. We would also go into training.

While we were talking, a Mexican army jeep with an officer and two soldiers pulled up across the road; they watched us for ten minutes. We had climbed high so we could not be overheard, but a group of people talking so earnestly there must have looked suspicious. I started singing "Happy Birthday" to Art, and everyone joined in lustily. Finally, the driver put the jeep in gear and pulled away.

M arjorie   We couldn't do any more until we found out what the peasant leaders thought. Before leaving Guatemala, Art and Tom had arranged meeting places with different leaders along the Mexican–Guatemalan border. Art and Tom separately made the eight-hundred-mile trip from Mexico City to the border.

They returned to tell us that many Guatemalan troops had arrived in Huehuetenango but there had been no reprisals; all was calm in the Maryknoll parishes. However, the peasants weren't sure if they were ready for us to help them. They had to decide if there was a possibility of organizing in greater numbers and if the risks were worth it.

At the time we left Guatemala, we had considered the idea of making public our expulsion and the reasons behind it as a means of publicizing the revolution. But we had decided it would be better to work quietly so as not to alert the government forces more than was inevitable. At times, we wondered whether we shouldn't have refused to leave, and made Maryknoll, the U.S. Embassy, and the Guatemalan government prove that a crime had been committed. However, we came to realize that a legal approach would have jeopardized the safety of the students and Indians involved. If we had lost in the courts, as we almost certainly would have, the identities of all the people involved would probably have been revealed, leaving them to face the vengeance of the oligarchy's army. Our retreat to Mexico, to examine there the possibilities of organizing, had been the only feasible alternative.

Our fears about reprisals were confirmed when we learned that other Maryknollers, some of whom hadn't even known of the Escuintla meetings, had been expelled. Father Blase Bonpane was handed his plane ticket three days after our departure. And within two weeks, Brother Augustine and Sisters Gail, Paula, and Cathy had been told to leave. We weren't sure but what some Maryknollers might even give out the names of Guatemalans to protect themselves.

Meanwhile, on January 12, Tom and I were married in Mexico City, in a private ceremony consisting of a simple exchange of vows, with Art as our witness. Since we couldn't reveal our names or our whereabouts, we had to forgo obtaining a civil marriage certificate. (Later, after returning to the

United States, we went through the formality of a civil ceremony.)

Before committing ourselves to this step, we had talked it over with the students, Tom had discussed it with two of the peasant leaders, and everyone but Art and one of the students strongly approved. We knew, of course, that from the standpoint of canon law, we would be incurring the penalty of automatic excommunication. But such a consideration now seemed virtually irrelevant to us, typical of the legalisms that in our church had taken precedence over Christian love. In fact, it was precisely in order to demonstrate our conviction that the spirit of the Church had been stifled by such legalistic concerns, that we deliberately refused to seek a Vatican dispensation for our marriage.

We had prepared a statement of these views; unfortunately, the news of our marriage reached the newspapers prematurely, because of a casual mention of it we had made in a letter to John Breen. Thereafter only Monsignor Ivan Illich's Center of Intercultural Documentation at Cuernavaca would publish our statement.

Even we, I think, were surprised by the overwhelming sense of peace and joy we felt in joining our lives to continue together our mission of serving "the people of God." We had anticipated some sort of guilt feelings, but they did not materialize—though there *was* a certain gnawing anxiety that perhaps our parents would be unable to understand what we had done (a fear that later proved groundless). Art had eventually accepted our decision, more out of fraternal good will than from conviction.

Tom On January 16 we heard that two U.S. military attachés, Colonel John Webber and Lieutenant Commander Ernest Munro, had been assassinated in Guatemala City by the FAR. The chief of the National Police claimed that "the plot was hatched at last year's meeting of the leftist Latin American Solidarity Organization in Havana," while the Associated Press quoted "informed sources" as suggesting that "FAR may have slain the Americans to get into the limelight again and put pressure on Castro to extend more help." Nobody seemed to pay much attention to the FAR's own reason for the assassinations: Its communiqué stated that the two Americans were killed "because the U.S. military mission was helping Guatemala in pursuing guerrillas."

Guatemala was in a state of civil war; the government forces were pitted against the revolutionaries, and there certainly was no more appropriate target for the guerrillas than Colonel Webber, who on more than one occasion had publicly boasted of the success of his counterinsurgency program and of the terroristic tactics that it employed.

Colonel Webber had taken command of the counterinsurgency program upon the installation of President Méndez Montenegro, and from that time on, the fighting had been intensified. Peasants, forcibly inducted into the army, now found themselves fighting against their own people and their own interests. One aspect of Webber's pacification program involved the payment of anywhere from one to fifty quetzals for the death of so-called Communist sympathizers and was thus responsible for the murder of countless peasants and their families.

Dragging Castro's name into the affair was a cynical attempt to make the killings appear to be part of an "international conspiracy." The people of Guatemala were fully capable of planning and executing their own revolution. Actually, Castro's aid to the revolutionaries has been largely moral and inspirational; the United States, on the other hand, has supported the established order with tens of millions of dollars.

Two days after the assassination, I went out to buy a paper. There on the display frame, glaring at me from the front pages of about five of Mexico City's dailies, were my photograph and Art's. I grabbed one of the papers, and the vendor yelled at me, "Those are for display. Get one over here, you dummy."

My hands shook as I tried to clip the paper back in place. I thought everyone would recognize me, even though it was my ordination picture and I looked like a kid.

GUERRILLA PRIESTS HIDING IN MEXICO, read the headline. We were dumfounded. It was almost a month since we had left Guatemala, and not a word had been publicly reported about our departure. Now, Maryknoll in New York announced to the press that we had "personally interfered in the internal affairs of a country where we were guests, thus violating a strict policy of the Order."

It was impossible for us to determine just why the story had been released now, so closely following the death of the two Americans. But in claiming that it is not a missionary's concern what a government or army does to its people, Maryknoll was obviously trying to disassociate itself from us to save its own face in Guatemala.

John Breen's statement in the Guatemalan press was a more personal attack. His accusations exaggerated our "guerrilla activity," but what I particularly resented was the charge that the three of us "were taking up collections and using the money for causes not connected with the Church." I had, in fact, withdrawn Q.2,300 from the bank; but I had left more than Q.3,500 in the form of my own new jeep pickup truck and several easily collectible IOU's. As for "Church" causes, Vatican II stated very clearly that the Church is the "people of God"—all the people. The Q.2,300 had been used for getting peasants and students out of the country—to save "people of God."

Shortly after we left, there was published a statement by an unidentified Maryknoller which read, in part: "These people may be misguided, but they should not be dismissed as isolated cases or neurotics who couldn't take it. Slowly, perniciously, the syndrome of despair is growing among many of us whose lives are spent in what seems a fruitless effort to alleviate this terrible misery."

Soon thereafter, however, a rebuttal appeared in the Mexican press, in the form of a denunciation of us said to have been signed by all our 102 Maryknoll confreres in Guatemala. Their statement said: "We wish to make known our opposition to the naïve, impetuous, individualistic and romantic reasoning which has now set back the authentic work of human and social development in Guatemala. . . . Here, guerrillas and revolution mean kidnapping, murder, machine-gunning, stealing, bombing of school buses."

Even as we read this, we realized that it represented an effort by the Maryknoll Superiors to prove their loyalty to the Guatemalan government, in answer to the demand of Vice-President Marroquín Rojas that the whole Order be expelled. Later, we learned that few Maryknollers had actually signed the statement or agreed with it.

The ambivalence of Maryknoll's position—supporting an oligarchic government yet claiming to be concerned for the welfare of the poor—must have been plain to some of the priests and sisters. Our sin was not that we mixed in politics as such, but that we were on the wrong side—one may respectably serve as a "dupe" of the landowners but not of the peasants.

Marjorie   Because of the publicity, we were being hunted by the governments of Guatemala, Mexico, and the United States. Our photos were published in Guatemala on the *Mano Blanca*'s (White Hand's) death list, and Father Blase Bonpane advised us by phone that the FBI was searching for us. My parents, living in Texas, were visited by two agents wanting to know my whereabouts; but I hadn't given my family any way to communicate with me.

Tom made another trip to the Guatemalan border, and this time I accompanied him. In Tapachula a Guatemalan told us that we were being hunted and advised us not to return to Guatemala at that time. Later, as we sat talking in a restaurant, Tom noticed a woman staring at me. I recognized her as the wife of the TACA Airline manager in Guatemala. She suddenly stood up and left. Tom told me to get out quickly while he paid the bill. As I was leaving the restaurant, I saw her coming back with two policemen. The sidewalk was crowded, and I had no trouble losing myself in the crowd. The next day we read that the "guerrilla nun," dressed in long white robes and carrying a typewriter, had been picked up by the Mexican police in Tapachula. Naturally, I was not going around dressed in a nun's habit. We hoped that the poor little nun, whoever she was, had no problem proving her identity. Mexico's jails are as bad as Guatemala's, and no place for a nun to spend even a minute. "Tom," I said, "can you imagine her trying to explain that to her Mother Superior!"

Tom One reason for the turmoil produced by our expulsion was that the university students who left with us were all from well-known families. Their parents demanded that the Church pressure them to return. Neither the parents nor the archbishop recognized the students as free agents whose decisions were based on their personal convictions.

Archbishop Mario Casariego had sent to all the churches of the archdiocese of Guatemala a letter to be read at Sunday Masses which denounced us as Communists who had seduced Guatemalan young people into following that "insidious doctrine." Laughing, I said to Art, "I'm going to write to the archbishop and to Maryknoll telling them we've given up on the bombing of school buses and have decided that a campaign of sex education in the schools and fluoridation of drinking water is the best way to subvert the flower of Guatemala's youth."

Art said, "You'll be taken seriously. Let's get off the defensive and do what we have to do."

Marjorie   Maryknoll's Superior General had accused us of trying to lead a revolution. This indicated a lack of understanding on his part: Only a Guatemalan will lead a Guatemalan Revolution, and only an Indian will lead the Indians in that revolution. John Breen (notwithstanding his accusations) had tried to explain our activities by saying that we wanted to "Christianize the guerrilla movement" and to "get the guerrillas to give up their use of violence." But Tom had years before stopped trying to "Christianize" even the people of his parish, when he decided that his true vocation was to be a Christian to the people. Keeping our "Christian identity" was only meant to assure the peasants and students that we were not atheists and devils. For ourselves, we had long since rejected labels as a way of judging people. Christ said: "By their fruits you shall know them." Many people guided by the writings of Marx lived like Christians, and many others starved and killed peasants while professing Christ at Mass and in Holy Communion. We had not tried to get the guerrillas to give up violence, because for the most part they did not practice it—their actions were aimed, rather, at countering the institutionalized violence, both socioeconomic and paramilitary, to which the people were perpetually subjected.

We contacted members of the Guatemalan FAR in Mexico to see how we could cooperate, and they invited three of us to go to Cuba. We refused, not because we didn't agree with the Papal Nuncio in Havana that Fidel is "politically a Marxist and ethically a Christian," but because such an association would have only confused the people we wanted to reach with our message.

One morning we were surprised to read that Archbishop Casariego was returning to Guatemala after spending four days in Mexico City, where, he claimed, he had gone to look for us and the students. He had visited the Intercultural Center in Cuernavaca and had also made inquiries of the Mexican government about us. Reporters quoted him as saying that if the Fathers Melville "had not come down from their priestly pedestals, but had read and preached the papal encyclicals, there would now be peace and justice in Guatemala."

I wished I had been there, just to ask him, "Monseñor, if *you* had read and preached them, would there now be peace and justice?"

The next morning, March 17, as he was being driven from the airport in Guatemala City to his palace, Monseñor Casariego was kidnapped in full view of dozens of police and soldiers. The FAR was blamed for the deed, motivated allegedly by the rumor that he had brought back twenty-five students on his plane. Four days later, he reappeared. His kidnappers had been the right-wing White Hand and high-ranking military personnel. They had expected that the people would blame the FAR and consider the kidnapping the last straw of terrorism. The situation might have been ripe for a coup.

But the strategy backfired. Everyone kept calm, and there were even some snickers among Catholics at the archbishop's plight. After his release, President Méndez Montenegro removed the minister of defense, Colonel Arriaga Bosque; the commander of the Zacapa military base, Colonel Carlos Arana Osorio,* who had worked closely with Webber; and the national police chief, Colonel Sosa Avila. Right-wing terrorism subsided.

Tom Art heard that some of the peasants in his parish had been killed. This report later proved to be unfounded; but he was anxious to make another trip to the border to see if he could check the story out. It was also essential to decide whether there were enough committed people to go back over the border to begin our movement.

* *In March 1970 Arana Osorio was elected president of Guatemala for a four-year term.*

Art had dyed his blond hair black and grown a mustache, and we were in the process of obtaining false identification papers for him. However, since we had all entered Mexico legally and he was in a hurry, he decided that his own passport and visa were good enough, even though the Mexican government was looking for us. He left for the Guatemalan border. Margie and I went north to Chihuahua, where we were to meet Father Blase Bonpane, who had collected some money in American universities to keep us going. We were living on a shoestring, since without residence papers we couldn't get jobs.

When Blase didn't appear, we called him in California. He told us that he had heard from a friend in Washington that Art had been picked up by the Mexican police in Comitán, near the border, and was being held incommunicado.

I immediately telephoned Mexico City to advise the students who were living with Art to move. This was the procedure if any one of us were arrested, so no one else would be jeopardized.

Blase came the next day, but he had no further news. Margie and I hurried back to Mexico City and started trying to find Art through some Mexican and Guatemalan lawyer friends. Officials of the Mexican Ministry of the Interior denied any knowledge of him. Finally, two Mexican lawyers reached the minister of the interior himself, who said he would personally try to locate Art. We were becoming desperate by this time and were also trying to contact ex-President Cárdenas, who we thought might help us. Finally, the minister told our intermediaries that Art had been put across the border at Laredo, Texas, at five o'clock that morning.

Art had demanded to see the American consul, once he had been transferred to Mexico City, but this request had been refused. The police had beaten him badly, torn hair from his head in large bunches, twisted a wire around his throat to cut off his breathing, boxed both ears simultaneously with open palms until he could no longer hear, beaten him around the head with his own shoe, breaking a tooth in the process, and repeatedly threatened to kill him. They wanted to know where Marjorie and I were. Art, of course, couldn't have told them, even if he had wanted to.

The four men who questioned Art were not Mexicans—a Mexican accent is easily distinguishable. In Guatemala, Cubans, Puerto Ricans, and Mexican-Americans are used for undercover work; perhaps these were more of the same. After giving up on their "interrogation," the men drove Art to the American border. On the way they told him they intended to kill him. In desperation, he tried to run the car off the road in hopes of escaping, but was unsuccessful and was beaten unconscious.

Before releasing Art at Laredo, the secret police, or whoever they were, took all his documents and money. The U.S. immigration officials in Laredo were apparently expecting him and waved him across, even without papers. Art went to two Catholic churches in Laredo and identified himself, but the priests refused to help him. One told him that he had gotten what he deserved for abandoning his mission of saving souls. At the St. Vincent De Paul charity center he was told, "We only help people, not priests—go back to the rectory."

Finally a Mexican-American, noticing his bloody and haggard look, stopped Art on the street, and asked if he could help. When Art identified himself, the man opened his wallet and gave him his last dollar for breakfast, then told Art he would get money for his watch. When the man returned with money from pawning the watch, he took Art to the telegraph office and then found him a room at a small hotel. Art wired our family for funds. I wondered how often the priests who refused to help Art had told the story of the Good Samaritan to Mexican-Americans.

Art later went to see Covey T. Oliver, assistant secretary of state for Latin America, to get an explanation for the Mexicans' conduct. The Mexican government claimed that Art had been in the country without papers, and that he had asked them to send him either to Cuba or North Vietnam so that he could continue to fight U.S. imperialism. None of this was true, but no satisfaction was obtained from Mr. Oliver.

Meanwhile, some friends in the Mexican government told us that it was believed in the Ministry of the Interior that we might have as many as five thousand peasant guerrillas training in Mexico to invade Guatemala. Though this was patently absurd—where could we have hidden five thousand guerrillas? —thousands of Guatemalan troops had taken up positions along the border. The Mexican authorities wanted desperately to find us, and as soon as the full police force was back on duty after Holy Week, an all-out effort was due to be made.

M arjorie We had been in Mexico nearly four months now and we seemed farther away from our goal than ever. We had even received word that Father Denny Kraus had denounced us publicly and told his parishioners that those who agreed with us had better leave and go to Mexico immediately. This strong reaction and that of other Church authorities served to frighten the peasants and stop all organizing activities inside Guatemala. Our money was running out, and prospects of getting the guerrilla front moving in the near future were becoming dimmer and dimmer.

The loss of Art and his contacts was a big blow. Tom and I talked it over with the students and a peasant leader who had come to Mexico City to consult with us. All agreed that the two of us should return to the United States to take the heat off those still in Mexico. Some had already returned and gone underground in Guatemala. We would try to raise money and publicize Guatemala's plight among the people of the United States.

The two of us left on Easter Saturday and rode the bus across Mexico and into California. Art had warned us that he had seen our pictures posted by the police in the customs office in Nuevo Laredo, Mexico, so we decided to go by way of

Tijuana, where the border has always been relatively loosely guarded.

In San Diego, as we rode past mile after mile of every type of warship imaginable tied up along the docks, Tom nudged me and murmured, "Look. That's what we're fighting against. The U.S. thinks God has appointed it the earth's policeman."

I thought to myself, *Those warships are powerless without sailors to man them and without armament-plant workers to outfit them. What if they called a war and nobody came?*

I turned to Tom: "We've got to do something so that the U.S. people can understand what they're doing to the Guatemalan peasants. We've got to stop them from sending counterinsurgency experts, helicopters, and guns. If we can convince young Americans not to seek their manhood in the Green Berets, or even better, persuade the American people not to finance counterinsurgency efforts in Latin America, we can save countless innocent people."

"I know, I know," he muttered. "But let's not kid ourselves. There really isn't a hell of a lot we can do."

XXIII

To Burn Papers, Not People

Tom Margie and I flew from San Diego to Washington, D.C., where Father Blase Bonpane had gone only a few weeks before in the hope of meeting Congressmen to whom he could explain the realities of United States policy in Latin America. He invited Margie and me to join him in this task. But we simply did not believe that our government policy-makers were unaware of the true nature of U.S. activities in Latin America. That true nature was obvious from the record: roughly a score of imperialistic invasions of Latin American nations by the United States since the turn of the century.* Nevertheless, we went to Washington, expecting to stay only for a short visit, to think things out for ourselves and to determine what our next step should be.

The two of us found a place to stay in a community house in northwest Washington, where we were joined by my brother Art, and shortly thereafter, by John Hogan, formerly Brother Augustine, who had just resigned from the Maryknoll Order. The community had been established by George Mische to support the movement against United States participation in the Vietnam War. George was a former employee of the Alliance for Progress program in Honduras and the Dominican Republic and had returned to aid his brother, Jerry, in founding a Catholic lay missionary organization in

---

* *World Almanac* 1970: "U.S. Military Actions 1900–1970," p. 169.

Paterson, New Jersey, for volunteer work in Latin America. As the war in Vietnam developed, George turned his attention to peace efforts. Among the people working with him in his peace campaign was a five-foot-five, slender, red-headed woman of boundless energy, Mary Moylan. Mary had worked a number of years in Uganda, Africa, as a volunteer nurse, and her Irish temperament went with the color of her hair.

Two weeks after we arrived, Father Phil Berrigan came down from Baltimore one night to speak to George. I had read about Father Berrigan while I was in Guatemala—how he and three others had entered a Selective Service office in Baltimore about six months before and poured blood over the 1-A draft files. He had been convicted in Federal Court, and was now awaiting sentencing.

I was very impressed by Phil Berrigan's determination and commitment. A tall, good-looking, silver-haired man, he laughs easily and his eyes are crinkled and smiling. Tremendously self-disciplined, he holds himself very straight in almost a military manner. During World War II he had won a battle-field commission in Europe; but now, he spoke with a fierce hate for the war in Vietnam; he seemed agonized by his inability to stop it, and to bind up that nation's wounds. As a civil rights activist, Phil had been in many of the freedom marches in the South. He had now concluded that the war in Vietnam itself was the result of white supremacist attitudes, and he denounced the hypocrisy of those men who cry loudest for the freedom of the South Vietnamese, while denying the black man freedom to live and work where he wants, to be black and different in his native land.

"The Riverses and the Eastlands and the Stennises would not have a South Vietnamese eat at the same table with them, but they'll send black men and brown men and white men, other men's sons, to die for the freedom of people they neither understand nor care about."

The words came out softly, almost like a prayer—first a statement of facts and then an analysis of them. Phil's strongest words of indictment were not for these men, however—or even for Johnson or Rostow or Rusk—but for Cardinal Spellman of New York, Archbishop Lucey of San Antonio, Bishop Furey of San Diego, and other leaders of the Catholic Church who had declared the Vietnam War to be a holy crusade.

No one in the room contested his charges. Only when he got to the problem of what to do, was there any controversy. From an indictment of the Catholic hierarchy, not only for its support of the war but for fostering divisiveness among the Vietnamese, he turned the conversation to a public examination of conscience as to the status of our own Catholicism. He asked how we felt about the prowar stand or the evasion of any stand which alternatively characterized, almost universally, the American Catholic hierarchy. Mary and George had no problem with their answer—by this time, both were agreed on the irrelevance of most Catholic bishops in today's world.

John Hogan, Art, Margie, and I discussed the parallels between the Church's actions in Guatemala and in Vietnam. Then, Father Phil asked us: "What are you going to do about it?"

During the first week of May 1968, we met in the basement of a friend's house in Washington. There were perhaps twenty-five people present from different parts of the country, all connected in a ministerial capacity with one or another of the Christian churches. One of the participants came right to the point. There was going to be a raid on a draft board in Catonsville, Maryland, in a few weeks. The 1-A files were to be burned with napalm, with a minimum possibility of physical harm to either the raiders or the clerks in the office. The people making the raid would turn themselves in for arrest, explain the motivation for their action, and take the consequences. Two- or three-year jail sentences would probably be the result after a prolonged period—say, two years, more or less—of appeals and public dialogue. How many were interested in joining the action?

From the stunned silence it was obvious that many were not prepared for such a confrontation.

The spokesman then added, "We only have two weeks—it must be done before Tom and Phil are sentenced for their first project." He was referring to Tom Lewis, the artist from Baltimore who had joined Father Berrigan in pouring blood on the Baltimore draft files.

George Mische immediately said, "Those who will join in this action, raise your hands."

Father Phil, George, Tom Lewis, Mary Moylan, John Hogan, my brother Art, myself, and David Darst, a young Christian Brother from St. Louis—all raised our hands. A low murmur erupted into open protests:

"You're trying to high-pressure us into this without any discussion."

"We were invited here for a meeting on antiwar protest and church participation, not to decide on how many years we're willing to spend in jail!"

"No one is pushing anybody. Those who want to take part are welcome; those who don't can simply refuse."

One of those opposing the plan as masochistic was Blase Bonpane. He did not live at the community house and was unprepared for the proposal. I was surprised at his opposition, because I thought we had all agreed that something had to be done to bring Guatemala's message home to the people of the United States. Although he had often admitted that talking to Congressmen was a long, slow process and that other answers had to be found, he just didn't see burning draft files and going to jail as being among them. I was surprised and angry with Blase, and defended the proposal. I tried to relate what was going on in Guatemala to Vietnam to show that Vietnam was not an isolated blunder, but had resulted from a policy consistent with America's view of the world and its place in it. Blase understood this, of course, but that argument got nowhere with most of those present:

"We can't even convince people of the horror and immorality of the Vietnam War, and now you want to drag in Guatemala."

So it went, back and forth, with the original lines of opposition unchanged. The meeting lasted from nine in the morning until three in the afternoon.

I noticed that Margie had been silent almost from the beginning of the meeting but attributed this to the tension that had been generated in all of us. I took it for granted that she agreed with the action.

The three of us from Guatemala who had volunteered decided that John Hogan and I would burn the draft files if it were indicated that our action was related to Guatemala and Latin America. Art would not take part, since we felt one of us had to stay free to publicize our message. Blase, now in a conciliatory mood, said he would continue to explain the message but would not try to justify the action. Although he had no moral qualms about it, he thought it unwise from a tactical political standpoint.

When the meeting broke up, there were seven people pledged to participate in the Catonsville action. Those who had rejected the idea from the beginning were angry in varying degrees for having been brought to the meeting under "false pretenses." Phil claimed to have explained the meeting's purpose in a letter inviting the participants, but it was obvious that many had not understood him. I should add, however, that those most vociferously opposed at the time have since taken part in similar acts of witness and are, as I write, in jail or under indictment.

Marjorie   I was angry and hurt. Tom had committed himself without talking it over with me at all. We hadn't been married even four months and it seemed to me he was taking our dreams of united action in Guatemala's liberation struggle into something I was not a part of. His act would mean years in jail, of separation. I couldn't see how such a raid would emphasize the immorality of the war or bring about any understanding of the situation in Guatemala. I withdrew into myself to meditate again on the meaning of my life. When I thought I wouldn't be missed at the meeting, I slipped out and walked to a nearby park. I was ready to cry.

Through my anguish, two ideas were dominant. I dreaded being separated from Tom, yet felt guilty at my unwillingness to permit him this expression of his convictions. But I also had an intense need to affirm my own aims, to determine what I was going to do now that we were back in the States, and I felt unable to face this problem alone. I wanted us to face it together—I wanted us to love our fellow humans together, to bridge misunderstanding together.

Tom When Margie later told me of her thoughts on the matter, I was confused. We had discussed this problem over and over in Guatemala. I had struggled for years with the celibacy question, realizing that the supposed aim—love for all mankind—often means love for no one and subserves the subtlest of egotisms. Then Margie and I had had to deal with the question of whether our love for each other could detract from our love for Guatemala's people and stand in the way of our dedication to them.

We had argued, discussed, fought, and prayed over that a thousand times.

Finally we had reached a conclusion that resulted in Escuintla. To me, Catonsville and jail were a logical extension of that same decision, and as far as I was concerned, Margie's reaction was inconsistent, and it upset me. But those were difficult days for her in many ways that I did not grasp at first.

We were meeting all kinds of people interested in the issues of war, peace, and revolution. Often, when we were introduced, people would say, wide-eyed, "The Melvilles?—From Guatemala?" This bothered her very much. She was uncomfortable when someone wanted to make a heroine out of her.

Often, her distress was heightened by people insisting that we provide all the answers to the problems of U.S. foreign policy. Or someone would want us to prescribe his role in straightening out the world's ills. Many simply could not see that we were searching too. And, since Margie's background has been almost exclusively Latin American, she was not accustomed to the harsh and unguarded talk of North American revolutionaries or of those posturing as revolutionaries. In Guatemala, someone who thinks about revolution meditates long and deeply before revealing it even to his best friend. There it is not a game, but a matter of life and death. Some of the people we were now meeting talked as if they weren't ready to change themselves and as if revolution were a lark. We knew that a true revolutionary is born of suffering, both his own and that of others, and acts from a desire to alleviate it, not increase it.

Marjorie

Tom believed the act of civil disobedience and disruption at Catonsville might shake the complacency of Americans who disliked the war but weren't willing to make personal sacrifices to end it. He had enthusiastically committed himself, and this had created a gap between us so big that I couldn't think about anything else. He'd agreed to something that would earn him years in jail. I couldn't begin to think what I would do meanwhile. My life had been utterly uprooted in the space of a few months, and I didn't know where and how to plant my feet firmly again. I couldn't go back to Guatemala, and publicizing the cause without Tom here in the United States would be too difficult for me alone.

We talked about it, and when I was calm, I was able to understand his point of view somewhat better. I went off for another long walk. Suddenly I recognized that I too had to accept jail as testimony of my opposition to my country's military intervention in Latin America and Southeast Asia. I repudiated its policies; but if I remained silent, I would in effect be acquiescing in them. Nuremberg came to mind. My first judgment of the Catonsville action had been pragmatic: How can the destruction of a few files end a war or get the Green Berets out of Guatemala? But now I saw the symbolic strength of the action—this was the best way for me to speak to people in the United States, which was precisely what I wanted to do. I couldn't understand why I hadn't thought of this before.

I went to look for Tom. I told him, "I'm going with you to Catonsville." He looked at me and then hugged me. We were back at Escuintla.

Father Dan Berrigan, who had not been at the original meeting, had joined us, so now there would be nine of us. Mary Moylan and I would be the two women. As soon as I made the decision, I was filled with joy, even peace; I was back with Tom, and we were once again on the road to helping the people of Guatemala, to whom we had dedicated ourselves and our marriage.

Tom   On May 17, 1968, we drove to Baltimore, where the nine of us met. We had printed press releases explaining our action and had informed a Baltimore television station that an antiwar protest was going to take place at Selective Service Local Board No. 33, in Catonsville. When we realized that all who had finally agreed to act were Catholics, we decided to aim our statement primarily at the Catholic Church, as we believed it was the most culpable of all the Christian churches in providing a moral rationale for war and exploitation.

Tom Lewis was to enter the draft board at 12:30 p.m., when most of its employees would be at lunch, and only two or three clerks would be there. He was to announce that he represented a group of clergy and laymen concerned over the Vietnam War and the United States's militaristic and imperialistic policies. He was to tell them that we were going to stage a demonstration and that they needn't be alarmed. The moment came; but when we followed him two minutes later, he was still standing at the office doorway on the second floor of the small wooden building, saying, "Excuse me, I represent some people. . . . Pardon me, can I have your attention?" In his nervousness, he hadn't raised his voice enough to get more than momentary notice.

We pushed on past him and seized the files of the 1-A registrants, which we carried in our arms and in two wire baskets to a parking lot next to the local board's office. There we doused them with napalm we had made ourselves according to specifications in a U.S. Special Forces handbook, and set them on fire. One of the women working in the office tried to stop us from removing the files, saying angrily with the outrage of a small shopkeeper who had caught a boy stealing a bunch of bananas, "You can't take those—where are you going with my files?" I still wonder if she ever worried or even thought about what happened to the boys whom those files represented.

Marjorie   We made it clear that we wished to demonstrate a better use for napalm than burning human beings to death. That we were arrested for destroying property, and specifically government property, by the same government which used identical methods of destruction against human beings—that made a symbolic equation. It is noble, patriotic, and worthy to use napalm to burn *people*, "enemy people." It is ignoble, unpatriotic, and unworthy to use napalm to burn "our paper," our *property*. Property is important; life is expendable.

This is what the struggle in Guatemala is about. Land is the key issue. Those who own land have power, and they expect the majority to live on starvation diets. When the poor insist on a fair share of the national resources, they are charged with subversion, and are repressed, persecuted, killed.

We believe this is what the struggle in Vietnam is about. Liberation Front struggles all over the world, whether their leaders follow the philosophy of Marx or Rousseau, are putting human beings ahead of privileged property. The United States takes the side of privilege in every struggle, and usually the Catholic Church does likewise. This achieves two results, besides causing many useless and tragic deaths. It limits uncommitted peoples to a choice between Communism and capitalism, with no way to seek viable alternatives beyond both; and it convinces the Third World that the United States is the main enemy of human development and freedom, forcing people to join with Communist countries they might otherwise prefer to avoid. We are like the Spanish conquistadores, who claimed they were delivering the heathen into the arms of Christ, by forcing people to embrace a pseudo-Christianity. When the Indians of ages past fought for their freedom, they too were portrayed as rejecting God and siding with the Devil.

The nine of us waited in the parking lot while the napalm burned furiously and the files were destroyed. We recited the Lord's Prayer and sang freedom songs. The local police took us to the Catonsville police station. They hardly seemed to know what to do with us. After a time, federal agents arrived on the scene. We were photographed, fingerprinted, and marched off to jail in Towson, Maryland.

Tom   We spent a week in jail at Towson, where we fasted on liquids to symbolize our desire to identify with the world's poor whose cheap labor makes it possible for Americans to enjoy ever more affluent lives.

After we posted bail and were released, we wrote to every Catholic bishop in the United States explaining our action. We said that we wished to test publicly in the courts the right of our country to oppress—economically and militarily—the weaker peoples of this earth. "Why has patriotism replaced religion, law replaced justice, order replaced rights, power replaced greatness, wealth replaced dignity?" we asked.

We also stated our conviction that when a bishop or other religious leader says he is unqualified to make moral judgments on the issues of the day, as did Cardinal Cooke of New York, he disqualifies himself as a moral leader. The bishops were asked to explain to their flocks the theory of a just war which demands that a moral judgment be made before an individual can fight in a war. "My country, right or wrong," is simply unchristian.

To the more than two hundred such letters we sent out, we received exactly three answers: An auxiliary bishop in Chicago told us that the government would give us what we deserved; an auxiliary bishop in Rhode Island sent us $25 toward legal fees; an auxiliary bishop in the Midwest wrote that he felt that even more than burning draft files had to be done to wake up the country, but he could not say so publicly without forfeiting his position.

We went on trial in October 1968. The judge was a grandfatherly man who let us address the jury but felt that our motivation made no difference as regarded our guilt. He sentenced some of us to three years: Margie, and the rest of the group, to two years. He could have given us much more; still, the prospect of those years in prison is grim. But if our going to jail can help in any way to shake into awareness some portion of the American public, and thereby contribute to saving some innocent lives in Guatemala and elsewhere, we deem it time well spent. These, nevertheless, are the equations that are balanced in the scales of Eternity, and all we can do is to try and to hope.

The tragedy of Guatemala, and our feelings of responsibility to its people, loom large in our motivation. We lived long and fully among these people and feel we have promises to keep. Catonsville is by no means the fulfillment of these promises—it is merely the beginning. And it is little enough for us to do, to repay them for the lessons of life that they taught us.

A Note on the Type

This book was set on the Linotype in Electra, *a type face designed by* W. A. Dwiggins. *The Electra face is a simple and readable type suitable for printing books by present-day processes. It is not based on any historical model, and hence does not echo any particular time or fashion.*

Composed, printed, and bound by
The Haddon Craftsmen, Inc., Scranton, Pa.
Typography and binding design by
Bonnie Spiegel